MAITREYA'S SUTRAS AND PRAYER

WITH COMMENTARY BY PADMA KARPO

BY TONY DUFF AND TAMÁS AGÓCS
PADMA KARPO TRANSLATION COMMITTEE

First edition, February 2013
ISBN paper book: 978-9937-572-62-0
ISBN e-book: 978-9937-572-63-7

Janson typeface with diacritical marks and
Tibetan Classic Chogyal typeface
designed and created by Tony Duff,
http://www.pktc.org/pktc/

Produced, Printed, and Published by
Padma Karpo Translation Committee
P.O. Box 4957
Kathmandu
NEPAL

Committee members for this book: translation and composition, Lama Tony Duff; translation of the Maitreya Sūtras, Agócs Tamás; cover design, Christopher Duff.

Web-site and e-mail contact through:
http://www.pktc.org/pktc
or search Padma Karpo Translation Committee on the web.

CONTENTS

Introduction v

Two Sūtras Petitioned by Maitreya in *The Noble Great Stack of Jewels* vi

About *The Noble Great Stack of Jewels* vi

Reading the Sūtras vii

Authoritative Statement viii

The General Story of the Two Sūtras x

Maitreya's Prayer xii

Overview: Five Important Prayers of the Great Vehicle xii

Detail: A Commentary on Maitreya's Prayer xiv

About the Author of the Commentary xv

About the Commentary xvi

Related Matters xix

Translation Methods and Issues xix

Sanskrit and Diacriticals xxi

Supports for Study xxi

❖ ❖ ❖

Of *The Great Stack of Jewels'* hundred thousand chapters of dharma enumerations, the forty first chapter, An Authoritative Statement Petitioned by Noble Maitreya 1

Of *The Great Stack of Jewels'* hundred thousand chapters of dharma enumerations, the forty-second chapter, An Authoritative Statement Concerning Eight Dharmas Petitioned by Maitreya 39

Maitreya's Prayer 51

A Commentary to Noble One Maitreya's Prayer; Asaṅga's Understanding Clearly Shown by All-Knowing Padma Karpo 55

❖ ❖ ❖

Glossary of Terms 96

About the Author, Padma Karpo Translation Committee, and Their Supports for Study 119

Tibetan Texts

- Sūtra one: Noble Maitreya's Petition For the Presentation of Authoritative Statement 124
- Sūtra two: Noble Maitreya's Petition For Eight Dharmas 147
- Maitreya's Prayer 152
- Padma Karpo's Commentary 155

Index 173

INTRODUCTION

The main aim of this book is to present a prayer by the great bodhisatva Maitreya and to present it in a way that makes it useful to Westerners. It is a prayer which, although popular amongst Great Vehicle followers in Asia over the centuries, has not become popular with Westerners. The main reasons for that are that there has been no authoritative translation backed by the necessary background information and explanation of the meaning of the prayer. This book provides all of that and translation of the sūtra in which the prayer appears so that the reader can gain the clearest possible understanding of the context of the prayer. In short, this book makes Maitreya's prayer available in the most complete way possible so that Westerners could use it in their own practice or at least be fully informed about it.

The prayer is contained in one of two sūtras petitioned by Maitreya and found in a very large collection of Great Vehicle sūtras named *The Noble Great Stack of Jewels*. Thus, the second aim of this book is to present a selection of the two sūtras from that collection petitioned by Maitreya; this will be the first time that these sūtras have been seen in English.

Altogether, the book consists of background information given in this introduction, followed by the two sūtras petitioned by Maitreya, then the prayer itself extracted from the sūtra, and finally a commentary to the prayer by the famous Tibetan Buddhist author, All-Knowing Padma Karpo.

1. Two Sutras Petitioned by Maitreya in *The Noble Great Stack of Jewels*

1.a. About *The Noble Great Stack of Jewels*

The sūtras presented in this book represent all of the sūtras petitioned by Maitreya and preserved in a very large collection of Great Vehicle sūtras named the *Ārya Mahāratnakūṭa* or *Noble Great Stack of Jewels*. First, a little about that collection.

The word *Noble* at the beginning of the name indicates that it contains sūtras of the Great Vehicle. This use of "noble" is a convention that was settled on when the Buddhist sūtras were compiled; placed at the beginning of a sūtra's name, it shows the sūtra is a Great Vehicle sūtra as opposed to a Lesser Vehicle sūtra. In this context, it has often been translated into English as "sublime" which is not the meaning at all; sublime in its true sense means that which is so deep that it *sub* goes below *lime* the level at which the normal mind can access it. The actual meaning of "noble" in this context is that the teachings of the Great Vehicle are superior and special compared to those of the Lesser Vehicle and sit high above them in the same way as the nobility of a country have a special position above the common people.

The words *Stack of Jewels* in the name means that the collection houses a great *stack* or pile *of* the Buddha's teachings and that those teachings encompass all of the Three *Jewels*—buddha, dharma, and saṅgha.

The Great Stack of Jewels is comprised of forty-nine chapters, each one a sūtra of the Great Vehicle. The sūtras petitioned by Maitreya are the forty-first and forty-second chapters of *The Great Stack of Jewels*.

The forty-nine chapters begin and end with the words "chapter such and such of *The Noble One, The Great Stack of Jewels'* dharma enumerations in a hundred thousand chapters". If there are only forty-nine chapters in *The Great Stack of Jewels*, why does each chapter begin and end with the statement that it has one hundred thousand chapters of dharma enumerations? It is because each of the forty-nine chapters contains many smaller teachings in which specific classifications of the dharma are enumerated by the Buddha, so that *The Great Stack of Jewels* contains an enormous number—a hundred thousand, so to speak—of these little sections or chapters of teaching in which classifications of dharma are shown or enumerated. You will clearly see this style of presentation in the sūtras presented in this book.

1.b. Reading the Sutras

In general, the sūtras are not easy to read because they contain substantial amounts of the technical vocabulary of enlightenment as the Buddha presented it and because the actual intent behind the questions, answers, and doings of the people involved is often less than obvious. To overcome these difficulties, two things are needed. First, one needs a good understanding of the vocabulary and style of expression of dharma, at least as it is used in a sūtra. Secondly, it is necessary to have experience with the sūtras and how to interpret them. Traditionally, and for good reason, a person has always gained that experience and knowledge by going to a Buddhist master and requesting that he transmit his knowledge to the person.

Specifically, the two sūtras petitioned by Maitreya do contain a great deal of technical vocabulary and to help the reader with that I have provided extensive notes and a glossary. However, the meaning of the sūtras is straightforward and does not require further interpretation. (For an example of a sūtra from *The Great Stack of Jewels*. that does require considerable interpretation, see our translation of *The Sūtra Petitioned by the Householder*, the nineteenth chapter of *The Great Stack of Jewels*.)

1.b.1. Authoritative Statement

The very first words of the title of each sūtra petitioned by Maitreya are "An Authoritative Statement ..." On reading these two sūtras, you should be able to understand from context that this term "authoritative statement" is important within the Buddha's teaching. What then is "authoritative statement"?

The Buddha taught that his transmission of the dharma occurs in two ways: one through what is known as "authoritative statement" and the other as "realization". The first is the transmission of his word through person-to-person contact, though written scripture is not excluded. The second is the direct transmission from one mind to another through realization.

Most Tibetan Buddhists will know of a something called a "lung" in Tibetan. It is more fully called "imparting a lung", a process in which someone who belongs to an unbroken transmission of a certain piece of scripture will impart it to the audience by reading it to them. Having done so, the audience now has the transmission of the scripture. Note the person-to-person quality of this. If the mere reading of the scripture was sufficient, then the audience would simply be given the text to read for themselves, but that is not how it is done. Personal transmission from someone who has received it from someone else, and so on, in an unbroken line is important.

The word "lung" translates the Sanskrit word "āgama". Āgama means exactly something which is a verbal statement made by someone who is a true authority. In English, it comes to mean "authoritative statement". Authoritative statement was a very important part of the Buddha's teaching. As mentioned above, it was one of the two ways in which the Buddha himself said that his teaching was transmitted.

The importance of this term cannot be understated. Many of the forty-nine chapters of *The Great Stack of Jewels* are entitled "the authoritative statement petitioned by such and such" where such and such was a person who came before the Buddha and petitioned him for his authoritative statement on some matter. The two sūtras here go so far as to mention in the title that they arose because Maitreya was seeking authoritative statement of the Buddha.

The Buddha was a person who had total and unimpeded knowledge of all things both in terms of their reality and their surface appearances. Thus, his statements always would be correct and exactly applicable to the situation; they were authoritative statements given at the highest level. The petitioners could have gone elsewhere in the search to have their questions answered. However, by coming into the presence of a truly complete buddha, whatever statements they might hear would be guaranteed to be authentic statements made by a person who had the ultimate capacity to inform his listeners. Remember that in India, at the time of the Buddha, there were many teachers who had founded religious movements. Each of them claimed to be the one who had authentic statement. When you have investigated carefully and come to understand what a buddha actually is, you will understand that only a buddha—whoever that might be—can give the ultimate authentic statement to his listeners.[1]

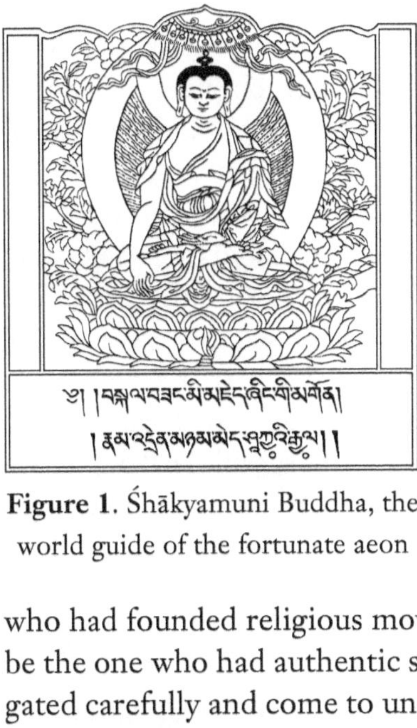

Figure 1. Śhākyamuni Buddha, the world guide of the fortunate aeon

[1] An excellent place to start with understanding what a buddha is is to read the Buddha's own explanation of it. You will find this laid out with commentaries to it in the book *Unending Auspiciousness, the Sutra*

(continued...)

1.b.2. The General Story of the Two Sutras

Thus, we know even from the title that these two sūtras are cases of the next world-leading buddha, who is present in the sūtras as the bodhisatva mahāsattva[2] Maitreya, coming before the current world-leading buddha Śhākyamuni and requesting of him answers from a truly complete buddha. In a sense, this is an amazing event: we have a truly complete buddha giving instruction to the great bodhisatva whom he has named as the next buddha. Even to see the interchange should be of interest.

The sūtra which is the forty-first chapter is not a long sūtra by any means, though it is much longer than the sūtra which is the forty-second chapter. It seems that Maitreya's question that results in the sūtra which is the forty-first chapter gave the Buddha the opportunity he needed to make some important points about differing styles of progression along the bodhisatva's path. In essence, it contains a comparison between the ways followed by Śhākyamuni and Maitreya on their respective journeys to enlightenment. Śhākyamuni Buddha points out that, while Maitreya was very skilful in the way that he went along the bodhisatva path, he progressed slowly in comparison with himself. It becomes a very personal story in which Śhākyamuni Buddha details the sacrifices that he was willing to undergo in order to achieve truly complete enlighten-

---

[1](...continued)
of the Recollection of the Noble Three Jewels by Tony Duff, published by Padma Karpo Translation Committee, 2010, ISBN: 978-9937-8386-1-0. This book contains many of the definitions needed to understand the terminology of the sūtras, so is particularly useful as background reading to go together with this book.

[2] For the important term bodhisatva mahāsattva, see the glossary. Here, it has the second meaning, specifically indicating a bodhisatva dwelling on the highest, non-regressing bodhisatva levels.

ment, sacrifices which Maitreya skilfully avoided in his lives as a bodhisatva.

The general details of Śhākyamuni's progression of lives as a bodhisatva is well-known from the *Birth Tales* in which the Buddha told many stories of his former incarnations. However, the sūtra which is the forty-first chapter has new information on his progress to enlightenment which does not appear in any other sūtra and which is fascinating to hear as he compares his approach with Maitreya's approach.

At some point in this story, Ānanda asks a question as he tries to understand what the Buddha has been explaining about the approach of Maitreya. In reply, the Buddha uses his extra-perceptions[3] to present a prayer which Maitreya had composed and recited every day in a former life. Having recited the prayer word-for-word out of his total knowledge of events of the past, the Buddha continues by explaining how this prayer was a crucial factor in Maitreya's progress as a bodhisatva. With the presentation of the prayer, we arrive at a central message of this sūtra. With this we now not only have Maitreya's prayer for our own use but also have the Buddha's explanation of its overall meaning—we understand the context for the prayer, making it considerably more accessible for our own use.

The sūtra which is the forty-second chapter is a discourse that occurred at a separate time from the discourse that is the basis for the forty-first chapter; we can tell that from the location in which each sūtra was taught. However, it does add to the meaning of the sūtra which is the forty-first chapter. In it, Maitreya again asks for instruction that will give him authoritative information on how to

---

[3] The extra-ordinary or we could say extra-sensory knowledges or perceptions are those knowledges which are beyond the range of the ordinary person's six senses and which come with taming the mind.

continue his path to enlightenment so that he does not slip back from his current position in any way and only continues to go forward[4]. The single answer given by the Buddha to Maitreya's single question seems to function as an adjunct to the answers given in the forty-first chapter. Once the forty-first chapter has been read and understood, the forty-second chapter is easy to read and understand.

So far, I have discussed the source for the two sūtras presented in this book—*The Great Stack of Jewels*—and given an overview of both sūtras. In doing so, we have seen that the sūtra which is the forty-first chapter is of greatest interest here because it gives Maitreya's prayer and also gives the context for the prayers as explained by the Buddha himself. Next, we look at Maitreya's prayer in detail.

2. Maitreya's Prayer

2.a. Overview: Five Important Prayers of the Great Vehicle

The Great Vehicle tradition of Buddhism in general demarcates a group of five prayers that are most important to its followers. All five prayers are either in daily use by individuals or in regular use by individuals and groups. The five are: Samantabhadra's Prayer, Maitreya's Prayer, Mañjuśhrī's Prayer, the Sukhāvatī Prayer, and the chapter of prayers in Śhāntideva's famous guide to the bodhisatva's conduct.

Of the five prayers, the first three are connected with the three most senior bodhisatva sons of Śhākyamuni Buddha: Samantabha-

[4] Not that he had far to go—he was already a bodhisatva known as a "master of the tenth level", a bodhisatva who has not only arrived at the last bodhisatva level prior to the achievement of truly complete enlightenment but who had mastered that level completely and is now awaiting final attainment of truly complete enlightenment.

dra, Maitreya, and Mañjuśhrī. All three were bodhisatvas dwelling on the tenth bodhisatva level. Samantabhadra was regarded as the senior-most bodhisatva who was in many ways more advanced than all the others. It is mentioned in the sūtras that he was regarded as the chief of all of Śhākyamuni Buddha's bodhisatva sons because of being senior in age, training, good qualities, and wisdom. He was also known for his expertise in composing prayers and it is true that the most important prayer of his in the sūtras is a masterpiece of composition. Despite his position, the Buddha predicted him as one who would not show the deeds of a world-leading buddha for a very long time. Mañjuśhrī, the next most senior bodhisatva, was regarded as equivalent to Samantabhadra in his capacities and was predicted by the Buddha to be the sixth world-leading buddha of this good age of one thousand and two buddhas. Maitreya was appointed by the Buddha as his regent, meaning that he would be the next world-leading buddha to appear after Śhākyamuni Buddha, the fifth world-leading buddha of this good age of one thousand and two buddhas. In sum, these three bodhisatvas are regarded as the most advanced amongst Śhākyamuni Buddha's bodhisatva disciples and, as a consequence, the prayers associated with them are the most prominent prayers amongst followers of the Great Vehicle.

Of the three prayers composed by those three great bodhisatvas, the one spoken by Samantabhadra is not only the most well-known but without doubt the most used amongst followers of the Tibetan Buddhist tradition. It is also the longest and most complex of the three prayers, having an enormous amount of meaning packed into its sixty verses. The prayer was spoken aloud by Samantabhadra to a bodhisatva called Sudhana who had come to him for teachings. It is recorded in the fifty-third and last chapter of the *Gaṇḍavyūha Sūtra*, which itself is a sūtra at the end of the very large compilation of Great Vehicle sūtras called the *Flower Ornament* or *Avataṃsaka Sūtra*. There are many explanations of Samantabhadra's prayer available in the *Translated Treatises*,[5] with several from Indian masters such as Nāgārjuna, and many by Tibetan masters[6].

Maitreya's prayer whose source has already been described above, consists of twenty-four four-line verses. Essentially, it starts with the seven limbs for accumulating merit, proceeds to an explanation of emptiness as taught in the Great Vehicle which it then sets as the ground for all bodhisatva activity, and finally explains the practice of the six pāramitās as the path to supreme enlightenment. The prayer reads easily and its literal meaning can be understood by anyone with a basic knowledge of the Great Vehicle teachings. However, it also contains many less obvious meanings that can only be understood through an explanation given by someone conversant with the details of the Great Vehicle. There are very few explanations of Maitreya's prayer available. Of them, I have chosen one by the Tibetan master Padma Karpo.

The prayer of Mañjuśhrī is not used as much as those of Samantabhadra and Maitreya, so no more will be said about it here.

2.b. Detail: A Commentary on Maitreya's Prayer

To understand Maitreya's prayer more fully, it is necessary to have a commentary on it. As mentioned above, there are very few explanations of Maitreya's prayer available. Of them, I have chosen one by the Tibetan master Padma Karpo because it is medium-sized and very succinct. It is short enough that a sense of the whole prayer can easily be kept in mind as one reads through it, yet its wording is very concise, so a depth of meaning is available at the same time.

---

[5] Tib. bstan 'gyur. Tangyur.

[6] A major book on Samantabhadra's Prayer, including commentaries by Nāgārjuna and others called *Samantabhadra's Prayer and Commentaries* by Tony Duff has been published by Padma Karpo Translation Committee, ISBN 978-9937-572-60-6.

2.b.1. About the Author of the Commentary

All-Knowing Padma Karpo [1527–1592 C.E.] was the fourth Drukchen or hierarch of the Tibetan Drukpa Kagyu tradition. He was known for his extraordinary level of knowledge and unusual abilities at written composition. With his knowledge and erudition, Padma Karpo became one of the greatest authors of the Tibetan Buddhist tradition. His explanations are so valued that I have translated a number of them and, together with longer explanation of his capabilities and works, published them in a series of books.[7]

Because of the first quality mentioned above, he came to be known as "All-Knowing", a title reserved in Tibet for those rare individuals—one or two in each century—who just seemed to "know it all". Because of the second quality, he became famous for his ability to weave many threads of meaning into very tight explanations. His writings can seem deceptively simple because of it and Drukpa Kagyu teachers warn that his works must be read very carefully so as not to miss the subtle but important threads of meaning woven into them. This quality of many levels of detail in a short space is very evident in his commentary on Maitreya's prayer, and the warning of the Drukpa Kagyu lineage to read carefully so as not to miss the threads of meaning and implications involved is highly applicable!

Padma Karpo did not hide his capabilities; he was very sure of himself and said so in many of his writings, though he reputedly was not at all proud. There is an example of this in the closing verse of his commentary here; it says:

> This, which I was able to compose in just a few lines of
> well-considered verse,

---

[7] If you would like to know more about him or find yourself drawn to his style of explanation, look at the listing of books containing his works in the Supports for Study chapter of this book.

Brings the clever understanding of bloated learned
people to a halt;
Is there any way that these people who know all topics of
knowledge
And comment on the meaning of hundreds of texts can
be fitted into the region of becoming?[8]

There have been Tibetan commentators who wrote extensively on this prayer and many other things; their writings are clever but also long-winded. Padma Karpo says that his commentary might appear to be only middling in length but is equivalent if not better than their much longer writings. With that, he is saying that he is smarter than these other very learned people, but this is not mere pride talking—it happens to be true. His commentary might not be very long, but it packs all of the needed meaning into a short space and does so using just the right wording. In fact, it is remarkably erudite because the whole commentary is given in reference only to the works of Maitreya, as you will see from the citations that he makes.

2.b.2. About the Commentary

The commentary was given verbally by All-Knowing Padma Karpo whilst visiting a monastery in central Tibet called "The Dharma Sanctuary of Great Maitreya". He was asked for it by someone from a place called Dromo who had meditative realization. Padma Karpo used quotations from the texts of Maitreya's teachings on the Great Vehicle—the *Five Dharmas of Maitreya* as they are known—as the basis for his commentary. He supplemented them with quotations mainly from third turning of the wheel sūtras, which is fitting; Maitreya is known for being the bodhisatva who was given the responsibility by the Buddha of carrying forward the very profound teaching of view and meditation taught in the third turning of the

[8] They have become so bloated with their pride and their endless words of concepts that you have to wonder how they could possibly fit into something as large as even becoming, meaning saṃsāra, itself.

wheel. Thus, All-Knowing Padma Karpo crafted an explanation of Maitreya's prayer that had many connections with Maitreya. Even the title of the commentary—A Commentary to Noble One Maitreya's Prayer, Asaṅga's Understanding Clearly Shown—shows this, given that Asaṅga was the Indian master who was later primarily responsible for spreading Maitreya's teachings in India.

The commentary packs an enormous amount of very detailed and often technical information into a very short space. To fully understand it requires a high level of familiarity with the Buddha's Mind-Only and Other Emptiness presentations given in the third turning of the wheel of dharma and Maitreya's own presentations of the same which are found in his *Five Dharmas of Maitreya* texts.

I am sure that some readers will want a commentary that is less technical and more general. Unfortunately, the few commentaries to the prayer which are available all go into even deeper technical explanations and do so at great length, as Padma Karpo alludes to in his verses at the end of his commentary. In short, Padma Karpo's commentary is the best available for those who are not master scholars.

To give a hint of the depth of understanding that one could enter in relation to Maitreya's prayer, we can say that the prayer is worded in such a way that it can be understood according to the approach that the Buddha expounded in the Prajñāpāramitā sūtras of the second turning of the wheel or according to the approach that he expounded in the Mind-Only sūtras and the sūtras which the Tibetans later called the profound essence sūtras or the sūtras connected with Other Emptiness, all of which are found in sūtras of the third turning of the wheel. Padma Karpo has mainly explained it through the approach of the Mind-Only sūtras of the third turning and Maitreya's later commentaries on that. Other Tibetan commentators have done otherwise. An explanation of the differences and similarities between the approaches of the second and third turnings of the wheel of dharma and how they can be understood through Maitreya's prayer are outside the scope of this volume, though Padma Karpo Translation Committee has published several books on these matters, all of which would help with understanding Padma Karpo's commentary here.

As mentioned at the beginning of the introduction, the aim of this book was to make Maitreya's prayer accessible to English-speaking Buddhists so that they could use the prayer if they found it useful. Therefore, let's put behind us the complications and difficulties that could be entered in relation to the prayer and focus on how it could be useful for those who without great Buddhist scholarship. For this, the first thing to point out is that the prayer is written so that it reads easily. It is not like Samantabhadra's prayer which, in using all of the capabilities of the Sanskrit language, becomes quite difficult to read even if it is a masterpiece of composition. Maitreya's prayer was written in a very straightforward way that makes it very easy to read. I have found that people enjoy it for that reason alone. Nevertheless, there is a profound depth of knowledge that can be inferred from the seemingly easy to understand wording of the prayer, so it is important to ensure that one does not make the mistake of assuming that one has correctly understood the meaning of the words of the prayer simply because they are easy to read.

A good approach to studying Maitreya's prayer would be to first read the sutra containing the prayer, then to read the prayer itself a few times, and finally to look at it in more detail by taking it a verse or two at a time while reading the relevant section of the commentary. You will find that the commentary will give you a deeper understanding of the words of the prayer, but if you find that the commentary is becoming too technical, simply leave it there for those verses and move on. That way, it will not take long to get a basic yet correct understanding of the words of the prayer.

3. Related Matters

3.a. Translation Methods and Issues

We used the Derge Edition of the *Translated Word*[9] as the source for the two sūtras of Maitreya. It is well known that there are several editions of the *Translated Word*, none of which is perfect. Therefore, it was not surprising that we found a number of errors in the Tibetan text of the sūtras. We corrected the Tibetan texts as we went; the corrected editions of the two sūtras are given in this book and the corrected electronic editions are also available on the Padma Karpo Translation Committee web-site.

A new edition of both the *Translated Word* and *Translated Treatises* was published in Beijing, China, about two years ago. It is a comparative edition which uses the Derge edition as the basis and then meticulously notes every difference with the seven other major editions of the *Translated Word* and *Translated Treatises*. It is a truly excellent reference. With it, we were able to examine the eight main editions of the Tibetan *Translated Word*. We found that there were differences between editions here and there throughout the prayer, though, fortuitously, most of them did not change the meaning. All in all, we were able to prepare a translation from the Derge edition which was consistent with the other editions.

Padma Karpo's commentary proceeds by citing from a few words to a few lines of the prayer at a time and then explaining that. Not so fortuitously, the prayer as quoted in the commentary does not match any of the editions in the Kangyur and has several obvious errors in it. This led me to check the three editions of Padma

---

[9] Tib. bka' 'gyur. Kangyur.

Karpo's *Collected Works*[10] to see whether the edition I had first examined was perhaps a bad edition, but all editions read the same. This does not indicate that Padma Karpo's text is particularly faulty; on the one hand, this kind of corrupted citation of earlier works is endemic in Tibet literature and, on the other, the commentary portion of the text was very well done and free of errors. Most likely Padma Karpo relied on memory to quote the prayer as he gave the commentary and mis-quoted it here and there or the written edition of the prayer available to him at the time was slightly corrupt.

Many of the places where the prayer as cited in Padma Karpo's commentary differs from the prayer as written in the *Translated Word* can be resolved as obvious mistakes in the commentary's citation of the prayer. However, there are a few places where there is a real difference. To solve this in a way that I thought would lead to faith and minimize confusion, the prayer as seen in the *Translated Word* was used for the final translation of the prayer and the lines of the prayer as they have been cited in the commentary have been translated as they appear in the commentary. The final result is a translation of the prayer which fits with the *Translated Word*; This has been left without notes so that it makes a nice basis for recitation. And then, there is the translation of the commentary which is internally consistent and which has copious notes added to make any discrepancies clear.

The Tibetan text of All-Knowing Padma Karpo's commentary has been provided in this book and also made available electronically on our web-site. Note that the lines of the prayer cited in the Tibetan commentary are highlighted in colour in the electronic edition of the commentary for ease of study.

---

[10] These were all editions made last century: the Lhasa and Bhutanese editions from the turn of the twentieth century, and an edition made in Darjeeling in the 1970's.

3.b. Sanskrit and Diacriticals

Sanskrit terms are an important aspect of the technical explanations found in the commentary. They are properly rendered into English with diacritical marks, therefore, for the sake of precision, diacritical marks have been used with them throughout this book.

The IATS system of transliteration of Sanskrit, which is the one generally in use in academic circles is hard for non-scholars to read. Therefore, we have modified that system slightly to make the transliterated Sanskrit more readable even when the meaning of the diacritical marks is not understood. This same approach seems to be commonplace amongst translators of Tibetan Buddhism. In it:

ś is written the way it sounds, as śh
ṣ is written similarly as ṣh
ṛ is written similarly as ṛi
ca is written as cha
cha is written as chha

The other letters for transliteration are used in the same way as they are used in the IATS scheme. In general, if you do not understand the system, simply read the letters as though they did not have the diacritical marks and, with our modified system, you will be have a good approximation to the actual pronunciation.

3.c. Supports for Study

Padma Karpo Translation Committee has amassed a range of materials to help those who are studying this and related topics. In particular, several books on Other Emptiness have been published, all of which support each other and each of which clarifies another important aspect of the teaching. Please see the chapter containing information on supports for study at the end of the book for the details.

Lama Tony Duff, director
Agócs Tamás, translator
Christopher Duff, manager
Padma Karpo Translation Committee
Swayambunath, Nepal,
February 2013

Sutra One:

The forty-first chapter of The Great Stack of Jewels' dharma enumerations in a hundred thousand chapters:

An Authoritative Statement Petitioned by Noble Maitriya

The forty-first chapter of *The Great Stack of Jewels'* dharma enumerations in a hundred thousand chapters: Authoritative Statement[11] Petitioned by Noble Maitriya[12]

A single bundle[13].

In Sanskrit: ārya maitriya paripṛicchā nāma mahāyāna sūtra

In Tibetan: 'phags pa byams pas zhus pa zhes bya ba theg pa chen po'i mdo

In English: The Great Vehicle Sūtra Called "Petitioned by Noble Maitreya"[14]

---

[11] Authoritative statement is explained in the introduction.

[12] Here, the Tibetan text spells the Sanskrit out as "Maitriya", which is a metrical version used mainly in verse of the usual spelling "Maitreya".

[13] Indian Buddhist texts were written on palm-leaves which were then stitched together into bundles. When they were translated, there was often an indication of how many bundles the text had come as. This text was in a single bundle.

[14] The system for translating texts from other languages into Tibetan included adding this header before the actual translation, giving the

(continued...)

Homage to every buddha and bodhisatva.

I heard these words at one time. The bhagavan[15] was residing in the country of Varga, in a forest dwelling place of animals, on a fearsome mountain that was like a child-killing crocodile, together with a great community of monks[16] consisting of about five-hundred monks made up exclusively of the great elder hearers[17] who had attained the extra-perceptions[18]. Among these about five

---

[14](...continued)
name of the text as written in the source language followed by the name of the text as it had been translated into the Tibetan language. We think that the system should be extended by adding the translation of the original name in the target language as a third item, as done here for this translation into English.

[15] "Bhagavan" is a term of respect used throughout Indian religions for a person who is regarded to be very advanced spiritually. The term literally means "one who has overcome the defilements" preventing enlightenment and is also explained to mean "one who has good qualities". Very extensive explanations of the meaning of "bhagavan" are given in *Unending Auspiciousness, the Sutra of the Recollection of the Noble Three Jewels*; see note 1.

[16] Skt. bhikṣhu. "Monk" in this translation refers only to full monks, not to śhrāmaṇeras or novices.

[17] Skt. mahā sthavira śhrāvakas. The first five in the list are the first five disciples of the buddha. The rest include the other five who were included as the ten closest śhrāvaka disciples, and the various Kāśhyapas all of whom played an important role in the transmission of the Buddha's teaching, and the two foremost śhrāvaka disciples Śhāriputra and Maudgalyayāna, the Buddha's personal attendant Ānanda, the Buddha's son Rāhula, and so on.

[18] "Extra-perceptions" here indicates a level of spiritual attainment.

hundred monks were the Vitality-filled[19] all-knowing Kauṇḍinya, the Vitality-filled Aśhvajit, the Vitality-filled Vāṣhpa, the Vitality-filled Mahānāma, the Vitality-filled Bhadrika, the Vitality-filled Vimala, the Vitality-filled Pūrṇa, the Vitality-filled Gavampati, the Vitality-filled Mṛigaśhīr, the Vitality-filled Uruvilva Kāśhyapa, the Vitality-filled Nāḍī Kāśhyapa, the Vitality-filled Gaya Kāśhyapa, the Vitality-filled Dāna Kāśhyapa, the Vitality-filled Great Kāśhyapa, the Vitality-filled Amogharāja, the Vitality-filled Sumati, the Vitality-filled Śhāriputra, the Vitality-filled Great Maudgalyayāna, the Vitality-filled Meru, the Vitality-filled Nanda, the Vitality-filled Upananda, the Vitality-filled Ānanda, the Vitality-filled Rāhula, and so forth.

He was also together with Maitreya and others, ten thousand bodhisatva mahāsattvas[20] who had attained the extra-perceptions, and among these ten thousand bodhisatvas were bodhisatva Vardhamānamati, bodhisatva Sumati, bodhisatva Sthiramati, Viśhālamati, Pratibhānakūṭa, Avalokiteśhvara, Mahāsthāmaprāpta[21], Ketuśhrī, Mañjuśhrī, Abhijñāpuṣhpavaipulya, Anālambanamanasikārin, Śhraddhavatī, Ratnapāṇi, Indradeva, Varuṇa, Nirghośhākarṇa, Kṣhetraviśhuddhin, Merukūṭa, Pratibhānasaṃpannaḥ, Indraśhrī, Dharaṇiṃdhara, Gandhāraḥ, Narakātapta, Apāyajaha, Ratnakeśharaṃ, and so forth.

Then the bhagavan, surrounded by a retinue of many hundreds of thousands and looking straight ahead, was teaching dharma. At that point, the bodhisatva Maitreya joined and became present in that retinue. Then the bodhisatva Maitreya, aware of that assembled

---

[19] Skt. āyuṣhmat. This is a standard honorific term used in the monastic community when addressing other monks. It means that the other person is full of life, full of vitality, because of having abandoned worldly pursuits and taken up training in virtue.

[20] For bodhisatva mahāsattva, see the glossary.

[21] This is another name for Vajrapāṇi.

great retinue of bodhisatvas[22], rose from his seat and, having draped his outer robe over one shoulder, knelt down on his right knee. Then, bowing with joined palms in the direction of the bhagavan, he supplicated the bhagavan in these words:

"Were the bhagavan to give me the opportunity to petition him for authoritative statement, I would ask the tathāgata, arhat, truly complete buddha about some matters[23]."

He supplicated in those words and the bhagavan advised the bodhisatva mahāsattva[24] Maitreya in these words:

"Maitreya, the tathāgata has always given the opportunity to answer questions asked for the purpose of authoritative statement. Maitreya, ask me whatever you wish! And, through that question and its authoritative statement, your mind will be set at ease."

Then, as the bhagavan had given him the opportunity, the bodhisatva mahāsattva Maitreya supplicated the bhagavan in these words:

---

[22] The sense here is that he had realized the extent of the assembly that he had joined and was in awe of it and that he therefore proceeded in the most respectful way possible.

[23] "Tathāgata, arhat, truly complete buddha" is the standard, most respectful way of referring to or addressing a truly complete buddha. It addresses him by referring to three of his attainments. The phrase is fully explained in *Unending Auspiciousness, the Sutra of the Recollection of the Noble Three Jewels*; see note 1.

[24] The phrase "bodhisatva mahāsattva" is explained in the introduction. It is mostly used in this sūtra with the common meaning of "a bodhisatva who is, generally speaking, a greater type of being", though here it could also have the uncommon meaning because of showing the very high position of Maitreya amongst all bodhisatvas.

"Bhagavan, how many dharmas[25] would a bodhisatva have to have for him to abandon all bad migrations and not fall into the clutches of degrading companions, and to quickly achieve unsurpassed, truly complete enlightenment, manifest complete buddhahood?[26]"

He supplicated in those words and the bhagavan instructed the bodhisatva mahāsattva Maitreya in these words:

"Maitreya, as you have rendered outstanding service to the conquerors of the past, developed roots of virtue, remembered past lives, attained knowledgeability[27], and have for a long time practised chastity, and Maitreya, as you have fully taken on benefit for many beings and ease for many beings[28] and heartfelt love for the world, and the aims, benefit, and ease of ordinary beings and of gods and men, and the sons and daughters present and future of the bodhisatva vehicle family, it is good, it is good that you have thought to ask this question of the tathāgata! Therefore, Maitreya,

---

[25] The word "dharma" is accepted in Buddhism as having ten distinct meanings. In the sūtras and texts in this book, it either refers, as it does here, to "feature" or "quality", or to dharma being the teaching of the Buddha, or to phenomena.

[26] "Truly complete enlightenment, manifest complete buddhahood" is a description of the enlightenment of a person who has followed the bodhisatva path to enlightenment. An arhat is referred to as enlightened, someone who has manifested buddhahood. However, his degree of enlightenment is not truly complete. This phrase distinguishes the attainment of unsurpassed enlightenment, truly complete buddhahood from lesser types of enlightenment, lesser attainments of buddhahood.

[27] For knowledgeability, see the glossary.

[28] "Benefit and ease" is a standard phrase in Buddhist teaching. Benefit means to help sentient beings in a worldly way, assisting them as much as possible. Ease means to help sentient beings in a transcendent way, bring them into the ease of unsurpassed enlightenment.

listen well with your fullest attention, retain it in mind, and I will explain!"

The bodhisatva mahāsattva Maitreya said to the bhagavan "Very well!" then listened in accord with the bhagavan, and the bhagavan instructed him in these words:

"Maitreya, if a bodhisatva has one dharma, he will abandon all bad migrations[29] and not fall into the hands of degrading companions, and will quickly achieve an unsurpassed truly complete enlightenment, manifest complete buddhahood. 'What is that one dharma?' It is: the enlightenment mind of perfect special intention[30]. Maitreya, if a bodhisatva possesses that single dharma, he will abandon all bad migrations and not fall into the hands of degrading companions, and will quickly achieve an unsurpassed, truly complete enlightenment, manifest complete buddhahood.

"Maitreya, furthermore, if a bodhisatva has two dharmas, he will abandon all bad migrations and not fall into the hands of degrading companions, and will quickly achieve an unsurpassed, truly complete enlightenment, manifest complete buddhahood. 'What are the two?' They are: seeking calm-abiding and being skilled in insight[31]. If a bodhisatva has those two dharmas, he will abandon all bad migrations and not fall into the hands of degrading companions and will quickly achieve an unsurpassed, truly complete enlightenment, manifest complete buddhahood.

---

[29] Bad migrations are births in the hells, preta realms, or animal realms.

[30] For special intention, see the glossary. Here it means a perfect, very pure intention of enlightenment mind or bodhichitta, for which see the glossary.

[31] For calm-abiding and insight see the entries under their Sanskrit names, śhamatha and vipaśhyanā respectively, in the glossary.

"Maitreya, furthermore, if a bodhisatva has three dharmas, he will abandon all bad migrations and not fall into the hands of degrading companions, and will quickly achieve an unsurpassed, truly complete enlightenment, manifest complete buddhahood. 'What are the three?' They are: to have attained great compassion, to have ascertained the dharma of emptiness, and because of that also to be not bloated[32]; Maitreya, if a bodhisatva has those three dharmas, he will abandon all bad migrations and not fall into the hands of degrading companions, and will quickly achieve an unsurpassed, truly complete enlightenment, manifest complete buddhahood.

"Maitreya, furthermore, if a bodhisatva has four dharmas, he will abandon all bad migrations and not fall into the hands of degrading companions, and will quickly achieve an unsurpassed, truly complete enlightenment, manifest complete buddhahood. 'What are the four?' They are: abiding within discipline, not being sceptical about all the dharmas, taking true delight in solitude, and to have entered the authentic and not be wavering from being in the authentic[33]. Maitreya, if a bodhisatva has those four dharmas, he will abandon all bad migrations and not fall into the hands of degrading companions, and will quickly achieve an unsurpassed, truly complete enlightenment, manifest complete buddhahood.

"Maitreya, furthermore, if a bodhisatva has five dharmas, he will abandon all bad migrations and not fall into the hands of degrading companions and will quickly achieve an unsurpassed, truly complete enlightenment, manifest complete buddhahood. 'What are the

---

[32] A person who has not realized the absence of self, which is done through realizing its emptiness, will be bloated with the pride that comes of thinking that one truly exists.

[33] To have entered and not be wavering from the authentic means that the person has entered and is staying firmly within a genuine approach to life and also can mean that the person has entered and is staying firmly within reality, which is also known as "the authentic".

five?' They are: abiding in emptiness, not seeking the confusion of others[34], examining oneself, taking real delight in the dharma, and being engaged in working to benefit others. Maitreya, if a bodhisatva has those five dharmas, he will abandon all bad migrations and not fall into the hands of degrading companions, and will quickly achieve an unsurpassed, truly complete enlightenment, manifest complete buddhahood.

"Maitreya, furthermore, if a bodhisatva has six dharmas, he will abandon all bad migrations and not fall into the hands of degrading companions, and will quickly achieve an unsurpassed, truly complete enlightenment, manifest complete buddhahood. 'What are the six?' They are: being free from desire, being free from anger, being free from stupidity, replying to questions immediately with an appropriate answer, being not difficult to approach, and be conducting oneself within emptiness. Maitreya, if a bodhisatva has those six dharmas, he will abandon all bad migrations and not fall into the hands of degrading companions, and will quickly achieve an unsurpassed, truly complete enlightenment, manifest complete buddhahood.

"Maitreya, furthermore, if a bodhisatva has seven dharmas, he will abandon all bad migrations and not fall into the hands of degrading companions, and will quickly achieve an unsurpassed, truly complete enlightenment, manifest complete buddhahood. 'What are the seven?' They are: being skilled in mindfulness, being skilled in the dharma, having undertaken perseverance, having attained joy, having attained thorough processing[35], being skilled in

---

[34] "Not seeking the confusion of others" means to be working on oneself using one's own intelligence rather than seeking answers to the unsatisfactoriness of saṃsāric existence by looking outside oneself and following other people's confused ideas about life.

[35] "Thorough processing" is the final outcome of the perfect develop-
(continued...)

concentration and being skilled in utmost discernment using prajñā[36]. Maitreya, if a bodhisatva has those seven dharmas, he will abandon all bad migrations and not fall into the hands of degrading companions, and will quickly achieve an unsurpassed, truly complete enlightenment, manifest complete buddhahood.

"Maitreya, furthermore, if a bodhisatva has eight dharmas, he will abandon all bad migrations and not fall into the hands of degrading companions, and will quickly achieve an unsurpassed, truly complete enlightenment, manifest complete buddhahood. 'What are the eight?' They are[37]: to have right view, to have right thought, to have right speech, to have right extremes of action[38], to have right livelihood, to have right effort, to have right mindfulness, and to have right concentration. Maitreya, if a bodhisatva has those eight dharmas, he will abandon all bad migrations and not fall into the hands of degrading companions, and will quickly achieve an unsurpassed, truly complete enlightenment, manifest complete buddhahood.

---

[35](...continued)
ment of calm-abiding or shamatha. It includes bliss of body and mind, lightness of body and mind, utter workability of mind, the ability to fly, and many other features.

[36] In general, one discerns what is from what is not using prajñā—that is the function of prajñā. When the Buddha taught the path to enlightenment, he pointed out that one needs one-pointedness of mind as a basis followed by an unrelenting examination of phenomena and oneself using prajñā so that all phenomena without exception and oneself as well are known to be empty. In other words, the use of the word "utter" has meaning in terms of how the Buddha taught the path.

[37] The eightfold path of the noble ones, which he will now enumerate.

[38] The "extremes of action" are good and bad karmic actions. One has to know which is which and then practise right action accordingly. Although this has usually been translated simply as "right action", that misses some of what the Buddha actually said.

"Maitreya, furthermore, if a bodhisatva has nine dharmas, he will abandon all bad migrations and not fall into the hands of degrading companions, and will quickly achieve an unsurpassed, truly complete enlightenment, manifest complete buddhahood. 'What are the nine?' They are as follows[39]. Maitreya, in regard to this a bodhisatva has accomplished and is abiding in the first absorption which is isolated from desirables and isolated from the evil actions of the non-virtuous dharmas, and which has with it examination, analysis, and joy and bliss born from the isolation[40]. He has accomplished and is abiding in the second absorption, in which, being divorced from examination and analysis[41] and inwardly having utmost lucidity, the stream of mind has been integrated into a whole, so there is no examination, there is no analysis, and it has with it joy and bliss born from concentration. He has accomplished and is abiding in the third absorption when he has abandoned the desire for joy, so there is abiding in equanimity, and it has with it mindfulness and alertness, and while bodily bliss is experienced, it is without joy in what the noble ones have called "mindful equanimity abiding in bliss". He has accomplished and is abiding in the fourth absorption in which bliss also has been abandoned and, since suffering also has previously already been abandoned and bliss of

---

[39] The nine are: to have accomplished and be abiding in: the four absorptions (Skt. dhyāna) of the formless realm; the four āyatanas of the formless realm; and the non-analytical cessation. The Buddha explains them in that order, with full information how each one leads to the next stage. The presentation of each one is very brief; more information on them is available in other texts.

[40] Tib. dben pa. Isolation means "to be completely removed from" or "to have completely removed oneself from". For example, to abide in the first absorption, one has to have completely removed oneself from the phenomena of and the coarse non-virtuous actions associated with the desire realm, as mentioned here.

[41] Examination and analysis are two functions of coarse dualistic mind. They are eliminated by the development of the absorptions.

mind and non-bliss of mind also have subsided, there is neither bliss nor is there suffering, just completely pure equanimity and mindfulness. He has accomplished and is abiding in the āyatana of infinite space in which the perceptions of form have been truly transcended in every way, so the perceptions of tangibility have subsided and there is no mental involvement with the variety of perceptions because of which one thinks, 'There is infinite space'. He has accomplished and is abiding in the āyatana of infinite consciousness in which the āyatana of infinite space has been truly transcended in every way, so one thinks, 'There is infinite consciousness'. He has accomplished and is abiding in the āyatana of nothing at all in which the āyatana of infinite consciousness has been fully transcended in every way, so one thinks, 'There is nothing at all'. He has accomplished and is abiding in the āyatana of neither absence of perception nor non-absence of perception in which the āyatana of nothing at all has been truly transcended in every way. Having truly transcended in every way the āyatana of neither absence of perception nor non-absence of perception, he has accomplished then abides in the cessation of perception and feeling. Maitreya, if a bodhisatva has those nine dharmas, he will abandon all bad migrations and not fall into the hands of degrading companions and will quickly achieve an unsurpassed, truly complete enlightenment, manifest complete buddhahood.

Maitreya, furthermore, if a bodhisatva has ten dharmas, he will abandon all bad migrations and not fall into the hands of degrading companions, and will quickly achieve an unsurpassed, truly complete enlightenment, manifest complete buddhahood. 'What are the ten?' They are: to have the vajra-like concentration[42]; to have the concentration in which one visibly strives at the topics and non-

[42] This is one of several important absorptions that the Buddha taught for bodhisatvas.

topics[43]; to have the concentration in which one proceeds via method; to have the concentration which completely illuminates; to have the concentration of total illumination; to have the concentration that makes visibility everywhere; to have the concentration of the precious moon; to have the concentration of the moon lamp; to have the concentration of being without afflictions; and to have the concentration of the army's ornament atop the king's standard[44]. Maitreya, if a bodhisatva has those ten dharmas, he will abandon all bad migrations and not fall into the hands of degrading companions, and will quickly achieve an unsurpassed, truly complete enlightenment, manifest complete buddhahood.

Then the bodhisatva mahāsattva Maitreya, being appeased and gratified, rejoiced; his utter joy gave rise to joy and mental happiness, so he rose from his seat and, having draped his outer robe over one shoulder, knelt down on his right knee, then, bowing with joined palms in the direction of the bhagavan, extolled the bhagavan with these fitting verses:

> You who performed giving up till now,
> Have given up your beautiful son, food and drink,

---

[43] Topics and non-topics are those things which have become topics for discussion and not. Things which have become topics for discussion are, for example, the doing of bad karmic actions because the Buddha has to explain to his followers why the action is faulty, what should be done to purify it, and so on. Non-topics are those things which require no further discussion on the Buddha's part. A thorough treatment of topics and non-topics is given in the book *The Six Topics that All Buddhists Learn* by Tony Duff, published by Padma Karpo Translation Committee, 2012, ISBN: 978-9937-572-13-2.

[44] In ancient India and elsewhere, a king would go into battle with someone carrying the king's standard at the head of the troops. In ancient India, the insignia of his armed force was an ornament at the top of the standard.

And even your head and eyes;
The Buddha has gone to the other shore of total
generosity[45].

Like a yak and its tail, for a long time[46]
You have kept uncorrupted discipline.
In terms of discipline you are incomparable;
The Buddha has gone to the other shore of good
discipline.

Having developed the strength of patience,
You endure the mistaken doings of the childish[47];
Possessing all the strengths of patience,
The Buddha has gone to the other shore of good
patience.

Having developed the strength of perseverance,
You have gained the unsurpassed peace[48];
Possessing strength due to the strength of perseverance,
The Buddha has gone to the other shore of good
perseverance.

---

45 Gone to the other shore is the literal translation of pāramitā, so this is saying that the Buddha has totally achieved the pāramitā of generosity. The same idea applies to the subsequent verses.

46 The Tibetan yak is famous for protecting its magnificent tail to the utmost. It is used as an example of how one's vowed disciplines should be guarded.

47 The childish are the confused beings in saṃsāra who have yet to mature and develop spiritual knowledge.

48 … of enlightenment …

Having burnt away all evil deeds,
The great being who is a guide cherished absorption[49];
Possessing strength due to the strength of absorption,
The Buddha has gone to the other shore of good
absorption.

Those dharmas are empty of nature[50],
Not being something born by way of an entity;
Having reached the other shore by prajñā,
The Buddha has gone to the other shore of good prajñā.

One of great knowing, at the foot of the bodhi-tree,
You tamed māra together with his regiments[51],
And gained the most excellent goal;
The Buddha has defeated the bad māra hordes.

The great being did in Vāranāsi
Utterly turn the wheel of dharma,
Scaring the bad tīrthika groups;
The Buddha has defeated the groups with tīrthika ways.[52]

---

[49] Skt. dhyāna, Tib. bsam gtan.

[50] "Those dharmas" refers to the previous five pāramitā, all of which must be known to be empty by being conjoined with prajñā pāramitā in order to be the true forms of pāramitā.

[51] The four regiments of māra's army which attacked the Buddha in his final approach to enlightenment.

[52] "Tīrthikas" is a kindly way of referring to the followers of other spiritual systems. Rather than saying that they are, for example, non-Buddhists and imply with it that they have no spiritual path at all, this term refers to someone who has made a start on a spiritual path other than the Buddha's path, so, even if their path is not a true path, they are at the brink of being on the true path to enlightenment.

You of unsurpassed great prajñā
That has no match anywhere
Teach the precious dharma;
The Buddha-Guide is the maker of light.

No one compares to you in generosity,
Discipline, patience, and perseverance;
Having gone to the other shore of them all,
The Buddha is by many good qualities raised aloft.

Then the bodhisatva mahāsattva Maitreya, having extolled the bhagavan with those fitting verses, sat down to one side. Then the Vitality-filled Ānanda supplicated the bhagavan in these words:

"Bhadanta[53] bhagavan, that this bodhisatva mahāsattva Maitreya is such that he has perfect knowledgeability, such that he teaches dharma using words of precise ascertainment, such that he teaches dharma using apt words and letters, such that he teaches dharma using words of the profound, such that he teaches dharma using well-related words, and such that he teaches the dharma using words of recollection, is indeed wonderful!"[54]

---

[53] Bhadanta is the common term used in the Buddhist tradition when a layman addresses a monk. It comes to mean "virtuous one".

[54] "Words of precise ascertainment" means nouns, adjectives, and so on which are the exact ones needed when identifying something; "apt words and letters" means that words and letters in general which are suited to the needs of the explanation being given; "words of the profound" are not common words but words used specifically to explain the profound; "well-related words" are words which have been correctly linked to each other using the correct grammatical parts of speech such as appropriate conjunctions, and so on, and done so while observing all changes of morphology that are required with their application; and "words of recollection" are phrasings and the like which make it easy for the listener to recollect what has been said for later contemplation.

The bhagavan instructed:

"Ānanda, it is so! Just as you have said, that the bodhisatva Maitreya has perfect knowledgeability and that he teaches the dharma using words of exacting ascertainment down to teaches the dharma using words of recollection is wonderful!

"Ānanda, now is not the only time that the bodhisatva Maitreya has praised me with fitting verses. Why is that? Ānanda, in the events of the past, there was a point in time a full ten countless kalpas[55] ago when the tathāgata, arhat, truly complete buddha, possessor of knowledge and its feet, the sugata, knower of the world, unsurpassed driver who tames beings, and teacher of gods and men, the buddha bhagavan[56] called Ālokavikrīditābhijñāna appeared in the world. At that time, there was a brahman boy called Bhadrau, who was of finer form, handsome, lovely to behold, and of good colour and excellent build. He went off to a park and, having gone as far as the village, saw the tathāgata, arhat, truly complete buddha Ālokavikrīditābhijñāna—handsome; faith-inspiring; senses pacified; mind pacified; having the excellences of being tamed and calmly abiding; whose faculties were protected; who was like an elephant with his senses tamed; their being clearly evident like a lake limpid and free of contamination, his body was nicely adorned with the thirty-two marks of a great being and his body was fully decorated

---

[55] Skt. kalpa. "Kalpa" is the general term for a long period of time. Indian culture defined many degrees of kalpa, going from thousands of years up to cosmic ages.

[56] The string of terms from "tathāgata" down to the "buddha bhagavan" is a string of nine epithets of a buddha. The string was taught by Śhākyamuni Buddha under the name "Recollection of the Buddha". A very thorough presentation of this recollection, with extensive explanations of each of the terms in it can be found in the book *Unending Auspiciousness, the Sutra of the Recollection of the Noble Three Jewels*; see note 1.

with the eighty excellent insignia, fully bloomed like the fully-blossomed flower of the king Sāla tree, and strongly projecting, like the king of mountains Sumeru[57]; his face like the disc of the moon was peaceful; like the disc of the sun he was dazzling, striking, conspicuous, and his body well-proportioned like a Nyagrodha tree[58] blazed with light, blazed with great glory. And on seeing him, his mind turned to having faith in the bhagavan. Due to his mind having turned to faith, he thought this, 'Oh how good! This body of the tathāgata which is fully decorated and is colourful and brilliant, and which is blazing with glory and the marks and is dazzling, striking, and conspicuous is wonderful!' Having thought that, the brahman boy Bhadrau said, 'Oh how good! May I also have a body like this in a future time! May I become blazing like this with colour, brilliance, glory, and the marks and become dazzling, striking, and conspicuous like this!' Having made that prayer in those words, he lay down on the ground and thought, 'If I shall in a future time come to have a body of this sort, blazing like this with colour, brilliance, glory, and the marks and become dazzling, striking, and conspicuous like this, may the foot of the tathāgata touch my body!'

"Ānanda, then that tathāgata, arhat, truly complete buddha Ālokavikrīditābhijñāna, knowing the brahman boy Bhadrau's special intention, went to where the brahman boy Bhadrau was and touched the brahman boy Bhadrau with his foot. As soon as that tathāgata, arhat, truly complete buddha Ālokavikrīditābhijñāna touched the

---

[57] "Fully blossomed" and "visibly projecting" are the way that the Buddha described the appearance of the thirty-two marks and eighty insignia.

[58] A Nyagrodha tree is a large tree with a visually perfect symmetry. It is used as an example of a buddha's body with its perfect symmetry.

brahman boy Bhadrau with his foot, at that very time, the boy attained forbearance with respect to the unborn dharma[59].

"Ānanda, then the tathāgata Ālokavikrīditābhijñāna, looking back towards the monks, instructed them, saying, 'Monks, none of you should step on the brahman boy Bhadrau's body with your feet! Why? It is because this bodhisatva mahāsattva has attained forbearance with respect to the unborn dharma. Then, right at that point, the brahman boy Bhadrau attained the knowledges which come as extra-perceptions—the god's eye, the god's ear, the knowing of the mind of others, and the knowledge that makes evident the recollection of past circumstances. He also actually accomplished miraculous powers. He, in the presence of the tathāgata Ālokavikrīditābhijñāna, also praised him openly with the following, fitting verses:

> Though one may travel around the cardinal and
> intermediate directions and search,
> No-one in the worlds who is a ruler amongst men like
> you will be found.
> Amongst all migrators[60], the complete buddha is
> evidently superior;
> Self-arising universal guide[61], to you I prostrate!
>
> Like for example, the sun shining up in space,
> Its light brightening all these worlds in the world realms
> In all the cardinal and intermediate directions;

---

[59] "Attained forbearance with respect to the unborn dharma" means that he gained acceptance of the fact that all phenomena are unborn, that is empty of a nature.

[60] For migrator, see the glossary.

[61] "Universal guide" is one of the many epithets of a Buddha. Buddhas are guides. The universal guide is the supreme nirmāṇakāya type of Buddha, like Śhākyamuni Buddha.

Buddha, brilliant beam of good qualities, to you I
prostrate!

Just as a lion roaring in the jungle will subdue
With its magnificence all the major packs of jackals,
So the holy one among men who has great power also
Will subdue with his magnificence all the many having
tīrthika ways.

Tathāgata, the white urna[62] at the point between your
eyebrows,
Which glitters with infinite brilliance like grains of silver
or flakes of snow,
Has illuminated all these worlds;
In all worlds, you Buddha are equal to being unequalled.

Leader of beings you have on your feet a divine wheel,
Clear and beautiful with a full thousand spokes and
encircling rim;
These make these lands with their mountains and forests
Utterly move; the Capable One is a person without
equivalent[63]!

You have discarded all of the mass of afflictions to be cast
off,
And utterly gained the noble path of certain deliverance;
Possessing all riches and abounding in good qualities,

---

[62] The urna is a small hair at the point between the eyebrows of a buddha. It is one of the thirty-two major marks. Miraculous events emanate from it, such as the all-illuminating light rays of this verse.

[63] For Capable One, see the glossary.

You display the riches of the noble ones[64] in accordance
with intentions[65].

You are analogous to the earth and have become a place
of generosity without analogy,
Have gained possession of all good qualities, and have
completely pure discipline;
Just as a hand is unhindered, unattached in space,
You have no attachment or anger in the worlds.

With patience that has reached the endpoint, all facts and
phenomena[66]
Have been known as having no essence, as sustainable,
and as accumulated[67];
For all the migrators of becoming[68] whoever they are,
The sentient beings with bloated mind do not gain
vitality and things.[69]

Knowing their constituents, conducts, applications, and
intentions[70],

---

[64] The riches of the noble ones are the many excellent qualities of the noble ones.

[65] Intentions here means the specific thoughts and wishes of sentient beings who the Buddha will tame.

[66] "Facts" here means phenomena as they are known by mind.

[67] "Sustainable" here means that phenomena are things which come into being because of the force of karma.

[68] For becoming, see the glossary.

[69] For bloated, see note 32. Because they do not follow the training in virtue that leads to enlightenment, they do not have vitality. Because they do not follow virtuous ways, they do not gain what they want.

[70] This is a standard listing of what a buddha knows of sentient beings
(continued...)

You have become a lamp that produces marvels and
complete discernment;

Having come to look on migrators driven by the great
river,[71]
From the past till now you acted to develop the power of
a steady force of perseverance.

Having abandoned birth and possessing a mind pacified
of the afflictions,
You, vast-minded one have brought forth the end of
birth, aging, and death;
Moving about without defilement, as would happen in
the depths of space,
You move in the three worlds not shrouded by the things
of the world.[72]

Great Soul[73], by your prajñā you do the act of
illuminating;
All darkness—pitch-black darkness—is completely
dispelled.

---

[70](...continued)
and, because of knowing it, is able to teach them dharma in a way that is exactly tailored to their needs. Constituents are the eighteen dhātus, conducts is their way of doing things, applications is what they apply themselves to in order to achieve their goals, and intentions is their thoughts and wishes about how they should proceed.

[71] … of saṃsāra …

[72] Defilements of saṃsāric mind are hindrances. Buddha does not have defilements in his mind, so he moves around unhindered, as one would move around in space …

[73] Skt. mahātma. For example, as in Mahatma Gandhi but here referring to the Buddha.

You alleviate the perspiration of desire and remove the darkness
Of the various stains of anger and delusion—to you I prostrate!

"Ānanda, since then, the brahman boy Bhadrau's miraculous powers and extra-perceptions have not diminished. Ānanda, should you have concern or be of two minds or entertain doubts in which you think, 'The one who, at that point, at that time, was the brahman boy called 'Bhadrau' is someone else', then do not view it that way! Why is that? Because it was this very bodhisatva mahāsattva Maitreya who at that point, at that time, was born as the brahman boy called 'Bhadrau'; he was the one who openly extolled the tathāgata, arhat, truly complete buddha Ālokavikrīditābhijñāna with these verses."

He instructed with those words and the Vitality-filled Ānanda supplicated the bhagavan in these words:

"Bhagavan, if it were the case that this bodhisatva mahāsattva Maitreya indeed attained forbearance with respect to the unborn dharma a long time ago, then on what account did he not quickly achieve unsurpassed, truly complete enlightenment, manifest complete buddhahood?"

He supplicated in those words and the bhagavan instructed the Vitality-filled Ānanda in these words:

"Ānanda, the bodhisatvas' arrangements and ownerships are twofold. What are the two? They are arrangement of sentient beings and ownership of sentient beings, and arrangement of a field and ownership of a field. If these are the two, then the bodhisatva mahāsattva Maitreya, when performing the bodhisatva's activities in the past, had totally purified the arrangement of a field and had owned the ownership of a field. Ānanda, when I was performing the bodhisatva's activities in the past, I had totally purified the arrangement of sentient beings and had owned ownership of sentient beings, and I also had totally purified the arrangement of a field and had owned the ownership of a field.

"Ānanda, I know through extra-perceptions that it was not until forty-two kalpas after the bodhisatva mahāsattva Maitreya had entered the authentic that I first aroused the mind for unsurpassed, truly complete enlightenment. Ānanda, ninety-four kalpas after this good kalpa has passed it will be suitable for him to attain unsurpassed, truly complete enlightenment, manifest complete buddhahood. Ānanda, it is because I made blazing perseverance that I quickly achieved unsurpassed, truly complete enlightenment, manifest complete buddhahood. Ānanda, I, through tremendous perseverance, quickly achieved unsurpassed, truly complete enlightenment, manifest complete buddhahood. Ānanda, it is through these ten dharmas that I quickly achieved unsurpassed, truly complete enlightenment, manifest complete buddhahood. 'What are those ten?' I completely stopped caring about loss of any and all possessions; completely stopped caring about loss of goods; completely stopped caring about loss of son; completely stopped caring about loss of head; completely stopped caring about loss of eyes; completely stopped caring about loss of dominion over a kingdom; completely stopped caring about loss of possessions; completely stopped caring about loss of blood; completely stopped caring about loss of bone and marrow; and completely stopped caring about loss of limbs. Through that, I quickly achieved unsurpassed, truly complete enlightenment, manifest complete buddhahood.

"Ānanda, furthermore, I quickly achieved unsurpassed, truly complete enlightenment, manifest complete buddhahood by a set of ten dharmas. What are the ten? Ānanda, I quickly achieved unsurpassed, truly complete enlightenment, manifest complete buddhahood by abiding in the dharma of the good quality of discipline. Ānanda, I quickly achieved unsurpassed, truly complete enlightenment, manifest complete buddhahood by having strength of patience. Ānanda, I quickly achieved unsurpassed, truly complete enlightenment, manifest complete buddhahood by undertaking blazing perseverance. Ānanda, I quickly achieved unsurpassed, truly complete enlightenment, manifest complete buddhahood by abiding in the good quality of absorption. Ānanda, I quickly achieved unsurpassed, truly complete enlightenment, manifest complete buddhahood by abiding in the Prajñāpāramitā. Ānanda, I quickly achieved unsurpassed, truly complete enlightenment, manifest complete buddhahood by not rejecting any sentient being at all. Ānanda, I quickly achieved unsurpassed, truly complete enlightenment, manifest complete buddhahood by staying within skilful means. Ānanda, I quickly achieved unsurpassed, truly complete enlightenment, manifest complete buddhahood by having an even mind towards all sentient beings. Ānanda, I quickly achieved unsurpassed, truly complete enlightenment, manifest complete buddhahood by realizing the dharma of emptiness. Ānanda, I quickly achieved unsurpassed, truly complete enlightenment, manifest complete buddhahood by realizing the dharmas of signlessness and wishlessness[74]. Ānanda, it is by those ten dharmas that I quickly achieved unsurpassed, truly complete enlightenment, manifest complete buddhahood.

"Ānanda, if you were to know the sorts of raw, intense pain I went through to achieve unsurpassed, truly complete enlightenment, manifest complete buddhahood, you could not believe it. How could that be? Ānanda, in the events of the past there was a point in time when there was a young prince called 'Giver of All Wealth' who was of finer form, handsome, lovely to behold, of good colour and excellent build, great royal wealth and great royal power. He went off to a park and, having gone as far as the village, saw a man

---

[74] The three doors of emancipation taught in the Prajñāpāramitā sūtras as a summary of the bodhisatva's approach to enlightenment are: emptiness, signlessness, and wishlessness.

who was afflicted by and suffering from harm, who had been stricken with a severe disease. On seeing the man, he felt compassion, so he went over to him and asked, 'Hey! Man, why are you suffering?' He said, 'Divine One, I am stricken by an llness.' The prince asked him, 'Hey! Man, what would alleviate your disease? What could I give you?' He said, 'If I could drink as much of the blood from the Divine One's body as it would take to satisfy me, then my disease would be alleviated.' Ānanda, then the young prince called Giver of All Wealth took a sharp weapon and, piercing his own body, let his blood run out, then gave it to that man to drink. Ānanda, as soon as the man drank it, the disease of the man was cured. Ānanda, although the young prince Giver of All Wealth pierced his own body and let all his blood run out, he had not a single mind of regret. Ānanda, should you have concern or be of two minds or entertain doubts in which you think, 'The one who, at that point, at that time, had become the young prince Giver of All Wealth is someone else', then do not view it that way! Why is that? It was I who, at that point, at that time, had become the young prince called 'Giver of All Wealth'. Ānanda, the mass of water in the four great oceans is measurable, but the blood I have given to sentient beings during the quest for this unsurpassed, truly complete enlightenment is immeasurable.

"Ānanda, in the events of the past there was a point in time when there was a young prince called 'Flower' who was of finer form, handsome, lovely to behold, of good colour and excellent build, great royal wealth and great royal power. He went off to a place where there was a park and, having gone as far as the village, saw a man who was afflicted by and suffering from the harm of being stricken by a very severe form of the disease oedema. On seeing the man, he felt compassion, so he went over to him and asked, 'Hey! Man, what would alleviate this disease of yours? What could I give you?' He said, 'If I could get as much of the marrow from the Divine One's body as it would take to satisfy me, then my disease would be alleviated.' Then that young prince Flower being appeased and gratified rejoiced, and his utter joy gave rise to bliss and mental bliss, so he beat his own body, extracted the marrow, then spread it on that man's body. Ānanda, as soon as he spread it, the disease of the man was cured. Ānanda, although the young prince Flower beat his own body and let the marrow run out, he had no regret in his mind. Ānanda, should you have concern or be of two minds or entertain doubts in which you think, 'The one who, at that point, at that time, had become the young prince called 'Flower' is someone else', then do not view it that way! Why is that? It was I who, at that point, at that time, had become the young prince called 'Flower'. Ānanda, the mass of water in the four great oceans is measurable, but the marrow I have given to sentient beings during the quest for this unsurpassed, truly complete enlightenment is immeasurable.

"Ānanda, in the events of the past, there was a point in time when there was a king called 'Moonlight' who was of finer form, handsome, lovely to behold, of good colour and excellent build, great royal wealth and great royal power. He went off to a park and, having gone as far as the village, saw a blind man without eyes, a poor, destitute man who begged to get by. On seeing the man, he felt compassion. Then that man went over to King Moonlight and having arrived before him said, 'Divine One, you are happy. You are glad. I am suffering. I am blind. I have no eyes. I am poor. I am destitute. I am a beggar. I am without a guardian.' Then the king Moonlight saw the man again and heard his words too, and wept. While shedding tears, he said this to him, 'Hey! Man, what do you need? Shall I give you food, drink, a mount, ornaments, gold, gems, pearls, or various precious things? Or, tell me what you need!' The man said, 'If you could give me your eyes, I would ask you for your eyes.' Ānanda, then King Moonlight took out his own eyes and gave them to the man. Ānanda, although King Moonlight took out his own eyes and gave them to that man, he had no regret in his mind. Ānanda, should you have concern or be of two minds or entertain doubts in which you think, 'The one who, at that point, at that time, had become the young prince called 'Moonlight' is someone else', then do not view it that way! Why is that? It was I who, at that point, at that time, had become the king called 'Moonlight'. Ānanda, the king of mountains Sumeru is measurable, but the eyes I have given to sentient beings during the quest for this unsurpassed, truly complete enlightenment are much greater, are immeasurable.

"Ānanda! When the bodhisatva mahāsattva Maitreya previously was performing the bodhisatva's activities, he genuinely accomplished unsurpassed, truly complete enlightenment using an easy vehicle, using an easy entry, using an easy path. Ānanda, when the bodhisatva mahāsattva Maitreya previously was performing the bodhisatva's activities, he did not give up his hands, did not give up his legs, did not give up his marrow, did not give up the loss of his wife, did not give up the loss of his son, did not give up the loss of his villages, his towns, his cities, his lands, his country, or his royal palace with retinue. Ānanda, when the bodhisatva mahāsattva Maitreya previously was performing the bodhisatva's activities, by fully concerning himself with means, he used an easy vehicle, easy entrance, and easy path, through which he truly accomplished unsurpassed, truly complete enlightenment."

Then the Vitality-filled Ānanda supplicated the bhagavan in these words:

"Bhagavan, the bodhisatva mahāsattva Maitreya based himself in skilful means to truly accomplish unsurpassed, truly complete enlightenment, and what indeed was that skilful means?"

He supplicated with those words and the bhagavan instructed the Vitality-filled Ānanda in these words:

"Ānanda, in regard to this, previously, when the bodhisatva mahāsattva Maitreya was performing the bodhisatva's activities, he would three times in the day and three times at night drape his upper robe over one shoulder, kneel down on his right knee, join his palms, and making all the buddhas actually present, say these words[75]:

I prostrate to all the buddhas.
I prostrate to the bodhisatvas,
The ṛiṣhis having the god's eye,
And to the śhrāvakas as well.

I prostrate to the enlightenment mind which
Turns away all of the bad migrations and
Utterly shows the path to the higher strata,
And leads to absence of old age and death.

I have fallen under the control of mind[76]
And therefore have done evil deeds;
Going into the presence of the buddhas,
I lay aside all the ones I have done.

The accumulation of merit I have created
By any of the three types of karma,
Is the seed of my own all-knowing,
May it become my unending enlightenment.

Every offering to the buddhas made
In the fields of the ten directions
Is known by the buddhas who rejoice,
And I rejoice in that.

I will lay aside every evil.
I will rejoice in all merits.

---

[75] The following verses are what is called "Maitreya's Prayer". A full commentary to the meaning is provided in a later chapter.

[76] He is saying that he has fallen under the control of dualistic, that is, saṃsāric mind and because of that has done evil deeds. If he had not fallen under the control of dualistic mind, he would not have done evil deeds.

I prostrate to all buddhas.
May I obtain supreme wisdom.

I urge the bodhisatvas in the ten directions
Who are dwelling on the ten levels
To go to supreme enlightenment
By becoming buddhas.

Having subdued the māras with their regiments
And reached finest enlightenment, buddhahood,
In order to provide medicine for all living creatures
Please will you turn the wheel of dharma.

Please use the sound of the great drum of dharma
To end the unsatisfactoriness of sentient beings.
Please stay for unthinkable tens of millions of aeons
Doing the deed of teaching dharma.

Sunk in the mire of desire and
Bound tight by the rope of becoming,
I am totally bound by fetters.
You the best of bipeds, please look on me!

Oh buddhas, please do not berate us
Who have developed stains of mind;
With your minds of love for sentient beings
Please release us from the ocean of becoming.

Completed buddhas who are present and
Those who have passed and not yet come
May I train following you and
Course in the conduct of enlightenment.

May I complete the six pāramitās and then
Emancipate the six migrator sentient beings.
May I manifest the six extra-perceptions
Then contact unsurpassed enlightenment.

May I realize unproduced, unarisen,
Not with nature, not with dwelling,
Not with knowing superficies, not with things,
Empty phenomena.

May I realize like the buddhas, the great ṛiṣhis,
That phenomena are not with sentient being,
Not with life, not with a person,
Not with living being, not with a self.

Not remaining at all in the things
Of grasped I and grasped mine,
In order to provide ease for all sentient beings,
Without avarice may I perform generosity.

By not treating things as existent things
May my possessions arise spontaneously.
Through the total collapse of all things may I
Complete the pāramitā of generosity.

With rules of discipline free of fault and
Discipline which has complete purity,
Through discipline without conceit may I
Complete the pāramitā of discipline.

Like the elements of earth, water,
Fire and air are without aggression,
So too through patience without aggression may I
Complete the pāramitā of patience.

Through the perseverance of perseverance undertaken,
The steady and delighted applications, without laziness
And with body and mind having force may I
Complete the pāramitā of perseverance.

Through the Illusion-Like Concentration,
Going Like A Hero Concentration, and

Vajra-Like Concentration may I
Complete the pāramitā of absorption.

Through the three doors of complete emancipation,
And equality of the three times and also
Three knowledges seeing in direct perception, may I
Complete the pāramitā of prajñā.

Through what all the buddhas have commended, and
Light and blazing brilliance, and
The perseverance of a bodhisatva may I
Complete my intentions.

Through doing that sort of conduct
And through renowned loving kindness
May I complete the six pāramitās
Then utterly abide on the tenth level.

"Ānanda, as for what skilful means the bodhisatva mahāsattva Maitreya based himself in so that by the skilful means of using an easy vehicle, easy entrance, and easy path he accomplished unsurpassed, truly complete enlightenment, that was it.

Ānanda, when the bodhisatva mahāsattva Maitreya previously was performing the bodhisatva's activities, sentient beings had little desire, little aggression, little delusion, and had the path of the ten virtuous actions. Later, when I achieved unsurpassed, truly complete enlightenment, manifest complete buddhahood, the complete purification of a field in that way was something I could only wish for[77]. Ānanda, the time and circumstance for such will arise. There will be a point in time when sentient beings appear who have little desire, little aggression, little stupidity, and who have the path of

---

[77] The meaning here is that it such a thing was impossible at that time so one could only wish for such a thing, saying, "How nice it would be if that could happen!"

the ten virtuous actions, and when that has happened, the bodhisatva mahāsattva Maitreya will, because of his prayer, achieve unsurpassed, truly complete enlightenment, manifest complete buddhahood.

"Ānanda, when I previously was performing the bodhisatva's activities, a time of a world having the five dregs,[78] sentient beings had a large amount of desire, a large amount of aggression, a large amount of delusion; their desires had started up, their aggression had started up, their delusion had started up; they were attached and clung to what is not dharma, were overwhelmed by the anxiety of attachment, held to wrong dharma; they were hostile to their fathers, hostile to their mothers, hostile to their relatives, hostile to their brothers and sisters, hostile to their spouses, hostile to their kinsmen, hostile to the noble ones, hostile to the preceptors and to the masters, hostile to themselves, and hostile to other people; they were impure men, savages of men, men with no education at all. For me in the midst of such people to achieve unsurpassed, truly complete enlightenment, manifest complete buddhahood through the accomplishment in that way of such a prayer is something that one could only wish for, saying, 'How nice it would be if …'

"Living in such dreadful times, Ānanda, I have put great compassion to the fore. If, with that great compassion, I had taught the dharma while staying in my village, in my town, in my city, in my land, in my country, or in my royal palace with retinue, I would have been the subject of backbiting and criticism; I would have been talked about in coarse, negative ways that would never be voiced in public. Ānanda, I would have been called a nihilist and I also would have been called an eternalist. They would have discussed how my

---

[78] The five dregs refers to five degraded features of the later times in a human era which started with exceptionally good circumstances. They are: degradation of views, degradation into afflictions, degradation of the lot of sentient beings in general, degradation or shortening of life, and the dregs or bottom end of the era.

retinue was full of desires, and would have talked about 'having great desire'. Even if I stayed in a household, I would have had dirt thrown at me, I would have been give food mixed with poison, and they would even have tried their best to put me on a pyre[79]. It is like this: even though I have became a buddha, they would have denigrated me, saying that I had sexual relations, with words like, 'He is a buddha but he is with a beautiful woman'. Ānanda, I have put great compassion to the fore, and with great compassion I now teach dharma to them, sentient beings who are like that."

He instructed saying those words and the Vitality-filled Ānanda supplicated the bhagavan in these words:

"Bhagavan, the act of teaching dharma to them, sentient beings who are like that, is that the tathāgata, arhat, truly complete buddha indeed tames the untamed, carries the great burden, and does what is difficult!"

He supplicated with those words and the bhagavan instructed the Vitality-filled Ānanda in these words:

"Ānanda, it is like that. As with what you said Ānanda, so a tathāgata, arhat, truly complete buddha tames the untamed, carries the great burden, and, those who have all of the virtuous dharmas teaching the dharma to sentient beings like that is their doing of what is difficult. Why is that? It is because they fully adhere to great compassion."

He instructed in those words and the Vitality-filled Ānanda supplicated the bhagavan in these words:

---

[79] In ancient India, it was a cultural norm to burn undesirable elements of society on a blazing pyre.

"Bhagavan, this enumeration of dharma is beautiful, and my hearing this enumeration of dharma and hearing it in the place of the foremost among men, the bhagavan, makes 'my hair stand on end' as is said; it is indeed wondrous! Bhagavan, what should be the title of this enumeration of dharma? How should it be retained?"

The bhagavan instructed:

"Ānanda, for that, retain this enumeration of dharma as 'A Truly Noble Prayer of the Past'! Or retain it as 'The True Emergence of a Tathāgata'! Or retain it as 'The Emergence of the Intention of Enlightenment'! Or retain it as 'Petitioned by Maitreya'!"

The bhagavan instructed with those words then the Vitality-filled Ānanda, the bodhisatva Maitreya, those five-hundred monks, and all of their retinue, and the world with its gods and men, asuras, and gandharvas[80] rejoiced and openly praised what the bhagavan had said.

Of the hundred thousand chapters of dharma enumerations of the *Noble One The Great Stack of Jewels*, this is the end of the forty-first chapter called "The Chapter Petitioned by Maitreya".

———— ◆◆◆ ————

[80] This is a standard listing of the beings who were in the audience, listening to the Buddha. Gods who could be taught dharma directly were the ones living in the levels above humans in the desire realm and also in the form realm; asuras are gods of the lowest god level of the desire realm who constantly war with the gods of the upper levels in an attempt to be like them; and gandharvas are the equivalent of European fairies, and they too historically took an interest in dharma.

Translated and edited by the Indian preceptors Jinamitra and Surendrabodhi and by the chief editor translator Bande Yeshe De, this has been finalized.

Sutra Two:

The forty-second chapter of The Great Stack of Jewels' dharma enumerations in a hundred thousand chapters:

The Authoritative Statement Concerning Eight Dharmas Petitioned by Noble Maitriya

The forty-second chapter of *The Great Stack of Jewels'* dharma enumerations in a hundred thousand chapters:

The Authoritative Statement Concerning Eight Dharmas Petitioned by Noble Maitreya

Half a bundle.

In Sanskrit: āryamaitriya paripṛhcchā nāma mahāyāna sūtra

In Tibetan: 'phags pa byams pas zhus pa zhes bya ba theg pa chen po'i mdo

In English: The Great Vehicle Sūtra called "Petitioned by Noble Noble Maitreya"

Homage to every buddha and bodhisatva!

I heard these words at one time. The bhagavan was residing on Vulture Peak Mountain in Rājagṛiha, together with a great community of monks consisting of one thousand two hundred and fifty monks and with ten thousand bodhisatvas. Then the bhagavan, surrounded by a retinue of many hundreds of thousands and looking straight ahead, was teaching dharma. At that point, the great bodhisatva called "Maitreya" joined that retinue and became present in it. Then the bodhisatva Maitreya rose from his seat and, having draped his outer robe over one shoulder, knelt down on his right knee. Then, bowing with joined palms in the direction of the bhagavan, he supplicated the bhagavan in these words:

"Were the bhagavan to give me the opportunity to petition him for an authoritative statement, I would indeed ask the one who has become a tathāgata, arhat, truly complete buddha about some matters."

He supplicated in those words and the bhagavan instructed the bodhisatva mahāsattva Maitreya in these words:

"Maitreya, the tathāgata has always given the opportunity to answer questions asked for the purpose of authoritative statement. Maitreya, ask me whatever you wish!"

Then, as the bhagavan had given him the opportunity, the bodhisatva mahāsattva Maitreya supplicated the bhagavan in these words.

"Bhagavan, how many dharmas would a bodhisatva have to have for him to be someone who has the dharma of being irreversible from unsurpassed, truly complete enlightenment and be someone who does not slip back and does not slip back at all[81], and as such to be one who has a special attainment, who has defeated the attacking māras[82], who has when performing the bodhisatva's activities, because of having realized the essential character of all phenomena exactly as it is, the capacity to be in saṃsāra without being wearied

---

[81] "To not slip back" is part of the vocabulary of the Great Vehicle teaching. It is used when discussing the irreversibility of a bodhisatva's progress towards enlightenment. Here, irreversibility not only means not going backwards but also means not reverting into lesser approaches such as those of the śhrāvaka monks.

[82] For māra, see the glossary.

of it at all[83], and who, having become possessed of a mind that remains totally unwearied of it would, moreover, through the wisdom[84] which does not come from another place, quickly attain unsurpassed, truly complete enlightenment, manifest buddhahood?"

He supplicated in those words and the bhagavan instructed the bodhisatva mahāsattva Maitreya in these words:

"Maitreya, you have done well! For having thought to ask a question concerning this meaning to the tathāgata, you also have done well! Therefore, Maitreya, listen well with your fullest attention and retain it in mind, and I will explain it to you!"

He replied, "I will do as the bhagavan asks!" The bodhisatva mahāsattva Maitreya then listened in accord with the bhagavan, and the bhagavan instructed him in these words.

Maitreya, if a bodhisatva mahāsattva possesses eight dharmas, he will be someone who has the dharma of being irreversible from unsurpassed, truly complete enlightenment and be someone who does not slip back and does not slip back at all, and as such will be one who has a special attainment, who has defeated the attacking

---

[83] The bodhisatva undertakes the journey of remaining in saṃsāra for the sake of completing his own path and benefiting others despite the suffering nature of saṃsāra. To be able to do that, he develops a mind which never wearies of the task he has set himself.

[84] For wisdom, see the glossary. Wisdom is something that sentient beings have within and something which they discover by looking into their own being. It is not something that is found on the other side, in things or other sentient beings. The principal quality of wisdom is that it knows everything, knowing each of every one of all phenomena and knowing the actual nature of each of all of those phenomena all at once.

māras, who has when performing the bodhisatva's activities, because of having realized the essential character of all phenomena exactly as it is, the capacity to be in saṃsāra without being wearied of it at all, and who, having become possessed of a mind that remains totally unwearied of it would, moreover, through the wisdom which does not come from another place, quickly attain unsurpassed, truly complete enlightenment, manifest buddhahood."

"What are those eight? They are as follows. Maitreya, for this, the bodhisatva mahāsattva is someone who has perfect intention, perfect application, perfect giving, skill at thorough dedication, perfect loving kindness, perfect compassion, skilful means, and is one who has turned definitely to the Prajñāpāramitā.

"Maitreya, how is a bodhisatva mahāsattva someone of perfect intention? Maitreya, for this, whether a bodhisatva mahāsattva hears the approval or disapproval of buddha, he is definite in his intent for unsurpassed, truly complete enlightenment, whether he hears approval or disapproval of dharma, he is definite in his intent for unsurpassed, truly complete enlightenment, and whether he hears approval or disapproval of the sangha, he is definite in his intent for unsurpassed, truly complete enlightenment. Maitreya, that is how it is with a bodhisatva mahāsattva who has perfect intention.

"Maitreya, how is a bodhisatva mahāsattva someone who has perfect application? Maitreya, for this, a bodhisatva mahāsattva abstains from killing, abstains from taking what is not offered, and from desirous improper sexual conduct, lying, divisive speech, harsh speech, and gossip. Maitreya, that is how it is with a bodhisatva mahāsattva who has perfect application.

"Maitreya, how is a bodhisatva mahāsattva someone who has perfect giving? Maitreya, for this, a bodhisatva mahāsattva becomes generous in many ways, giving clothes, food, bedding, medicine to cure disease, and useful articles to spiritual seekers, brahmans, and the poor and beggars. Maitreya, that is how it is with a bodhisatva mahāsattva who has perfect giving.

"Maitreya, how is a bodhisatva mahāsattva someone who has skill at thorough dedication? Maitreya, for this, a bodhisatva mahāsattva makes an thorough dedication of the roots of virtue actually formed by body, speech and mind, whatever they might be, all of them, to unsurpassed, truly complete enlightenment; Maitreya, that is how it is with a bodhisatva mahāsattva who has skill at thorough dedication.

"Maitreya, how is a bodhisatva mahāsattva someone who has perfect loving kindness? Maitreya, for this, a bodhisatva mahāsattva has bodily actions of loving kindness, has verbal actions of loving kindness, and has mental actions of loving kindness; Maitreya, that is how it is with a bodhisatva mahāsattva who has perfect loving kindness.

"Maitreya, how is a bodhisatva mahāsattva someone who has perfect compassion? Maitreya, for this, a bodhisatva mahāsattva has bodily actions without any harmful intent, has verbal actions without harmful intent, and has mental actions without harmful intent; Maitreya, that is how it is with a bodhisatva mahāsattva who has perfect compassion.

"Maitreya, how is a bodhisatva mahāsattva someone who has skilful means? Maitreya, for this, the bodhisatva mahāsattva is skilled in the meaning of fictional reality, is skilled in the meaning of superfactual reality,[85] and is skilled in both; Maitreya, that is how it is with a bodhisatva mahāsattva who has skilful means.

---

[85] For fictional and superfactual, see the glossary.

"Maitreya, how is a bodhisatva mahāsattva someone who has turned definitely to the Prajñāpāramitā? Maitreya, for this, a bodhisatva mahāsattva trains in the authentic like this:[86]

> Because this exists, this becomes; because this has arisen, this arises. It is like this. By the condition of ignorance, formatives[87] arise. By the condition of formatives, consciousness arises. By the condition of consciousness, name and form arises. By the condition of name and form, the six āyatanas arise. By the condition of the six āyatanas, contact arises. By the condition of contact, feeling arises. By the condition of feeling, craving arises. By the condition of craving, appropriation[88] arises. By the condition of appropriation, becoming arises. By the condition of becoming, birth arises. By the condition of birth, aging and death, and misery, lamentation, suffering, sorrow, and disturbance arise. In that way, this which is only a great mass of suffering, originates.
>
> Because this does not exist, this does not originate, because this ceases, this also ceases. It is like this. If ignorance ceases, formatives cease. If formatives cease, consciousness ceases. If consciousness ceases, name and

---

[86] In what follows, first the Buddha explains the forward order of the twelve links of interdependent origination in the first paragraph and the reverse order of the same in the second paragraph. The forward order is the mode of perpetuating saṃsāra, the reverse order is the mode of ending saṃsāra, which results in nirvāṇa.

[87] Skt. saṃskāra, Tib. 'du byed. This term is usually called "formations", but a formation is the product of that which caused its formation, whereas this term refers to the agent which will cause a formation. The formatives, which are the contents of the fourth of the five aggregates, cause the production of a future set of aggregates for the mindstream involved.

[88] For appropriation, see the glossary.

> form cease. If name and form cease, the six āyatanas cease. If the six āyatanas cease, contact ceases. If contact ceases, feeling ceases. If feeling ceases, craving ceases. If craving ceases, appropriation ceases. If appropriation ceases, becoming ceases. If becoming ceases, birth ceases. If birth ceases, then old age and death, and misery, lamentation, suffering, sorrow, and disturbance cease. In that way, this which is only a great mass of suffering ceases.

Maitreya, that is how it is with a bodhisatva mahāsattva who has turned definitely to the Prajñāpāramitā.

"Maitreya, if a bodhisatva mahāsattva possesses eight dharmas, he will be someone who has the dharma of being irreversible from unsurpassed, truly complete enlightenment and be someone who does not slip back and does not slip back at all, and as such will be one who has a special attainment, who has defeated the attacking māras, who has when performing the bodhisatva's activities, because of having realized the essential character of all phenomena exactly as it is, the capacity to be in saṃsāra without being wearied of it at all, and who, having become possessed of a mind that remains totally unwearied of it would, moreover, through the wisdom which does not come from another place, quickly attain unsurpassed, truly complete enlightenment, manifest buddhahood."

The bhagavan instructed with those words then the bodhisatva mahāsattva Maitreya, those monks, those bodhisatvas, and the world with its gods, men, asuras, and gandharvas rejoiced and openly praised what the bhagavan had said.

Of the hundred-thousand chapters of dharma enumeration of the *Noble One The Great Stack of Jewels*, this is the end of the forty-second chapter called "The Eight Dharmas Petitioned by Maitreya".

Translated and edited by the Indian preceptors Jinamitra and Dānaśhīla and by the chief editor translator Bande Yeshe De, then also modified in accordance with the language revision, this has been finalized.

Maitreya's Prayer

and a

Commentary to it by
All-Knowing Padma Karpo

Maitreya's Prayer

From the forty-first chapter, petitioned by Maitreya, of the Stack of Jewels Sūtra …

I prostrate to all the buddhas.
I prostrate to the bodhisatvas,
The ṛiṣhis having the god's eye,
And to the śhrāvakas as well.

I prostrate to the enlightenment mind which
Turns away all of the bad migrations and
Utterly shows the path to the higher strata,
And leads to absence of old age and death.

I have fallen under the control of mind
And therefore have done evil deeds;
Going into the presence of the buddhas,
I lay aside all the ones I have done.

The accumulation of merit I have created
By any of the three types of karma,
Is the seed of my own all-knowing,
May it become my unending enlightenment.

Every offering to the buddhas made
In the fields of the ten directions
Is known by the buddhas who rejoice,
And I rejoice in that.

I will lay aside every evil.
I will rejoice in all merits.
I prostrate to all buddhas.
May I obtain supreme wisdom.

I urge the bodhisatvas in the ten directions
Who are dwelling on the ten levels
To go to supreme enlightenment
By becoming buddhas.

Having subdued the māras with their regiments
And reached finest enlightenment, buddhahood,
In order to provide medicine for all living creatures
Please will you turn the wheel of dharma.

Please use the sound of the great drum of dharma
To end the unsatisfactoriness of sentient beings.
Please stay for unthinkable tens of millions of aeons
Doing the deed of teaching dharma.

Sunk in the mire of desire and
Bound tight by the rope of becoming,
I am totally bound by fetters.
You the best of bipeds, please look on me!

Oh buddhas, please do not berate us
Who have developed stains of mind;
With your minds of love for sentient beings
Please release us from the ocean of becoming.

Completed buddhas who are present and
Those who have passed and not yet come
May I train following you and
Course in the conduct of enlightenment.

May I complete the six pāramitās and then
Emancipate the six migrator sentient beings.
May I manifest the six extra-perceptions
Then contact unsurpassed enlightenment.

May I realize unproduced, unarisen,
Not with nature, not with dwelling,
Not with knowing superficies, not with things,
Empty phenomena.

May I realize like the buddhas, the great ṛiṣhis,
That phenomena are not with sentient being,
Not with life, not with a person,
Not with living being, not with a self.

Not remaining at all in the things
Of grasped I and grasped mine,
In order to provide ease for all sentient beings,
Without avarice may I perform generosity.

By not treating things as existent things
May my possessions arise spontaneously.
Through the total collapse of all things may I
Complete the pāramitā of generosity.

With rules of discipline free of fault and
Discipline which has complete purity,
Through discipline without conceit may I
Complete the pāramitā of discipline.

Like the elements of earth, water,
Fire, and air are without aggression,
So too through patience without aggression may I
Complete the pāramitā of patience.

Through the perseverance of perseverance undertaken,
The steady and delighted applications, without laziness
And with body and mind having force may I
Complete the pāramitā of perseverance.

Through the Illusion-Like Concentration,
Going Like A Hero Concentration, and
Vajra-Like Concentration may I
Complete the pāramitā of absorption.

Through the three doors of complete emancipation,
And equality of the three times and also
Three knowledges seeing in direct perception, may I
Complete the pāramitā of prajñā.

Through what all the buddhas have commended, and
Light and blazing brilliance, and
The perseverance of a bodhisatva may I
Complete my intentions.

Through doing that sort of conduct
And through renowned loving kindness
May I complete the six pāramitās
Then utterly abide on the tenth level.

Translated, edited, and finalized by the Indian preceptors Jinamitra and Surendrabodhi and the Tibetan chief editor Lotsāwa Bandhe Yeshe. Translated into English by Lotsāwa Tony Duff.

A Commentary to Noble One Maitreya's Prayer, Asanga's Understanding Clearly Shown

By All-Knowing Padma Karpo

I prostrate at the feet of the holy guru.

Maitreya the guardian let fall a rain of nectar
Which drew out all the sickness of ignorance
Making him the supreme of great healers, a divine doctor;
Bowing to him one hundred times, I prostrate.

This rite of aid that was performed by
The tongue of that leader among conquerors
Was heard by those in the group with Ānanda,
And has been explained during the five-hundred year periods since
exactly as originally heard.[89]

The one who is outstanding compared to others because of his loving kindness for sentient beings is Maitreya whose name literally

[89] The bodhisatva who was Maitreya in the time of the Buddha composed a prayer in verse in one of his lifetimes long before that. It was a great composition that would benefit beings by leading them from the sickness of saṃsāra into the healthy state of enlightenment. Later, the Buddha recalled the words of that prayer when giving a discourse to a group that included Ānanda. It was a question of Ānanda that prompted the Buddha to recall the words of the prayer. That prayer has been faithfully passed on since then down to the present time.

is "Loving Kindness". Because this is his prayer and also because of what in this case the use of the term prayer is intended to convey, the term "king" additionally has to be joined to the word prayer and, on top of that, the final meaning to be understood in this usage of the word prayer is "a thorough dedication of the bodhisatva's conduct". Therefore, this prayer is understood to be "The Noble One Maitreya's King of Prayers". The explanation of it has three parts: the story behind it, the prayer itself, and the conclusion.

1. The Story Behind the Prayer

> "Ānanda, in regard to this, previously, when the bodhisatva mahāsattva Maitreya was performing the bodhisatva's activities, he would three times in the day and three times at night drape his upper robe over one shoulder, kneel down on his right knee, join his palms, and making all the buddhas actually present, say these words ..."

The provisional meaning heard at that time was that noble one Maitreya was a great bodhisatva empowered as the regent who had one life hindering him[90]. From that perspective, "previously" was understood to mean that there had been a time long ago when he had originally aroused the mind and that since then he had not become a buddha. The definitive meaning contained in the words is that Maitreya, having become a buddha in Akaniṣhṭha, is seated as a nirmāṇakāya in Tuṣhita where he was on the verge of descending into the worlds to show the act of becoming a buddha, and in that case, "previously" refers to the time when he was training as a bodhisatva.

---

[90] "One life hindering" is a Great Vehicle term meaning that a bodhisatva is in his last life before becoming a buddha.

2. The Prayer Itself

This has two parts: making a preliminary prostration and then making the prayer.

2.1. Making A Preliminary Prostration

The object of the prostration is the Three Jewels. Of the three, for the buddha, it says:

> ***I prostrate to all the buddhas.***

"***All***" makes the object referenced every buddha—those who have descended already, those who are present now, and those who will descend. For the saṅgha it says:

> ***I prostrate to the bodhisatvas,***
> ***The ṛiṣhis having the god's eye,***

which refers to the assembly of bodhisatvas, the ones who have gained the six extra-perceptions,

> ***And to the śhrāvakas as well.***

which refers to the saṅgha of the noble ones in four pairs with eight members. The prostration itself is made through speech by saying ***I prostrate*** while mind and body are bowing.

For the holy dharma there are two types of prostration: a provisional meaning one for making a good birth and a definitive meaning one for putting an end to birth.

> ***I prostrate to the enlightenment mind which***
> ***Turns away the path of the bad migrations and***[91]

---

[91] The prayer is misquoted here. It should say, "Turns away all of the bad migrations". However, the meaning is essentially the same.

Utterly shows the path to the higher strata,
And leads to absence of old age and death.

For the first, provisional meaning, there is "***turns away the path of the migrations***" with bad migrations being the three bad places, the path to them being non-virtue, and turning away from it being the abandoning of all evil deeds. ***And*** there is "***utterly shows the path to the higher strata***", where the higher strata are those abodes of gods and men in which there can be complete emancipation. The path to those higher strata is to course in conduct in which the two types of formatives[92] have been perfectly purified, which is called "the vehicle for manifesting the higher ones".

For the second, definitive meaning, there is "***and leads to absence of old age and death***". Absence of old age and death is nirvāṇa, which is of two types: peaceful nirvāṇa and non-dwelling nirvāṇa[93]. "***Enlightenment mind which leads to***" refers to the stages of the path of the journey to nirvāṇa and includes all the ways of going there—the śhrāvakas' arousing of the mind for enlightenment, the pratyekas' arousing of the mind for enlightenment, and the bodhisatvas' arousing of the mind for unsurpassable enlightenment. That is called "the vehicle of definite goodness".

---

[92] The formatives are the contents of the fourth aggregate, the aggregate of formatives. Formatives are of two types: mental events and external events both of which are the primary cause of the formation of future sets of samsaric aggregates. With a mind purified of those, there can be no production of the causes for birth in the lower realms.

[93] Peaceful nirvāṇa is the peaceful nirvāṇa of the arhats and non-dwelling nirvāṇa is the nirvāṇa of truly complete buddhas who neither dwell in saṃsāra nor the peace of the arhats.

2.2. Making the Prayer

This has two parts: making a prayer to hold the holy dharma of all the conquerors, and a thorough dedication of the bodhisatva conduct that will be used to accomplish that dharma.

2.2.1. *Making a prayer to hold the holy dharma of all the conquerors*

To apprehend the first of the vehicles of that vehicle of definite goodness, there is this:

> ***I have fallen under the control of mind***

The *Sūtra of Complete Purity of All Karmic Obscurations* says:

> Bhikṣhus! The mind which is totally afflicted will make sentient beings have total affliction and the mind of complete purity will make sentient beings into complete purity.

That teaches that whether there will be saṃsāra or nirvāṇa depends on mind[94]. Good and bad births in saṃsāra depend on the power of evil and virtue, and virtue and evil moreover depend on one's thought, thus Āryadeva said:

> Therefore, the five root thoughts
> Are present in meritorious and evil forms[95].

And the *Vinaya Āgama* says:

> Dharmas beforehand go in mind; mind is chief.

And in the *Treasury of Abhidharma* it says:

---

[94] Total affliction means saṃsāra and complete purity means nirvāṇa.

[95] The five root thoughts are the five mental events present in every instance of samsaric mind. They will become virtuous or non-virtuous depending on the rest of the mental events appearing with them.

From karma the various worlds have been produced.
Karma is both mind in operation and what it has done[96].

And therefore have done evil deeds;
Going into the presence of the buddhas,
I lay aside all the ones I have done.

If you do not want to go to a bad birthplace, it is necessary to lay aside[97] evils already done and take a vow not to do them henceforth, so laying aside has been taught here. Going further with that, laying aside is to be done with a complete set of the four types of force: the force of reliance, the force of complete rejection, the force of fully performing of the antidote, and the force of turning away from repeating the bad action. Moreover, what is to be laid aside is: what oneself did previously or is now engaged in or was pleased at others doing or instigated others to do or has delighted in others doing. Though note that, once these have been restrained by taking a vow against them, because they will not happen again in the future, there has been no statement of their needing to be laid aside.

The accumulation of merit I have created
By any of the three types of karma

The three karmas—meritorious karma which causes birth as a man, meritorious karma which causes birth as a god, and unfluctuating karma which causes birth in the upper realms—are mentioned because the tradition teaches a division into those three in relation

---

[96] These two lines are the famous opening of the fourth chapter of the text, a chapter on karma. "Karma is mind in operation" means that karma is produced by the actions (karma) of samsaric mind. "And what it has done" means that the operating mind also causes the actions of body and speech, which then also become karmic actions.

[97] For lay aside see the glossary.

to the vehicles which manifest the higher strata called "men's vehicle", "god's vehicle", and "Brahmā vehicle". There is no accumulation of wisdom for worldly beings, so all three are considered to belong to the accumulation of merit.

The vehicle of definite goodness is as follows:

> ***Is the seed of my own all-knowing;***
> ***May it become my unending enlightenment.***

The ***all-knowing*** of enlightenment is further taught[98] as knowledge of all, and due to what accompanies it, knowledge of the path and knowledge of superficies[99]. Those three are made out as seeds, leading to the four noble ones arising like shoots, through which there is the unending or manifold situation of accomplishment in the three levels of enlightenment. Thus, the two noble ones śhrāvaka and pratyeka are the fruition of knowledge of all. Then the bodhisatvas having knowledge of the path are non-final noble ones, and their finalized fruition[100] is the knowledge of superficies. The "***my***" connected to that means that bodhisatvas also train in that knowledge of all; as has been said[101]:

> There is no such thing as
> Bodhisatvas not training in that.

That continues:

> Nonetheless, it is because that is to be known;
> It is not because that is to be manifested.

---

[98] … in Maitreya's teaching which Asaṅga wrote down and published under the name *Ornament of Manifest Realization*.

[99] For superficies, see the glossary.

[100] Their finalized fruition is the buddha type of noble one. He has the buddha-knowledge that knows all superficies without exception.

[101] Unknown source.

In definitive meaning, ***all-knowing*** is the sugata[102]. The seed is the time when it is present in the enclosure of the nine stains, which is taught to be "the sugatagarbha", so it is the element[103]. Moreover, "sentient beings, bodhisatvas, and sugatas" are taught: there is no difference to be found in their entity but the first two situations are defined because they are the time when it has obscurations to the superficies associated with it and the last one is defined as the time when it has been freed of obscurations. Thus the text says:

> For suchness, there is no difference between
> Any of them, but when it has become pure,
> Because that is the tathāgata[104] itself,
> All migrators are ones having its garbha[105].

Because of the key point that the entity itself is the same, if it is totally cleansed, that entity itself will be manifested, so there is a single fruition and therefore a single, ultimate vehicle is taught. If through it one becomes a buddha, while doing so nothing will have been done for other sentient beings given that the appearances of self and other have to be regarded as "the phenomena of adventitious confusion". There is no confusion in the objects but they are grasped through the grasping style of rational mind, so they should be freed of that because of which the text says:

> The element[106] empty of the adventitious …

---

[102] This paragraph paraphrases the teaching of Maitreya and Asaṅga's *Highest Continuum* then quotes from it at the end of the paragraph.

[103] The element is another name for the sugatagarbha. It is the element of being which is the basis for enlightenment.

[104] Tathāgata means "gone to suchness"; with that knowledge, this line properly connects to the first line.

[105] That is, all migrators have the tathāgatagarbha.

[106] Tib. khams. "The element" is another name for the tathāgata-
(continued...)

However, it is not possible for the nature[107] to change to something else, so the text says:

> ... is not empty of the unsurpassed dharmas[108].

Although it is explained to have that nature, it is illustrated with the words "space-like" which prevents it from being grasped as an object.

Thus, this has been a prayer for holding all dharmas. Because it contains all of the thorough dedications of bodhisatvas it is, according to the explanations in commentaries to the *Excellent Conduct*[109], a synopsis of all prayers.

2.2.2. *A thorough dedication of the bodhisatva conduct that will be used to accomplish that*

This has three parts, the entering conduct, the accomplishing conduct, and the accomplished conduct.

---

[106](...continued)
garbha. It is empty of what is adventitious to it, which is all of the afflictions of dualistic mind. The name has the sense of the basis or fundamental element within sentient beings from which tathāgatahood occurs. For element, also see the glossary.

[107] "The nature" is yet another name for the tathāgatagarbha, in this case it has the sense of being the nature of sentient beings.

[108] "The unsurpassed dharmas" are the unsurpassed qualities of supreme enlightenment which are the unsurpassed of all good qualities. These lines are very famous. They indicate that the sugatagarbha, which eventually becomes the wisdom of a sugata or buddha, is never parted from the good qualities of enlightenment.

[109] ... that is, commentaries to Samantabhadra's prayer called "Excellent Conduct". Samantabhadra's prayer also has a section of prayer for holding the buddha's dharma, and the comments on that apply here, and vice versa.

2.2.2.1. The entering conduct

Every offering to the buddhas made
In the fields of the ten directions

Imagining that you have set out great clouds of offerings—ones manifested by mind and ones actually set out—in all of the field realms[110], there is a vast offering. In regard to ***every ... made*** it has been said:

Except for acting to please sentient beings
There is no other way to please the conquerors.

and, given that arousing the enlightenment mind for enlightenment itself is the supreme of all offerings, that is what this phrase is in fact showing.

Is known by the buddhas who rejoice in it,
And I rejoice in that.

These two lines speak of the unsurpassed offering, which is the offering made with the purity of the three spheres[111].

I will lay aside every evil[112].
I will rejoice in all merits.

The words ***all merits*** mean "all the merits of others".

I prostrate to all buddhas.

---

110 "In the fields of the ten directions" means within all the fields of saṃsāric existence.

111 The three spheres are the three main components of any action: the agent, action, and acted upon or the offerer, the act of offering, and the offering.

112 Tib. sdig pa. "Evil" means evil deeds or those actions which have karmically bad results.

May I gain supreme wisdom.

To be transformed in the way that the fourth line dedicates is for the roots of merit to become like the elixir which transforms things into gold.

I urge the bodhisatvas in the ten directions
Who are dwelling on the ten levels
To go to supreme enlightenment
By becoming buddhas.

Having subdued the māras with their regiments
And in finest enlightenment become buddhas,
In order to provide medicine for all living creatures
Please will you turn the wheel of dharma.

These lines fit with the transformation mentioned above. This is urging the bodhisatva mahāsattvas.

Please use the sound of the great drum of dharma
To end the unsatisfactoriness of sentient beings[113]*.*

This is urging the buddhas to turn the wheel of dharma.

Please stay for unthinkable tens of millions of aeons
Doing the deed of teaching dharma.

---

[113] Most Tibetan editions, including the Derge edition, have "mthar" meaning "end" instead of "thar" meaning "emancipation" in this line. Thus the line could either be "to end the unsatisfactoriness of sentient beings" or, slightly less likely, "to emancipate all sentient beings from their unsatisfactoriness". This is one of the few places in the prayer where the translation will noticeably change according to differences in edition.

This is supplicating the buddhas not to pass into nirvāṇa. It comes before the seventh limb[114].

Sunk in the mire of desire and
Bound tight by the rope of becoming,
I am totally bound by fetters;

These first three lines show who will be protected or given refuge—sentient beings. The next line shows who will give protection or refuge—it shows only the ultimate refuge, though includes dharma and saṅgha as well.

You the best of bipeds, please look on me![115]

The next three lines show the reason for the protection, which is like a mother having love for her son even if he is badly behaved:

Oh buddhas, please do not berate us
Who have developed stains of mind[116]***;***
With your minds of love for sentient beings

And next how will that protection be given:

---

[114] The prayer so far has been through the first to sixth of the seven limbs. He makes the comment about the sixth coming before the seventh not because there is a special relationship between the sixth and seventh limbs but because the seventh limb would be expected next but is not mentioned. Thus his comment means "Normally, the seventh limb would come next". The seventh limb is the limb of dedicating all one's merits to unsurpassed enlightenment for the sake of all other sentient beings.

[115] "Best of bipeds" is one of the many epithets of a buddha from the time of ancient India. It is often translated as "best of humans" but that is yet another epithet of the buddhas.

[116] A minority of Tibetan editions of the *Translated Word* have this line reading "Who have made (mental) stains with our minds". The Derge edition has the reading shown. The meaning does not really change.

Please release us from the ocean of becoming.

And next there is the liturgy for the special arousing of mind[117]:

Completed buddhas who are present and
Those who have passed and not yet come
May I train following you and
Course in the conduct of enlightenment.

May I complete the six pāramitās and then
Take the six migrator sentient beings to the end[118].

The arousing of mind which is not special is explained in the texts of the shrāvakas whereas this special one is not, something which can be understood from Nāgārjuna's statement:

The thorough dedication of conduct

---

[117] "Arousing of mind" is a generic phrase used in Sanskrit to mean the deliberate production of a specific frame of mind. Thus, there is the arousing of mind of ordinary beings following their aspirations whatever those might be. That sort of arousing of mind is purely worldly and is not considered here. Then, in Buddhism in particular, there are the arousings of mind of those training on the shrāvaka and pratyekabuddha paths and those training on the bodhisatva path. The latter is special compared to the former two because it has many special features such as referencing all sentient beings rather than oneself only, and so on. Maitreya taught seven specific ways in which the Great Vehicle is great compared to the Lesser Vehicle and these are applicable.

[118] Half of the Tibetan editions, including the Derge edition, have "thar" meaning "emancipation" instead of "mthar" meaning "end" in this line. Padma Karpo's commentary has the latter. Thus the line could either be "emancipate the migrator sentient beings" or, less likely, "take the six migrator sentient beings to the end". This is one of the few places in the prayer where the translation will noticeably change according to differences in edition.

Not explained in the śhrāvaka basket of teachings …

To rouse a mind that follows that absence of explanation of dedication found in those texts is mistaken. This[119] shows that the right understanding is that the arousing of the mind of enlightenment itself means that the vows of the enlightenment mind have happened:

> Intelligent ones know that immediately they have
> aroused the supreme mind for enlightenment,
> They have also utterly restrained the mind away from
> doing the infinite types of bad behaviour.

That arousing of the mind moreover, must be taken to its completion by perfectly accomplishing the conduct associated with it. Thus there is the second topic, the accomplishing conduct.

2.2.2.2. *Accomplishing conduct*

This has two parts: prajñā apprehending superfact and compassion apprehending fiction.

2.2.2.2.1. *Prajna which apprehends superfact*

This has two parts: preliminary śhamatha and vipaśhyanā present in that.

2.2.2.2.1.1. *Preliminary shamatha*

> ***May I manifest the six extra-perceptions***
> ***Then contact unsurpassed enlightenment.***

In regard to this, Atīśha said:

> The cause of completing the accumulation
> Whose nature is merit and wisdom
> Has been asserted by all the buddhas

---

[119] From the *Ornament of the Great Vehicle Sūtra Section* by Maitreya and Asaṅga.

To be the generation of the extra-perceptions.

Just as a bird whose wings are incomplete
Is not able to fly in the sky,
So anyone not having the force of the extra-perceptions
Is not able to work for the sake of sentient beings.

The merits of a night and day
Of having the extra-perceptions is that
There is no separation from the extra-perceptions
Even in one hundred births.

Extra-perceptions moreover come with the
accomplishment of the concentration of śhamatha,
So if śhamatha has not been accomplished,
The extra-perceptions will not be accomplished.
Therefore, you must make efforts again and again
In order to accomplish śhamatha.

And similarly:

The accumulation of merit must be truly completed.
After that, the intelligent will stabilize mind.
Then the mindstream will be thoroughly clothed
In faith, and so on, the virtuous dharmas.

For a countless aeon through renunciation
In order to accomplish the wisdom accumulation
They utterly engage in the level of conduct in which
The oral instructions for extra-perceptions are taught.

2.2.2.2.1.2. *Vipashyana present in that*

This has two parts: actual prajñā and what is taught within its functioning.

2.2.2.2.1.2.1. Actual prajna

It is as *The Condensed*[120] says:

> By prajñā one entirely knows the nature of dharmas
> Then one truly transcends the three realms without
> exception.

Thus the prayer says:

> ***May I realize unproduced, unarisen,***

Prajñā is defined as the part[121] which fully discerns dharmas. It is divided into three prajñās: the prajñās which arise from hearing, contemplating, and meditating. Based on the prajñā arising from hearing, the prajñā arising from contemplation analyses and, by remaining in that, the prajñā arising from meditation is acquired.

The first one, hearing, occurs through listening to the holy dharma taught by a spiritual friend. This is how a spiritual friend shows the oral instructions of the true path: at first you rely on the spiritual friend as someone who is expert in the bodhisatva sūtra section or at least able to transmit the true oral instructions and later, because of him, you meet with buddha in direct perception[122].

Contemplation is the proper dissection with thought of the words and meanings as they were heard. When through that an under-

---

[120] *The Condensed Prajñāpāramitā in Verse.*

[121] Śhamatha provides the calmness part needed for prana's factor of discernment to work properly.

[122] First he explains and guides you through the teachings of the Lesser and Great Vehicles, then he gives you the introduction to your own buddha-nature in direct perception needed to practise the Vajra Vehicle.

standing arises which is consistent with the path of statement and reasoning[123], that is referred to as "cutting exaggerations"[124].

When exaggerations have been cut, one knows that all things[125], because of depending on causes and conditions, are ***unproduced*** and because of that do not arise anywhere at all, so are ***unarisen***. And,

> ***Not with nature, not with dwelling***[126],

---

[123] Tib. lung dang rigs pa. Authoritative statement and correct reasoning are the two aspects of the way to come to an intellectually correct certainty about a subject being analyzed.

[124] Exaggerations are mental over- or under-statements of how something actually is. Removing all of them is called "cutting exaggerations", though it simply means "removing all one's incorrect understandings about a subject".

[125] The use of "thing" in this section of the prayer has a specific meaning. "Things" are the things invented by conceptual mind. Thus, this is saying "one knows that all the things that one normally considers to be solid and real are unproduced, and so on, that is, all these things are empty of what they seem to be before they are carefully analysed". Watch for this term "things" in the coming lines and perhaps substitute it with "conceived-of things", which will make the meaning clearer. For example, a little further on the prayer says "not remaining in the (conceived-of) things of grasped I and grasped mine ...", which is an important two-line introduction to the conduct needed in order for generosity and the others to become actual pāramitā. This is so because the true pāramitās are actions done while coursing in direct perception of the emptiness of things.

[126] One Western translator has tried to say that "unproduced" means was not produced in the past, "unarisen" means will therefore not be produced in the future, "not with nature" means does not have a nature in the present, and therefore it is always empty of being a solid entity. That is all very clever, but wrong—for instance, the construction for "unarisen" is in the present tense, not the future tense.

they are an illusion without ***nature***. And, because they have no centre and edge, they do ***not dwell*** anywhere with a factor of dimensionality. And,

> ***Not with knowing superficies, not with things,***

means that, being without consciousness[127] they are without ***knowing superficies***, and that, being divorced from all references of grasped-at and grasping, they are ***not with things***. It says,

> ***may I realize ... Empty phenomena.***

What has just been set in the preceding lines is emptiness, so now they have been determined to be empty. That emptiness is called "absence of a self in dharmas". A self of phenomena seems to be there in phenomena, but when the matter is examined, that seeming existence is not found. Doing that leads to the disintegration of all references[128], therefore doing that is called "making all things[129] disintegrate".

The tīrthika texts designate a self which is "permanent, solitary, and independent", then go on to refer to it as a sentient being, life, person, living being, and other similar names. Nevertheless, such a self is empty: it is empty in fact and the names used for it are empty of their suggested meaning. Therefore:

---

[127] The Sanskrit and Tibetan terms for consciousness mean "awareness of superfice", which explains this item.

[128] "References" are the concepts used to label something and the process of referencing that uses them is the very heart of dualistic mind. Therefore, to slay dualistic mind, stab it in the heart and then, when its heart of referencing stops dead, all of its references will disintegrate, and that will be the end of dualistic mind. The prajñā directly knowing non-dualistic wisdom is then born and becomes the basis for the practise of the pāramitās.

[129] "Things" again is a technical term meaning conceived-of things.

May I realize like the buddhas, the great ṛiṣhis,

meaning may I realize the actual nature of phenomena according to how they spoke about it, which has been:

That phenomena are not with sentient being,
Not with life, not with a person,
Not with living being, not with a self.

The words ***realize ... are not with a self*** mean "remain in that fact". Thus, the conceptually-imagined self of phenomena and self of persons have both been negated.

Grasped I and grasped mine
Do not abide in all things.

This teaches, "What is called 'self' is not a thing itself, is not something else, is not their entity, and also is not, like rice and a wheel[130], based on them. It does not reside in things, so if it were apprehended like that, that would be nothing but twisted." In that way it proves that the co-emergent self of the view of the perishable which is apprehended as a convention on the basis of cause and effect is non-existent.[131]

---

[130] These are two well-known examples from the sūtras of a self not being based on things.

[131] This is the one place in Padma Karpo's commentary where, because he has started with an incorrect edition of the prayer, his commentary goes askew. According to his version of the prayer, these two lines stand alone as a single sentence which says "grasped at I and mine are not present in any thing". His commentary makes perfect sense when the lines are understood that way. However, all versions of the prayer in the various editions of the *Translated Word* have these two lines reading "Not remaining at all in the things of grasped I and grasped mine" as the first clause of a set of lines. Because of the wrong reading, Padma Karpo's commentary does not go far enough. It should explain

(continued...)

2.2.2.2.1.2.1. *What is taught within its functioning*

The work of that prajñā is exactly that meditation. Because of it[132]:

> The bodhisatva's equipoise
> Not comprehending with the expressions of mental mind
> Utterly does not see any of all the facts.

That is saying that forbearance[133] with respect to conceptually ascertaining phenomena is gained. Then it says:

> In order to develop the appearances of phenomena,
> An unyielding perseverance must be thoroughly undertaken.

Through that cause, forbearance with respect to great phenomena is gained. At that time:

> The appearance of phenomena has been increased,
> And one will abide in mind only.

---

[131](...continued)
what it has explained, then additionally point out that the person making the prayer is saying that, since all phenomena are empty, "I will, in order to set the ground for the conduct of the bodhisatva's path, not remain any longer in any of the conceptually-created things with their superimposed I and mine. Having like that taken up the view of empty phenomena as the basis for the path, I will—as it says in the next two lines—in order to bring happiness to all sentient beings, start the practise of the six pāramitās with the practice of generosity". Thus, these two lines conclude the discussion of emptiness and set the stage for acting on the basis of emptiness in all of the bodhisatva's enlightened conduct which now becomes the main topic of the prayer.

[132] This and following quotes are from the *Ornament of the Great Vehicle Sūtra Section*.

[133] Forbearance here means that one has developed the knowledge and realization needed to withstand a certain situation on the path and then remain in it.

Then within fact all appearances
Will utterly appear within mind.

At that time, the distraction of those
Grasped at things will have been abandoned.
Then, only the distraction of grasping
At them will be left.

Then, the superficies of grasped-at and grasping are pacified by the awareness abiding in its own nature—self-knowing, self-illumination—which the same text refers to with:

At that time, he will quickly contact
An unimpeded concentration.

That has brought him to the verge of the Other Emptiness Middle Way, so he proceeds into it:

Then, by entering that luminosity
All karma and affliction is ended,
Due to which there is not even
Simple self-knowing appearing.

The self-knowing just referred to means consciousness itself[134]. The result of entering the luminosity is that the level beyond consciousness has been reached, which is given the sweet-to-hear name "wisdom". In *The Sūtra Petitioned by the King of Men or What* it says:

That luminosity is the nature of mind. What the nature of mind is, is entered. What will be entered has all concept tokens[135] suppressed[136]. What has all concept tokens

[134] That is, just pure knowing, saṃsāric consciousness having totally ended.

[135] For concept token, see the glossary.

[136] Luminosity or wisdom is the inner nature of the samsaric mind.
(continued...)

> suppressed is called "entrance into absence of fault". What the entrance into the bodhisatva's absence of fault is, is forbearance with respect to unborn phenomena; that being so, "the bodhisatva who has entered absence of fault has gained forbearance for unborn phenomena". That gaining of forbearance forbears everything. It forbears emptiness and it also forbears persons. Why is that so? There is no being empty other than a person; a person is empty ...
>
> Son of the family! The bodhisatva who has gained the forbearance like that for unborn phenomena has nothing contrary; there is nothing for him which is contrary to any of all phenomena.

That process has been explained in the *Descent into Laṅka* like this:

> In dependence on mind only
> External facts are not thought of.
> In dependence on abiding in suchness
> One also passes beyond mind only.
> In dependence on having passed beyond mind only
> One will abide in absence of appearance.
> The yogin who abides in absence of appearance
> Sees the Great Vehicle[137].

---

[136](...continued)
When it has been entered, dualistic mind and all of its paraphernalia, such as the fundamental bits of conceptual process called concept token, are dissolved back into the fundamental luminosity and cease to operate.

[137] The true Great Vehicle is the coursing in Prajñāpāramitā beyond speech and thought, the nature of wisdom. The yogin who goes beyond the normal appearances of dualistic mind into the illusory appearances of wisdom has truly entered the Great Vehicle.

And, similar to that, it has also been explained like this[138]:

> Rational mind having understood that there is nothing other than mind
> The non-existence even of mind is then understood.
> Those having a rational mind understand that both are non-existent,
> Then abide in dharmadhātu which does not have that.

2.2.2.2.2. *Compassion which apprehends fiction*

This has two parts: overview and the body of the text.

2.2.2.2.2.1. *Overview*

The Mother says:

> Coursing in the six pāramitās of mind which possesses knowledge of all superficies[139], he quickly arrives at manifest complete buddhahood.

Method is the enlightenment mind which does not discard sentient beings. It is included in the six pāramitās. The way that generosity is done, it works for others' sakes by having three patiences and works for one's own sake by having threefold perseverance, absorption, and prajñā[140]:

> Utterly persevering at the sake of sentient beings,
> Giving with the patience of no harm;

---

[138] This is from the *Ornament of the Great Vehicle Sūtra Section*. These four lines are very famous. They summarize the path of Mind Only which proceeds in four steps, going from normal dualistic consciousness only to self-knowing, self-illumining dharmadhātu wisdom, as shown.

[139] Mind which possesses knowledge of all superficies is non-dual wisdom.

[140] This is from the *Ornament of the Great Vehicle Sūtra Section*.

> Place and liberation together in the basis
> All of one's own sakes are coursed in.

And, the first three are the higher training in discipline, the fifth is the higher training in mind[141], and the last one is the higher training in prajñā, with perseverance assisting them all[142]:

> From the standpoint of the three trainings,
> The conqueror truly explained the six pāramitās;
> The first three, the last two making two types,
> And one also included in the three.

The first four manifest the higher levels and the last two accomplish definite goodness[143], so:

> Perfect possessions, body, and
> Perfect retinue to begin with are actually seen and
> There is perpetually not falling under the control of the afflictions
> And not going wrong in actions.

And their sequence is defined in this way as a progression from coarse to subtle: there is a sequence of their production as in generosity gives rise to discipline, and so on; and there is a progression from lesser to better; and generosity is easier to do and its characteristics are easier to understand, so it is taught first. Thus:

> Their steps are taught

---

[141] These are the three trainings: śhīla, samādhi, and prajñā. The Buddha called them higher trainings to distinguish them from the trainings of the non-Buddhists of his time who used the words "trainings" to refer to the trainings of their own systems. The higher training of samādhi is a training of dualistic mind, so is also called, as it is here, "higher training of mind".

[142] The next three quotations are from the *Ornament of the Great Vehicle Sūtra Section*.

[143] Definite goodness is the unchanging goodness of enlightenment.

> Because of the next one being produced in dependence
> on the previous one,
> Because of them sitting as lesser and better,
> And because of them being coarser and subtler.

The function of that method is that, amongst all the actions of body, speech, and mind, there will not be one which is not done—directly or indirectly—for the purpose of sentient beings. In regard to that, there are two parts: with and without referencing sentient beings.

2.2.2.2.2.1.1. *With referencing sentient beings*

A person who is a beginning bodhisatva applies the name "sentient being" to beings who have a self and because of that arouses compassion for their suffering. With that compassion he trains in generosity and the other pāramitās. As he familiarizes himself with the training, the so-called "sentient beings" are understood to be non-existent from the start and they end up being named "adventitious".

In relation to others he thinks that "There is nothing at all there except mere aggregates, dhātus, and āyatanas" and also that "Other ends up being no more than my own mind; this other is nothing at all", because of which he produces compassion for their sufferings. Having produced it, he engages in generosity, and so on.

2.2.2.2.2.1.2. *Without referencing sentient beings*

The superfactual and fictional truths are realized in just-that-ness as one taste, but various methods are used to entirely ripen sentient beings in whichever of the three vehicles is appropriate. A commentary on the *Inexhaustible Intellect Sūtra* says the same:

> According to what was taught earlier, he stays in equipoise in all avenues of conduct but, in order to entirely ripen sentient beings, he follows all the ways of the

world, of the kingly caste, and so on, so he also possesses the skilful means of conduct which accords with theirs. That skilful means is held by prajñā so he dwells among them but remains unmixed with the world[144]. In what way does he remain unmixed with the world? It is what was taught, "Having gone beyond the eight worldly dharmas, he remains unmixed with any of all the afflictions".

2.2.2.2.2.2. *The body of the text*

Now, in terms of performing generosity, that is,

> ***In order to provide ease for all sentient beings,***

the non-conducive side is abandoned:

> ***Without avarice ...***

and the conducive side is trained in:

> ***... may I perform generosity.***

In order that the things to be given do not become exhausted, or, in terms of the result:

> ***By not treating things as existent things***
> ***May my possessions arise spontaneously.***

In that way he acquires the "the space storehouse". However, this is not the sort of storehouse in which there are many treasures piled up; it is that anything he wants becomes immediately and perfectly available to him.

The last two lines are from the standpoint of a beginner. The next two are more advanced:

> ***Through the total collapse of all things may I***
> ***Complete the pāramitā of generosity.***

---

[144] In other words "he remains in but not of the world".

By dwelling in thorough pacification of all the references involved with the given, giver, object of giving, and action of giving, there is the performance of generosity as an illusory being. That transcends the world so, because it has gone across to the shore where it is has that sort of ability, it gains the name "pāramitā" or "gone across to the other shore", which is happening in this case through generosity[145]. In this case, it is to give up on one's "dhana" or wealth, that is, it is "generosity"[146]. Its characteristic is "giving completely" so

---

[145] The Sanskrit term pāramitā literally means *itā* gone across *pāram* to the other shore. Although it is translated often as "transcendent action" or something similar, transcendent is another term. It is so cumbersome to translate the Sanskrit correctly that it is left untranslated or, unfortunately, translated with "transcendent" or "perfection", both of which mislead the reader.

In the sentence here, Padma Karpo cleverly shows the meaning of pāramitā. He points out that a person who can remain in emptiness of the three spheres of an action—in this case giving—performs the action as a person who is not grasping at a self anywhere during the performance of the action. Therefore, his action is not a worldly one but one which has passed over to being non-worldly.

There are two types of pāramitā of the bodhisatva. There is the worldly pāramitā which is the action of a person who is not able to remain in absence of self while doing the action of the pāramitā and the pāramitā which has passed over to being non-worldly and is the action of a person who is able to do so. The one that has passed over to being non-worldly is the true meaning of pāramitā given that pāramitā means "that which has ceased to be part of the doings on this side or shore of the ocean of saṃsāra because it has gone across to the far side or shore of that ocean, the side of nirvāṇa". Thus, the prayer being made here is "may I complete the true pāramitā, which is to act in the world while being in the realization of nirvāṇa, via the action of being generous". The same understanding applies to the verses of the remaining five pāramitās.

[146] The Sanskrit term for "personal wealth" is "dhana" as shown. To

(continued...)

the Buddha taught that if it is done in a vast way, "giving completely" itself will be classified as one of the six pāramitās.

With rules of discipline …

"Rules of" here has to be understood to mean "rules of the buddhas", which are the bodhisatva vows comprised of all three of the dutiful vows of personal emancipation, gathering virtuous dharmas, and acting for the sake of sentient beings. Doing so is "śhīla"[147], meaning "that which gains the relief of being cooled from the oppression of afflictions"[148].

Next the non-conducive side is abandoned:

… free of fault and …

with "free of fault" meaning being without the faults of lax discipline. Then the conducive side is stated:

Discipline which has complete purity,

That sort of discipline has six aspects: keeping possession of the disciplines of personal emancipation; being bound by the vows one has; perfection of liturgy[149]; perfection of behaviour[150]; viewing with

---

[146](...continued)
be fearless in giving it away is what is meant here. Note that the Sanskrit term for generosity is "dāna".

[147] … which we translate as discipline.

[148] Śhīla is the correct Sanskrit for the name of this second pāramitā. It literally means "to cool" and was explained by the Buddha in relation to the vows in the way that Padma Karpo has just done.

[149] The various vows require various liturgies to be performed at certain times in order to maintain their purity and dispense with any infractions that might have occurred. Perfection of liturgy means that
(continued...)

fear even the slightest unmentionable[151]; and properly keeping and training in the bases of training[152]. Discipline which has those six limbs is called "accumulation of discipline" or "aggregate of discipline".

> ***Through discipline without conceit may I***
> ***Complete the pāramitā of discipline.***

First, one properly accepts the disciplines. After that, from the time one starts to observe them until the end when one reaches the wisdom of complete liberation, there should not be even the slightest corruption or loss of them. Through that absence of corruption and loss, discipline goes to its end and, when it has turned into un-outflowed discipline[153], the aggregate of discipline has been fully completed. Thus, through being without conceit and the single key point of not conceiving of the three spheres, that discipline gains the name "pāramitā" which is happening through discipline.

> ***Like the elements of earth, water,***
> ***Fire, and air are without aggression,***

---

[149](...continued)
one always does those liturgies fully and completely at the required times.

[150] Perfection of behaviour in relation to the conduct expected of a person who has the vows.

[151] "Unmentionable" is one of many names for wrongdoing. In the community of those keeping vows, any act of impurity is embarrassing to hear, which is how the name came about. The term covers every kind of infraction of a vow from small to large.

[152] The bases of training are the vows themselves, for example, a layman's set of vows, or a monk's set of vows, and so on.

[153] For un-outflowed, see the glossary. Un-outflowed discipline is discipline done within non-dual wisdom.

> ***So too through patience …***

There is no anger present in the four great elements because they have no mind. Not conceiving of the three spheres is equivalent to that, so there is "kṣhānti", literally meaning being peaceful without anger, and that is given the name "patience". The non-conducive side is abandoned:

> ***… without aggression …***

and the conducive side is trained in:

> ***… may I***
> ***Complete the pāramitā of patience.***

The Stack of Jewels Bodhisatva's Piṭaka Sūtra says:

> "Aggression" is that which "destroys the roots of virtue created during one hundred thousand aeons".

And *The Sport of Mañjuśhrī Sūtra* says:

> "Aggression" is that which "destroys the roots of virtue accumulated during one hundred aeons".

Aggression should be understood in terms of the root afflictions, the proximate afflictions, and the specifics of the object[154].

> ***Through the perseverance of perseverance undertaken,***
> ***The steady and delighted applications, …***

---

[154] There are several similar states of mind which are variations on the root affliction called "anger", for example the "aggression" listed here. They are stated in the listings of root and proximate afflictions found in the listings of mental events. How anger is unrealistic and so should be abandoned in favour of patience can be understood through an analysis of the object towards which anger is being expressed.

"Vīrya" is glossed as the "best" type[155] so it is called "perseverance". "Undertaken" means that it is being done, that effort has been started up. "Steady" refers to the "perpetual application" and "delight" to the "devoted application" types of perseverance[156]. Then, the non-conducive side is abandoned:

... without laziness

and the conducive side is trained in:

And with body and mind having force may I
Complete the pāramitā of perseverance.

Because he is armoured with the great armour and does not show off to others, his patience cannot be challenged by the non-conducive side. Thus, it ends up meaning that, no matter how much a person possessing force exerts himself, he ends up without fatigue,

---

[155] "Vīrya" is the Sanskrit name for this pāramitā. It means the best type of effort.

[156] Perseverance is defined as two fold in the Abhidharma sūtras: perpetual, meaning an unflagging type of perseverance, and devoted, meaning a faith-based type of perseverance such as inspired perseverance. Thus the verse here is saying that one should have perseverance which is not merely in name but which has been taken up and been engaged and then that that engaged perseverance should be of the two types just mentioned. Altogether, that perseverance will firstly be without what opposes it, laziness, and secondly will be with what supports it, a force of body and mind.

disenchantment, and idleness[157]. The pāramitā mode is the same as before.

"Dhyāna", because it means a steadiness of mind is called absorption[158]. Moreover, this is achieved:

Through the Illusion-Like Concentration,

about which the *Descent into Laṅka Sūtra* says:

> If he meditates by gradually entering the objects of the concentrations[159] of the stages of the levels which are great compassion and skilful means in connection with

---

[157] There is a point here. "Force" is defined in the Great Vehicle literature as having a strength which cannot be overcome by whatever would oppose it. His words here are a direct commentary on the third line of the verse which mentions having force of body and mind. By having the specific force connected with the pāramitā of perseverance—named "armour-like perseverance"—the bodhisatva in training cannot be stopped by any of the things—fatigue, disenchantment, any of the many forms of laziness such as idleness—which would normally oppose and prevent his persevering.

[158] The name of this fifth pāramitā has always been the hardest to translate into English. The Sanskrit term "dhyāna" means a state of mind which is held utterly steady. However, it is not a concentration but an absorption into a particular realm of mind. This "absorption into a realm of mind" is what is intended by the Tibetan translation which seems to be saying "steadiness of thought". It is not that thought is being eliminated, as is the case with concentration, but that one is entering into an absorption of mind. Because of this, the term "dhyāna" is also frequently used in Sanskrit, such as in the sūtras and tantras, to mean "meditation". Thus this pāramitā is actually the pāramitā of meditation in which one learns to absorb the mind into all those states of mind or contemplations, either way, which are useful to the path and to sentient beings.

[159] Skt. samādhi, Tib. ting nge 'dzin.

> spontaneous existence, and all sentient beings' realms being illusion, and reflection, and equality, and not begun by conditions, and being isolated from the superficies of outer and inner objects, and possessing the blessing of being without concept tokens due to viewing them as an externalized play of mind, and so utterly dedicates himself to the three realms being mind's illusion, he will fully gain the Illusion-Like Concentration.

That is saying that the concentration involved with viewing in direct perception all dharmas which have been defined from form up to knowledge of all as dream-like, illusion-like, is the illusion-like concentration. Then there is:

> ***Going Like A Hero Concentration, and***

The *Going Like A Hero Concentration Sūtra* says:

> The holy beings who have gained this, the Going Like A Hero Concentration, have indeed gone into the place of all buddhas. They have indeed gained control over independent wisdom[160].

And says:

> Sons of the family! That being so, in order for the bodhisatva who wants to definitely arise in all paths of

[160] Dualistic consciousness is dependent in that it is controlled by the objects that appear to it; non-dualistic wisdom is independent in that it is not controlled by the objects which appear to it.

> definite arising[161] to be without every mind of conceit, he is to train in the Going Like a Hero Concentration.

The concentration which has, like a heroic army commander, defeated to the point of no resistance all of the things to be abandoned, is called "Going Like a Hero".

Then there is:

> ***Vajra-Like Concentration may I***
> ***Complete the pāramitā of absorption.***

The *Descent into Laṅka Sūtra* says:

> Mahāmati! Because that is so, I enter my mind into mind-only without appearances whereby the post-attainment abiding in Prajñāpāramitā is born and the bodhisatvas free of activity have followed, following into a concentration of the tathāgata's body which is like the form of a vajra. It is adorned with the force of possessing the manifestations of suchness, extra-perceptions, controls, love, and compassion and method. And, by separating themselves from the mind and mental mind and mental consciousness[162] which strongly goes to the Tīrthika places of the fields of all buddhas, they will, gradually, gain the tathāgata's body which transfers to places. Mahāmati! Because that is so, the bodhisatva mahāsattvas who have fully gained following the body of the tathāgata, with the aggregates, dhātus, āyatanas, mind,

---

[161] "Definite arising" is what is often translated as "renunciation". The term does not mean renunciation but means, having renounced, that one proceeds in a positive direction towards that which will provide definite release. It is one of the factors of cessation, the third truth of the noble ones. Here it means "for the bodhisatva who definitely wants to turn towards enlightenment in all the ways possible".

[162] Tib. sems, yid, rnam shes. These are three terms all meaning dualistic mind of saṃsāra.

> movement, and function possessed will, freed of the elaborations of discursive thought with its birth, and dwelling, and disintegration, follow sentient beings.

That says that that concentration which has destroyed every obscuration, is called the "Vajra-Like Concentration".

"Prajñā" is a rational mind which utterly dissects dharmas that functions in regard to the aspect of knowing superfact; that aspect is part of method, forces, prayers, and wisdom.

> ***Through the three doors of complete emancipation,***

They are: the complete emancipation of emptiness, signlessness and wishlessness[163].

> ***And equality of the three times as well as …***

And, equality of the three times which refers to there being no time in superfact and there has to be as well with that:

> ***Three knowledges seeing in direct perception may I***
> ***Complete the pāramitā of prajñā.***

In terms of appearance, the three knowledges are defined[164] in relation to the three times; the *Petitioned by the King of Men or What Sūtra* says:

> A truly completed buddha has sight of the unimpeded wisdom. Why is that? Son of the family! In regard to

---

[163] Emptiness means "absence of a nature". Signlessness means "absence of concept tokens". Wishlessness means "absence of aspiration", for example, absence of aspiration to obtain the various levels of the paths.

[164] "Equality of the three times" refers to empty superfact, but because there has to be appearance, there also has to be more, so the three knowledges which know not only emptiness but also appearance also have to be mentioned.

> the past minds of all sentient beings, all of the endings, cessations, separations from, and transformations of the mindstream are utterly known by the tathāgata. The causes from which those mindstreams arose, and the causes by which their ending and being separated from was shown, and all of their virtue or non-virtue or determinacy or indeterminacy together with superficies, together with grounds, together with logical reasonings, are utterly known by the tathāgata.
>
> The mindstream of the minds of all sentient beings arisen in the present, whether virtuous or non-virtuous, whether determinate or indeterminate—all of those mental events which arose under any mind—and together with superficies, together with country and direction, together with the basis they came from, are utterly understood by the tathāgata.
>
> The mindstream of the mind of all sentient beings in the future, and the dharmas which are the events of the minds whether virtuous or non-virtuous or determinate or indeterminate, all of those mental events which will arise under that mind and, moreover, together with superficies, together with country and direction, together with which basis they came from, are utterly understood by the tathāgata.
>
> Son of the family! Being like that, the tathāgata, arhat, truly complete buddha is possessed of unimpeded wisdom.

Here, the non-conducive side to be abandoned has not been mentioned for either absorption or prajñā because they are carried into the equality of becoming and peace and it is understood that there is no abandonment-adoption in that.

In the context of individualized beings, the non-conducive side to absorption—which is a concentration of one-pointed mind—to be abandoned is distraction. For prajñā—which is complete dissection in accordance with fact—the non-conducive side is lax prajñā.

2.2.2.3. *The accomplished conduct*

This has two parts: non-ultimate and ultimate.

2.2.2.3.1. *Non-Ultimate*

There is this which refers to the good qualities of bodhisatvas in general:

> ***Through what all the buddhas have commended, and ...***

And there is this which refers to good qualities that specifically occur within the path of meditation:

> ***Light and blazing brilliance, and ...***

Thus, those two lines refer to the infinite good qualities that bodhisatvas gain in general and to the empowerment of great luminosity attained by bodhisatvas on the tenth level which brings them to the level of being a conqueror's regent[165].

2.2.2.3.2. *Ultimate*

> ***The perseverance of a bodhisatva may I ...***

For three or thirty-two or infinite numbers of countless great aeons a bodhisatva is to ripen those to be tamed, to complete prayers, and to cleanse a field, so it says may I

> ***Complete my intentions.***

---

[165] Which then refers back to Maitreya, given that he was a master of the tenth level and had been prophesied by Śhākyamuni Buddha as his regent.

That is, may I become a buddha with the activities of the three kāyas[166].

3. Conclusion

> ***Through doing that sort of conduct ...***

means "By conducting myself in a way which is consistent with the prayer that has just been made".

> ***And through renowned loving kindness[167] ...***
> ***May I complete the six pāramitās[168],***
> ***Then utterly abide on the tenth level.***

This teaches that, starting from first arousing of the mind of enlightenment, the bodhisatva journeys through the stages of the ten levels following the order of the six pāramitās.

---

[166] One Tibetan scholar read this commentary and thought that this sentence means that the first line of the verse refers to the dharmakāya, the second to the saṃbhogakāya, and the third to the nirmāṇakāya. However, that is not what Padma Karpo is saying.

[167] In the original Sanskrit Loving Kindness here was "maitrī". This line of the prayer is a prayer by the former incarnation of Maitreya that in future he would have loving kindness for others at a level which was highly renowned. Accordingly, in the future he became known as Maitreya, meaning "he of loving kindness". This line has been translated as "By Maitreya of great renown" but that is not possible because this prayer was spoken aeons before Maitreya appeared. The translation as given is correct.

[168] The prayer is to complete the six pāramitās, then to complete the remaining four pāramitās, then become a buddha by following the conduct which has been explained in the prayer and by basing oneself in a renowned level of loving kindness.

Altogether the meaning is that "This lordly, venerable being, as with our teacher[169], did not perform generosity and the others according to what pleased him, but by doing them with skilful means and a happy frame of mind accomplished enlightenment"[170].

❖ ❖ ❖

This, which I was able to compose in just a few lines of well-considered verse,
Brings the clever understanding of bloated learned people to a halt;
Is there any way that these people who know all topics of knowledge
And comment on the meaning of hundreds of texts can be fitted into the region of becoming?[171]

The virtue of the master of Tuṣhita's statements
Has entered all the worlds bringing with it

[169] The lordly, venerable being is Maitreya and our teacher is Śhākyamuni Buddha.

[170] This paragraph is not a commentary on the last verse but a distillation of what the Buddha explained was the meaning of this prayer as a whole. This can be known from reading the sūtra which contains the prayer, presented earlier in the book.

[171] There have been Tibetan commentators who wrote extensively on this and many other things. Their writings are clever but Padma Karpo says he is smarter than them so was able to accomplish the task here with an economy of words.

The vast sovereignty of a Capable One;
I dedicate this to its becoming even vaster.[172]

This composition of White Lotus, a lotus born together with the view of the transitory[173] *made in the Dharma Sanctuary of Great Maitreya, was written down by the Realized One of Dromo.*

---

[172] The master of Tuṣhita is Maitreya. Having attained full enlightenment, he remains there, awaiting the time to manifest as a world-leading, guide, a supreme nirmāṇakāya. The virtue of his prayer made in an earlier time has pervaded all the saṃsāric worlds, and with that has led beings to the total sovereignty over both saṃsāra and nirvāṇa that comes with their becoming buddhas. May the prayer become even more pervasive!

[173] White Lotus is Padma Karpo. He is a lotus born into a human body, that is as a person having the view of the transitory five aggregates.

GLOSSARY OF TERMS

Adventitious, Tib. glo bur: This term has the connotations of popping up on the surface of something and of not being part of that thing. Therefore, even though it is often translated as "sudden", that only conveys half of the meaning. In Buddhist literature, something adventitious comes up as a surface event and disappears again precisely because it is not actually part of the thing on whose surface it appeared. It is frequently used in relation to the afflictions because they pop up on the surface of the mind of buddha-nature but are not part of the buddha-nature itself.

Affliction, Skt. kleśha, Tib. nyon mongs: This term is usually translated as emotion or disturbing emotion, etcetera, but the Buddha was very specific about the meaning of this word. When the Buddha referred to the emotions, meaning a movement of mind, he did not refer to them as such but called them "kleśha" in Sanskrit, meaning exactly "affliction". It is a basic part of the Buddhist teaching that emotions afflict beings, giving them problems at the time and causing more problems in the future.

Alertness, Tib. shes bzhin: Alertness is a specific mental event that occurs in dualistic mind. It and another mental event, mindfulness, are the two functions of mind that must be developed in order to develop shamatha or one-pointedness of mind. In that context, mindfulness is what remembers the object of the concentration and holds the mind to it while alertness is the mind watching the situation to ensure that the mindfulness is not lost. If distraction does occur, alertness will know it and will inform the mind to re-establish mindfulness again.

All-Knowing One, Tib. kun mkhyen: Every century in Tibet, there were just a few people who seemed to know everything so were given the title "All-Knowing One". One of them was Longchen Rabjam and throughout this text All-Knowing One always refers to him. Moreover, of all the All-Knowing ones, Longchenpa was regarded as the greatest, therefore, he is also frequently referred to as the "great" or "greatest" All-Knowing One. Note that "All-Knowing" does not mean "omniscient one" even though it is often translated that way.

Appropriation, Skt. upādāna, Tib. nye bar len pa: This is the name of the ninth of the twelve links of interdependent origination. Tsongkhapa gives a good treatment of all twelve links in his interdependent origination section of the *Great Stages of the Path to Enlightenment*, a translation of which is available for free download from the PKTC web-site. It is the crucial point in the process at which a karma that has been previously planted is selected and activated as the karma that will propel the being into its next existence. In other words, it is the key point in a being's existence when the next type of existence is selected. There is the further point that, at the time of death, the particular place that the wind-mind settles in the subtle body, a place related to the seed syllables mentioned in the tantras, also determines the next birth. The two points are not different. The selection of the karma that will propel the next life then affects how the wind-mind will operate at the time of death.

Arousing the mind, Tib. sems bskyed: This is a technical term nearly always used to mean "arousing the enlightenment mind", though it is occasionally used to refer to the deliberate production of other types of mind, for example renunciation. There are two types of arousing the mind—fictional and superfactual; see under fictional enlightenment mind and superfactual enlightenment mind.

Authoritative statement, Skt. āgama, Tib lung. Although often translated as "scripture", authentic statement means statement made by someone who has the true knowledge needed to make fully reliable statements about a subject. It is often used to indicate dharma taught by the Buddha or his disciples which is authoritative because of its source. It is also used in the pair "authoritative statement and realization" which, the Buddha explained, summed up the ways of transmitting his realization.

Awareness, Skt. jñā, Tib. shes pa: "Awareness" is always used in our translations to mean the basic knower of mind or, as Buddhist teaching itself defines it, "a general term for any registering mind", whether dualistic or non-dualistic. Hence, it is used for both samsaric and nirvanic situations; for example, consciousness (Tib. rnam par shes pa) is a dualistic form of awareness, whereas rigpa, wisdom (Tib. ye shes), and so on are non-dualistic forms of awareness.

Becoming, Skt. bhāvanā, Tib. srid pa: This is another name for samsaric existence. Beings in saṃsāra have a samsaric existence but, more than that, they are constantly in a state of becoming—becoming this type of being or that type of being in this abode or that, as they are driven along without choice by the karmic process that drives samsaric existence.

Bliss, Skt. sukha, Tib. bde: The Sanskrit term and its Tibetan translation are usually translated as "bliss" but refer to the whole range of possibilities of everything on the side of good as opposed to bad. Thus, the term will mean pleasant, happy, good, nice, easy, comfortable, blissful, and so on, depending on context.

Bodhichitta, Tib. byang chub sems: See under enlightenment mind.

Bodhisatva, Tib. byang chub sems dpa': A bodhisatva is a person who has engendered the bodhichitta, enlightenment mind, and, with that as a basis, has undertaken the path to the enlightenment of a truly complete buddha specifically for the welfare of other beings. Note that, despite the common appearance of "bodhisattva" in Western books on Buddhism, the Tibetan tradition has steadfastly maintained since the time of the earliest translations that the correct spelling is bodhisatva; see under satva and sattva.

Bodhisatva mahasattva, Skt. bodhisatva mahāsattva, Tib. byang chub sems dpa' sems dpa' chen po: In general, "bodhisatva" refers to *satva*, a being, who is on the path to *bodhi*, truly complete enlightenment, and "mahāsattva" refers to a person who is *mahā* at a greater level of *satva* being, a higher kind of person. Thus, the usual explanation of *bodhisatva mahāsattva* is that it means "a being on the path to truly complete enlightenment, one who is a great type of being because of his intention to reach truly complete enlightenment for the sake of all sentient beings.

However, there is also a second, less common explanation, in which "mahāsattva" does not mean a great being in general but has the specific meaning of those bodhisatvas who, amongst all bodhisatvas, have attained a very great level of being. In this case, it particularly refers to bodhisatvas who have achieved and are dwelling on the highest bodhisatva levels, the eighth to tenth bodhisatva levels. Unlike bodhisatvas at all levels below that, these bodhisatvas have attained such a high level of purity that they cannot regress to a lower level. Their level of attainment is enormous and with it, they have many qualities which are very similar to those of a buddha. It is important to know of this second understanding of "bodhisatva mahāsattva", because when it is used with that meaning, it says something about the bodhisatvas being mentioned. For example, when any of the eight heart-sons of the Buddha are mentioned, they are often referred to as bodhisatva mahāsattvas to indicate their extreme level of attainment. In that case, they specifically are the bodhisatvas above all other bodhisatvas, ones who are close to truly complete enlightenment.

Capable One, Skt. muni, Tib. thub pa: The term "muni" as for example in "Śhākyamuni" has long been thought to mean "sage" because of an entry in Monier-Williams excellent Sanskrit-English dictionary. In fact, it has been used by many Indian religions since the times of ancient India to mean in general, a religious practitioner "one who could do it", one who has made progress on a spiritual path and thereby become able to restrain his three doors away from non-virtue and affliction.

Clinging, Tib. zhen pa: In Buddhism, this term refers specifically to the twofold process of dualistic mind mis-taking things that are not true, not pure, as true, pure, etcetera and then, because of seeing them as highly desirable even though they are not, attaching itself to or clinging to those things. This type of clinging acts as a kind of glue that keeps a person joined to the unsatisfactory things of cyclic existence because of mistakenly seeing them as desirable.

Complete purity, rnam dag: This term refers to the quality of a buddha's mind, which is completely pure compared to a sentient being's mind. The mind of a being in saṃsāra has its primordially pure nature covered over by the muck of dualistic mind. If the being practises correctly, the impurity can be removed and mind can be returned to its original state of complete purity.

Concept tokens, Tib. mtshan ma: This is the technical name for the structures or concepts which function as the words of conceptual mind's language. They are the very basis of operation of the third skandha and hence of the way that dualistic mind communicates with its world. For example, a table seen in direct visual perception will have no concept tokens involved with knowing it. However, when thought becomes involved and there is the thought "table" in an inferential or conceptual perception of the table, the name-tag "table" will be used to reference the table and that name tag is the concept token.

Although we usually reference phenomena via these concepts, the phenomena are not the dualistically referenced things we think of them as being. The actual fact of the phenomena is quite different from the concept tokens used to discursively think about them and is known by wisdom rather than concept-based mind. Therefore, this term is often used in Buddhist literature to signify that dualistic samsaric mind is involved rather than non-dualistic wisdom.

Confusion, Tib. 'khrul pa: In Buddhism, this term mostly refers to the fundamental confusion of taking things the wrong way that happens because of fundamental ignorance, although it can also have the more general meaning of having lots of thoughts and being confused about it. In the first case, it is defined like this "Confusion is the appearance to rational mind of something being present when it is not" and refers, for example, to seeing an object, such as a table, as being truly present, when in fact it is present only as mere, interdependent appearance.

Consciousness, Skt. vijñāna, Tib. rnam shes: The term means "awareness of superficies". A consciousness is a dualistic (jñā) awareness which simply registers a certain type of (vi) superfice, for example, an eye consciousness by definition registers only the superficies of visual form. A very important point is that the addition of the "vi" to the basic term (jñā) for awareness conveys the sense of a less than perfect way of being aware. This is not a wisdom awareness which knows every superfice in an utterly uncomplicated way but a limited type of awareness which is restricted to knowing one kind of superfice or another and which is part of the complicated—and highly unsatisfactory process—called (dualistic) mind. Note that this definition, which is a crucial part of understanding the role of consciousness in samsaric being, is fully conveyed by the Sanskrit and Tibetan terms but not at all by the English term.

Cyclic existence: See under saṃsāra.

Dharmadhatu, Skt. dharmadhātu, Tib. chos kyi dbyings: This is the name for the *dhātu* meaning range or basic space in which all *dharmas*, meaning all phenomena, come into being. If a flower bed is the place where flowers grow and are found, the dharmadhātu is the dharma or phenomena bed in which all phenomena come into being and are found. The term is used in all levels of Buddhist teaching with that base meaning but the explanation of it becomes more profound as the teaching becomes more profound.

Dharmakaya, Skt. dharmakāya, Tib. chos sku: In the general teachings of Buddhism, this refers to the mind of a buddha, with "dharma" meaning reality and "kāya" meaning body.

Dharmata, Skt. dharmatā, Tib. chos nyid: This is a general term meaning the way that something is, and can be applied to anything at all; it is similar in meaning to "actuality" *q.v.* For example, the dharmatā of water is wetness and the dharmatā of the becoming bardo is a place where beings are in a samsaric, or becoming mode, prior to entering a nature bardo. It is used frequently in Tibetan Buddhism to mean "the dharmatā of reality" but that is a specific case of the much larger meaning of the term. To read texts which use this term successfully, one has to understand that the term has a general meaning and then see how that applies in context.

Discursive thought, Skt. vikalpa, Tib. rnam rtog: This means more than just the superficial thought that is heard as a voice in the head. It includes the entirety of conceptual process that arises due to mind contacting any object of any of the senses. The Sanskrit and Tibetan literally mean "(dualistic) thought (that arises from the mind wandering among the) various (superficies *q.v.* perceived in the doors of the senses)".

Elaboration, Tib. spro ba: This is a general name for what is given off by dualistic mind as it goes about its conceptual business. The term is pejorative in that it implies that a story has been made up, un-necessarily, about something which is actually nothing, which is empty. Elaborations, because of what they are, prevent a person from seeing emptiness directly.

Freedom from elaboration or being elaboration-free implies direct sight of emptiness. It is important to understand that these words are used in a theoretical or philosophical way in the second turning sūtra teachings but are used in an experiential way in the final teachings of the third turning sūtras and in the tantras of Great Completion and Mahāmudrā. In the former, being free of elaborations is a definition of what could happen according to the tenets of the Middle Way, and so on; in the latter it is a description of a state of being, one which, because it is empty of all the elaborations of dualistic being, is the actual sphere of emptiness.

Enlightenment mind, Skt. bodhichitta, Tib. byang chub sems: This is a key term of the Great Vehicle. It is the type of mind that is connected not with the lesser enlightenment of an arhat but the enlightenment of a truly complete buddha. As such, it is a mind which is connected with the aim of bringing all sentient beings to that same level of buddhahood. A person who has this mind has entered the Great Vehicle and is either a bodhisatva or a buddha.

It is important to understand that "enlightenment mind" is used to refer equally to the minds of all levels of bodhisatva on the path to buddhahood and to the mind of a buddha who has completed the path. Therefore, it is not "mind striving for enlightenment" as is so often translated, but "enlightenment mind", meaning that kind of mind which is connected with the full enlightenment of a truly complete buddha and which is present in all those who belong to the Great Vehicle. The term is used in the conventional Great Vehicle and also in the Vajra Vehicle. In the Vajra Vehicle, there are some special uses of the term where substances of the pure aspect of the subtle physical body are understood to be manifestations of enlightenment mind.

Entity, Tib. ngo bo: The entity of something is just exactly what that thing is. In English we would often simply say "thing" rather than entity. However, in Buddhism, "thing" has a very specific meaning rather than the general meaning that it has in English. It has become common to translate this term as "essence" *q.v.* However, in most cases "entity", meaning what a thing is rather than an essence of that thing, is the correct translation for this term.

Equipoise and post-attainment, Tib. mnyam bzhag and rjes thob: Although often called "meditation and post-meditation", the actual term is "equipoise and post-attainment". There is great meaning in the actual wording which is lost by the looser translation.

Exaggeration, Tib. skur 'debs pa: In Buddhism, this term is used in two ways. Firstly, it is used in general to mean misunderstanding from the perspective that one has added more to one's understanding of something than needs to be there. Secondly, it is used specifically to indicate that dualistic mind always overstates or exaggerates whatever object it is examining. Dualistic mind always adds the ideas of solidity, permanence, singularity, and so on to everything it references via the concepts that it uses. Severing of exaggeration either means removal of these un-necessary understandings when trying to properly comprehend something or removal of the dualistic process altogether when trying to get to the non-dualistic reality of a phenomenon.

Expressions, Tib. brjod pa: According to Sanskrit and Tibetan grammar following it, expressions refers to mental and verbal expressions. Thus, for example, the phrase seen in translation of "word, thought, and expression" is mistaken. The phrase is actually "expressions mental and verbal".

Fact, Skt. artha, Tib. don: "Fact" is that knowledge of an object that occurs to the surface of mind or wisdom. It is not the object but what the mind or wisdom understands as the object. Thus there are two usages of "fact": fact known to dualistic and non-dualistic minds. The higher tantras especially use "fact" to refer to the actual fact known in direct perception of actuality. Thus, there are phrases such as "in fact" which do not mean that the author is speaking truly about something but that whatever is about to be said is referring to actual fact as known to wisdom. A further complexity is that phrases such as "in fact" in those contexts are often abbreviations of "in superfact" *q.v.* This brings a further difficulty for the reader because "superfact" can be used in a general way to indicate directly perceived non-samsaric fact or can be used according to its specific definition (for which see superfact). In Buddhist tradition, problems like this are solved by having the text explained by one's teacher. That might not be possible for some readers, so uses of the word "fact" should be looked at carefully to see whether they are indicating fact in general or the factual situation of knowing reality in direct perception.

Fictional, Skt. saṃvṛtti, Tib. kun rdzob: This term is paired with the term "superfactual" *q.v.* In the past, these terms have been translated as "relative" and "absolute" respectively, but those translations are nothing like the original terms. These terms are extremely important in the Buddhist teaching so it is very important that they be corrected, but more than that, if the actual meaning of these terms is not presented, then the teaching connected with them cannot be understood.

The Sanskrit term saṃvṛtti means a deliberate invention, a fiction, a hoax. It refers to the mind of ignorance which, because of being obscured and so not seeing suchness, is not true but a fiction. The things that appear to that ignorance are therefore fictional. Nonetheless, the beings who live in this ignorance believe that the things that appear to them through the filter of ignorance are true, are real. Therefore, these beings live in fictional truth.

Fictional and superfactual: Skt. saṃvṛiti, paramārtha: Fictional and superfactual are our greatly improved translations for "relative" and "absolute" respectively. Briefly, the original Sanskrit word for fiction means a deliberately produced *fiction* and refers to the world projected by a mind controlled by ignorance. The original word for superfact means "that *super*ior *fact* that appears on the surface of the mind of a noble one who has transcended saṃsāra" and refers to reality seen as it actually is. Relative and absolute do not convey this meaning at all and, when they are used, the meaning being presented is simply lost.

Field, Field realm, Tib. zhing, zhing khams: This term is often translated "buddha field" though there is no "buddha" in the term. There are many different types of "fields" in both saṃsāra and nirvāṇa. Thus there are fields that belong to enlightenment and ones that belong to ignorance. Moreover, just as there are "realms" of saṃsāra—desire, form, and formless—so there are realms of nirvāṇa—the fields of the dharmakāya, saṃbhogakāya, and nirmāṇakāya and these are therefore called "field realms".

Generic image, Tib. spyi don: Generic image is the technical name for one type of conceptual structure used in the operation of conceptual mind. A generic image is a concept that conceptual mind takes and uses instead of having a direct perception of the actual thing. For example, a person can have a concept of a table, a complicated operation one aspect of which is a generic image, or can have direct sight of a table, which has no operation of concept with it. Thus, for example, the process of rational, dualistic mind with its generic images can never get at something like rigpa which lies outside the reach of dualistic mind.

Grasped-at and grasping, Tib. gzung 'dzin: When mind is turned outwardly as it is in the normal operation of dualistic mind, it has developed two faces that appear simultaneously. Special names are given to these two faces: mind appearing in the form of the external object being referenced is called "that which is grasped" and mind appearing in the form of the consciousness that is registering it is called the "grasper" or "grasping" of it. Thus, there is the pair of terms "grasped-grasper" or "grasped-grasping". When these two terms are used, it alerts one to the fact that a Mind Only style of presentation is being discussed. This pair of terms pervades Mind Only, Middle Way, and tantric writings and is exceptionally important in all of them.

Note that one could substitute the word "apprehended" for "grasped" and "apprehender" for "grasper" or "grasping" and that would reflect one connotation of the original Sanskrit terminology. The solidified duality of grasped and grasper is nothing but an invention of dualistic thought; it has that kind of character or characteristic.

Great Vehicle, Skt. mahāyāna, Tib. theg pa chen po: The Buddha's teachings as a whole can be summed up into three vehicles where a vehicle is defined as that which can carry a person to a certain destination. The first vehicle, called the Lesser Vehicle, contains the teachings designed to get an individual moving on the spiritual path through showing the unsatisfactory state of cyclic existence and an emancipation from that. However, that path is only concerned with personal emancipation and fails to take account of all of the beings that there are in existence. There used to be eighteen schools of Lesser Vehicle in India but the only one surviving nowadays is the Theravāda of south-east Asia. The Greater Vehicle is a step up from that. The Buddha explained that it was great in comparison to the Lesser Vehicle for seven reasons. The first of those is that it is concerned with attaining the truly complete enlightenment of a truly complete buddha for the sake of every sentient being where the Lesser Vehicle is concerned only with a personal liberation that is not truly complete enlightenment and which is achieved only for the sake of that practitioner. The Great Vehicle has two divisions: a conventional form in which the path is taught in a logical, conventional way, and an unconventional form in which the path is taught in a very direct way. This latter vehicle is called the Vajra Vehicle because it takes the innermost, indestructible (vajra) fact of reality of one's own mind as the vehicle to enlightenment.

Kaya, Skt. kāya, Tib. sku: The Sanskrit term means a functional or coherent collection of parts, similar to the French "corps", and hence also comes to mean "a body". It is used in Tibetan Buddhist texts specifically to distinguish bodies belonging to the enlightened side from ones belonging to the samsaric side.

Enlightened being in Buddhism is said to be comprised of one or more kāyas. It is most commonly explained to consist of one, two, three, four, or five kāyas, though it is pointed out that there are infinite aspects to enlightened being and therefore it can also be said to consist of an infinite number of kāyas. In fact, these descriptions of enlightened being consisting of one or more kāyas are given for the sake of understanding what is beyond conceptual understanding so should not be taken as absolute statements.

The most common description of enlightened being is that it is comprised of three kāyas: dharma, saṃbhoga, and nirmāṇakāyas. Briefly stated, the dharmakāya is the body of truth, the saṃbhogakāya is the body replete with the good qualities of enlightenment, and the nirmāṇakāya is the body manifested into the worlds of saṃsāra and nirvāṇa to benefit beings.

Dharmakāya refers to that aspect of enlightened being in which the being sees the truth for himself and, in doing so, fulfils his own needs for enlightenment. The dharmakāya is purely mind, without form. The remaining two bodies are summed up under the heading of rūpakāyas or form bodies manifested specifically to fulfil the needs of all un-enlightened beings. "Saṃbhogakāya" has been mostly translated as "body of enjoyment" or "body of rapture" but it is clearly stated in Buddhist texts on the subject that the name refers to a situation replete with what is useful, that is, to the fact that the saṃbhogakāya contains all of the good qualities of enlightenment as needed to benefit sentient beings. The saṃbhogakāya is extremely subtle and not accessible by most sentient beings; the nirmāṇakāya is a coarser manifestation which can reach sentient beings in many ways. Nirmāṇakāya should not be thought of as a physical body but as the capability to express enlightened being in whatever way is needed throughout all the different worlds of sentient beings. Thus, as much as it appears as a supreme buddha who shows the dharma to beings, it also appears as anything needed within sentient beings' worlds to give them assistance.

Kayas and wisdoms, Tib. sku dang ye shes: Enlightened being might be empty of samsaric phenomena but it does have enlightened content. "Kāyas and wisdoms" or "bodies and wisdoms" is a stock phrase used to indicate either the content of enlightenment or to imply that it does have content.

Knowledgeability, Tib. spob pa: Knowledgeability is a quality of both mind and speech. It refers to having the ability to instantly recall the knowledge needed when something needs to be expressed verbally, for example when teaching, and therefore also a confidence of knowledge that comes with it. Knowledgeability can be developed by anyone but the knowledgeability in the case of a buddha is inconceivable: a buddha's wisdom knows all things throughout all times so he can recall an inconceivable array of knowledge and with that a buddha has an ultimate level of confidence that he can do so. This then means that a buddha's verbal presentation of his knowledge is inconceivable: his abilities of speech are miraculous and beyond the reach of ordinary being's spoken abilities. For example, with one instance of speech he can answer the questions of countless numbers of beings, with each answer appearing to each listener in a language that the listener understands, and in a way that the listener can comprehend.

Lay aside, Tib. bshags pa: This term is usually translated as "confession" but that is not the meaning. The term literally means to cut something away and remove it from oneself. In Buddhism, it is used in the context of ridding oneself of the karmic seeds sown by bad karmic actions.

Buddhism is a totally non-theistic religion, so it is very important to understand that one is not confessing wrongdoings to anyone, including oneself. There is no granting of absolution in this system. As the Buddha himself said, he has no ability to purify the karmic stains of sentient beings, he can only teach them how to do so. The practice that he taught for ridding oneself of karmic wrongdoings is the practice of realizing for oneself that they hold the seed of future suffering, rousing regret, and distancing oneself from them. In doing so, one lays them aside.

There is a longer phrase that indicates the full practice of laying aside. The Tibetan phrase "mthol zhing shags pa" literally means "admitting and laying aside". Note that "admitting" also does not entail confession; it refers to that fact that one first has to admit or acknowledge to oneself that one has done something wrong, karmically speaking, and that it will have undesirable consequences. Without this, one cannot effectively take the second step of distancing oneself from the actions. Therefore, it is explained that the process of "laying aside" has to be understood to include the practice of "admission" because, without that acknowledgement, the laying aside cannot be done.

Lesser Vehicle, Skt. hīnayāna, Tib. theg pa dman pa: See under Great Vehicle.

Luminosity or illumination, Skt. prabhāsvara, Tib. 'od gsal ba: The core of mind has two aspects: an emptiness factor and a knowing factor. The Buddha and many Indian religious teachers used "luminosity" as a metaphor for the knowing quality of the core of mind. If in English we would say "Mind has a knowing quality", the teachers of ancient India would say, "Mind has an illuminative quality; it is like a source of light which illuminates what it knows".

This term has been translated as "clear light" but that is a mistake that comes from not understanding the etymology of the word. It does not refer to a light that has the quality of clearness (something that makes no sense, actually!) but to the illuminative property which is the nature of the empty mind.

Note also that in both Sanskrit and Tibetan Buddhist literature, this term is frequently abbreviated just to Skt. "vara" and Tib. "gsal ba" with no change of meaning. Unfortunately, this has been thought to be another word and it has then been translated with "clarity", when in fact it is just this term in abbreviation.

Mara, Skt. māra, Tib. bdud: The Sanskrit term is closely related to the word "death". Buddha spoke of four classes of extremely negative influences that have the capacity to drag a sentient being deep into saṃsāra. They are the "māras" or "kiss of death": of having a samsaric set of five skandhas; of having afflictions; of death itself; and of the son of gods, which means being seduced and taken in totally by sensuality.

Migrator, Tib. 'gro ba: Migrator is one of several terms that were commonly used by the Buddha to mean "sentient being". It shows sentient beings from the perspective of their constantly being forced to go here and there from one rebirth to another by the power of karma. They are like flies caught in a jar, constantly buzzing back and forth. The term is often translated using "beings" which is another general term for sentient beings but doing so loses the meaning entirely: Buddhist authors who know the tradition do not use the word loosely but use it specifically to give the sense of beings who are constantly and helplessly going from one birth to another, and that is how the term should be read. The term "six migrators" refers to the six types of migrators within samsaric existence—hell-beings, pretas, animals, humans, demigods, and gods.

Mind, Skt. chitta, Tib. sems: There are several terms for mind in the Buddhist tradition, each with its own, specific meaning. This term is the most general term for the samsaric type of mind. It refers to the type of mind that is produced because of fundamental ignorance of enlightened mind. Whereas the wisdom of enlightened mind lacks all complexity and knows in a non-dualistic way, this mind of un-enlightenment is a very complicated apparatus that only ever knows in a dualistic way.

Mindfulness, Skt. smṛiti, Tib. dran pa: A particular mental event, one that has the ability to keep mind on its object. Together with alertness, it is one of the two causes of developing śhamatha. See under alertness for an explanation.

Mindness, Skt. chittatā, Tib. sems nyid: Mindness is a specific term of the tantras. It is one of many terms meaning the essence of mind or the nature of mind. It conveys the sense of "what mind is at its very core". It has sometimes been translated as "mind itself" but that is a misunderstanding of the Tibetan word "nyid". The term does not mean "that thing mind" where mind refers to dualistic mind. Rather, it means the very core of dualistic mind, what mind is at root, without all of the dualistic baggage.

Mindness is a path term. It refers to exactly the same thing as "actuality" or "actuality of mind" which is a ground term but does so from the practitioner's perspective. It conveys the sense to a practitioner that he has baggage of dualistic mind that has not yet been purified but that there is a core to that mind that he can work with.

Muni: See under capable one.

Noble one, Skt. ārya, Tib. 'phags pa: In Buddhism, a noble one is a being who has become spiritually advanced to the point that he has passed beyond cyclic existence. According to the Buddha, the beings in cyclic existence were ordinary beings, spiritual commoners, and the beings who had passed beyond it were special, the nobility.

Outflow, Skt. āsrāva, Tib. zag pa: The Sanskrit term means a bad discharge, like pus coming out of a wound. Outflows occur when wisdom loses its footing and falls into the elaborations of dualistic mind. Therefore, anything with duality also has outflows. This is sometimes translated as "defiled" or "conditioned" but these fail to capture the meaning. The idea is that wisdom can remain self-contained in its own unique sphere but, when it loses its ability to stay within itself, it starts to have leakages into dualism that are defilements on the wisdom. See also under un-outflowed.

Post-attainment, Tib. rjes thob: See under equipoise and post-attainment.

Prajna, Skt. prajñā, Tib. shes rab: The Sanskrit term, literally meaning "best type of mind" is defined as that which makes correct distinctions between this and that and hence which arrives at correct understanding. It has been translated as "wisdom" but that is not correct because it is, generally speaking, a mental event belonging to dualistic mind where "wisdom" is used to refer to the non-dualistic knower of a buddha. Moreover, the main feature of prajñā is its ability to distinguish correctly between one thing and another and hence to arrive at a correct understanding.

Provisional and definitive meaning, Skt. neyārtha and nītārtha, Tib. drangs don and nges don: This is a pair of terms used to distinguish which is an ultimate or final teaching and which is not. A teaching which guides a student along to a certain understanding where the understanding led to is not an ultimate understanding is called "provisional meaning". The teaching is not false even though it does not show the final meaning; it is a technique of skilful means used to lead a student in steps to the final meaning. A teaching which shows a student the final meaning directly is called "definitive meaning". The understanding presented cannot be refined or shown in a more precise way; it is the final and actual understanding to be understood. These terms are most often used in Buddhism when discussing the status of the three turnings of the wheel of dharma.

Rational mind, Tib. blo: Rational mind is one of several terms for mind in Buddhist terminology. It specifically refers to a mind that judges this against that. With rare exception it is used to refer to samsaric mind, given that samsaric mind only works in the dualistic mode of comparing this versus that. Because of this, the term is mostly used in a pejorative sense to point out samsaric mind as opposed to an enlightened type of mind.

This term has been commonly translated simply as "mind" but that fails to identify this term properly and leaves it confused with the many other words that are also translated simply as "mind". It is not just another mind but is specifically the sort of mind that creates the situation of this and that (*ratio* in Latin) and hence, at least in the teachings of Kagyu and Nyingma, upholds the duality of saṃsāra. In that case, it is the very opposite of the essence of mind. Thus, this is a key term which should be noted and not just glossed over as "mind".

Realization, Tib. rtogs pa: Realization has a very specific meaning: it refers to correct knowledge that has been gained in such a way that the knowledge does not abate. There are two important points here. Firstly, realization is not absolute. It refers to the removal of obscurations, one at a time. Each time that a practitioner removes an obscuration, he gains a realization because of it. Therefore, there are as many levels of realization as there are obscurations. Maitreya, in the *Ornament of Manifest Realizations*, shows how the removal of the various obscurations that go with each of the three realms of samsaric existence produces realization.

Secondly, realization is stable or, as the Tibetan wording says, "unchanging". As Guru Rinpoche pointed out, "Intellectual knowledge is like a patch, it drops away; experiences on the path are temporary, they evaporate like mist; realization is unchanging".

Reference and Referencing, Tib. dmigs pa: Referencing is the name for the process in which dualistic mind references an actual object by using a conceptual token instead of the actual object. Whatever is referenced is then called a reference. Note that these terms imply the presence of dualistic mind and their opposites, non-referencing and being without reference imply the presence of non-dualistic wisdom.

Refuge, Skt. śharaṇaṃ, Tib. bskyab pa: The Sanskrit term means "shelter", "protection from harm". Everyone seeks a refuge from the unsatisfactoriness of life, even if it is a simple act like brushing the teeth to prevent the body from decaying un-necessarily. Buddhists, after having thought carefully about their situation and who could provide a refuge from it which would be thoroughly reliable, find that three things—buddha, dharma, and saṅgha—are the only things that could provide that kind of refuge. Therefore, Buddhists take refuge in those Three Jewels of Refuge as they are called. Taking refuge in the Three Jewels is clearly laid out as the one doorway to all Buddhist practice and realization.

Samsara, Skt. saṃsāra, Tib. 'khor ba: This is the most general name for the type of existence in which sentient beings live. It refers to the fact that they continue on from one existence to another, always within the enclosure of births that are produced by ignorance and experienced as unsatisfactory. The original Sanskrit means to be constantly going about, here and there. The Tibetan term literally means "cycling", because of which it is frequently translated into English with "cyclic existence" though that is not quite the meaning of the term.

Satva and sattva: According to the Tibetan tradition established at the time of the great translation work done at Samye under the watch of Padmasambhava not to mention one hundred and sixty-three of the greatest Buddhist scholars of Sanskrit-speaking India, there is a difference of meaning between the Sanskrit terms "satva" and "sattva", with satva meaning "an heroic kind of being" and "sattva" meaning simply "a being". According to the Tibetan tradition established under the advice of the Indian scholars mentioned above, satva is correct for the words Vajrasatva and bodhisatva, whereas sattva is correct for the words samayasattva, samādhisattva, and jñānasattva, and is also used alone to refer to any or all of these three satvas.

All Tibetan texts produced since the time of the great translations conform to this system and all Tibetan experts agree that this is correct, but Western translators of Tibetan texts have for the last few hundreds of years claimed that they know better and have "satva" to "sattva" in every case, causing confusion amongst Westerners confronted by the correct spellings. Recently, publications by Western Sanskrit scholars have been appearing in which these great experts finally admit that they were wrong and that the Tibetan system is and always has been correct!

Shamatha, Skt. śhamatha, Tib. gzhi gnas: This is the name of one of the two main practices of meditation used in the Buddhist system to gain insight into reality. This practice creates a one-pointedness of mind which can then be used as a foundation for development of the insight of the other practice, vipaśhyanā. If the development of śhamatha is taken through to completion, the result is a mind that sits stably on its object without any effort and a body which is filled with ease. Altogether, this result of the practice is called "the creation of workability of body and mind".

Special intention, Tib. lhag bsam: This term is used in general to refer to all specially pure intentions. In Great Vehicle literature it will more often refer specifically to enlightenment mind but even then, it can be used to mean bodhichitta in general or an especially pure instance of enlightenment mind.

Sugata, Tib. bde bar gshegs pa: This term is one of many names for a buddha. It has the twofold meaning of someone who has gone on a good, pleasant, easy journey and who has arrived at a place which is good, pleasant, and full of ease. The meaning in relation to buddhahood is explained at length in *Unending Auspiciousness, the Sutra of the Recollection of the Noble Three Jewels* by Tony Duff, published by Padma Karpo Translation Committee, 2010, ISBN: 978-9937-8386-1-0.

Sugatagarbha, Tib. bde bar gshegs pa'i snying po: This one of a pair of terms for the potential existing in all sentient beings that makes the attainment of buddhahood possible, also called the buddha-nature. The other term is tathāgatagarbha. The sanskrit term "garbha" primarily means something which is potent but contained in an outer shell, like a seed, and is also used to mean a matrix or womb from which something can be produced. Both meanings are applicable. Tibetans translated garbha with "snying po" which has many meanings but in this case means "an essence or core", which was their take on the meaning of buddha-nature. The meaning altogether is a seed contained within the obscurations of samsaric being, which makes it possible to become a sugata or tathāgata, that is, a buddha.

Sugatagarbha has the same basic meaning as tathāgatagarbha but is a practical way of talking where tathagātagarbha is theoretical. Sugatagarbha is used when an author is talking about the practical realities of an essence that can be or is being developed into enlightened being. For example, in the sūtras of the third turning of the wheel, the Buddha speaks of tathāgatagarbha when laying out the theory of buddha-nature but switches to sugatagarbha when speaking of wisdom as what is to be actually attained. Similarly, the tantras, which are mainly concerned with the practical attainment of wisdom mainly, use the term sugatagarbha and rarely use the term tathāgata garbha. See also under sugata.

Superfactual, Skt. paramārtha,Tib. don dam: This term is paired with the term "fictional" *q.v.* In the past, the terms have been translated as "relative" and "absolute" respectively, but those translations are nothing like the original terms. These terms are extremely important in the Buddhist teaching so it is very important that their translations be corrected but, more than that, if the actual meaning of these terms is not presented, the teaching connected with them cannot be understood.

The Sanskrit term literally means "the fact for that which is above all others, special, superior" and refers to the wisdom mind possessed by those who have developed themselves spiritually to the point of having transcended saṃsāra. That wisdom is *superior* to an ordinary, un-developed person's consciousness and the *facts* that appear on its surface are superior compared to the facts that appear on the ordinary person's consciousness. Therefore, it is superfact or the holy fact, more literally. What this wisdom knows is true for the beings who have it, therefore what the wisdom sees is superfactual truth.

Superfactual truth, Skt. paramārthasatya, Tib. don dam bden pa: See under superfactual.

Superfice, superficies, Tib. rnam pa: In discussions of mind, a distinction is made between the entity of mind which is a mere knower and the superficial things that appear on its surface and which are known by it. In other words, the superficies are the various things which pass over the surface of mind but which are not mind. Superficies are all the specifics that constitute appearance—for example, the colour white within a moment of visual consciousness, the sound heard within an ear consciousness, and so on.

The authentic, Tib. yang dag: A name for reality, that which is real. For example "the view of the authentic" means "the view of reality" not a correct view.

The element, Skt. dhātu, Tib. khams. The Sanskrit term has many meanings; the meaning here is "a fundamental substance from which something else can be produced". When the Buddha explained the tathāgatagarbha or buddha nature in the third turning of the wheel, he used several names for it, each one showing a specific aspect of it. He called it the element with the meaning "that basis substance from which buddhahood can be produced". He called it "the type" meaning that it was the same sort of thing as buddhahood and therefore could lead to buddhahood; this term is also translated as "family" and "lineage". He also called it "the seed" meaning the seed of enlightenment. He also called it "the garbha"; see under sugatagarbha for the meaning.

Three kayas: See under kaya.

Tirthika, Skt. tīrthika, Tib. mu stegs pa: This is very kind name adopted by the Buddha for those who did not follow him but who, because they followed some other spiritual path, had at least started on the path back to enlightenment. The Sanskrit name means "those who have arrived at the steps at the edge of the pool". A lengthy explanation is given in the *Illuminator Tibetan-English Dictionary* by Tony Duff and published by Padma Karpo Translation Committee.

Un-outflowed, Skt. aśhrāva, Tib. zag pa med pa: Un-outflowed dharmas are ones that are connected with wisdom that has not lost its footing and leaked out into a defiled state; it is self-contained wisdom without any taint of dualistic mind and its apparatus. See also outflowed.

Unsatisfactoriness, Skt. duḥkha, Tib. sdug bngal: This term is usually translated into English with "suffering" but there are many problems with that. When the Buddha talked about the nature of samsaric existence, he said that it was unsatisfactory. He used the term "duḥkha", which includes actual suffering but means much more than that. Duḥkha is one of a pair of terms, the other being "sukha", which is usually translated as, but does not only mean, bliss. The real meaning of duḥkha is "everything on the side of bad"—not good, uncomfortable, unpleasant, not nice, and so on. Thus, it means "unsatisfactory in every possible way". The real meaning of its opposite, sukha, is "everything on the side of good"—not bad, comfortable, pleasant, nice, and so on. Therefore, that he is completely liberated from the sufferings actually means that he has completely liberated himself from the unsatisfactoriness of samsara, which includes all types of suffering and happiness, too.

Vipashyana, Skt. vipaśhyanā, Tib. lhag mthong: This is the Sanskrit name for one of the two main practices of meditation needed in the Buddhist system for gaining insight into reality. The other one, śhamatha, keeps the mind focussed while this one looks piercingly into the nature of things.

Wisdom, Skt. jñāna, Tib. ye shes: This is a fruition term that refers to the kind of mind—the kind of knower—possessed by a buddha.

Sentient beings do have this kind of knower but it is covered over by a very complex apparatus for knowing, that is, dualistic mind. If they practise the path to buddhahood, they will leave behind their obscuration and return to having this kind of knower.

The Sanskrit term has the sense of knowing in the most simple and immediate way. This sort of knowing is present at the core of every being's mind. Therefore, the Tibetans called it "the particular type of awareness which is there primordially". Because of the Tibetan wording it has often been called "primordial wisdom" in English translations, but that goes too far; it is just "wisdom" in the sense of the most fundamental knowing possible.

Wisdom does not operate in the same way as samsaric mind; it comes about in and of itself without depending on cause and effect. Therefore it is frequently referred to as "self-arising wisdom" *q.v.*

ABOUT THE AUTHOR, PADMA KARPO TRANSLATION COMMITTEE, AND THEIR SUPPORTS FOR STUDY

I have been encouraged over the years by all of my teachers to pass on the knowledge I have accumulated in a lifetime dedicated to study and practice, primarily in the Tibetan tradition of Buddhism. On the one hand, they have encouraged me to teach. On the other, they are concerned that, while many general books on Buddhism have been and are being published, there are few books that present the actual texts of the tradition. Therefore they, together with a number of major figures in the Buddhist book publishing world, have also encouraged me to translate and publish high quality translations of individual texts of the tradition.

My teachers always remark with great appreciation on the extraordinary amount of teaching that I have heard in this life. It allows for highly informed, accurate translations of a sort not usually seen. Briefly, I spent the 1970's studying, practising, then teaching the Gelugpa system at Chenrezig Institute, Australia, where I was a founding member and also the first Australian to be ordained as a monk in the Tibetan Buddhist tradition. In 1980, I moved to the United States to study at the feet of the Vidyadhara Chogyam Trungpa Rinpoche. I stayed in his Vajradhatu community, now called Shambhala, where I studied and practised all the Karma Kagyu, Nyingma, and Shambhala teachings being presented there and was a senior member of the Nalanda Translation Committee. After the vidyadhara's nirvana, I moved in 1992 to Nepal, where I have been continuously involved with the study, practise, translation, and teaching of the Kagyu system and especially of the Nyingma system of Great Completion. In recent years, I have spent extended times in Tibet with the greatest living Tibetan masters of Great Completion, receiving very pure transmissions of the ultimate levels of this teaching directly in Tibetan and practising them there in retreat. In that way, I have studied and practised extensively not in one Tibetan tradition as is usually done, but in three of the four Tibetan traditions—Gelug, Kagyu, and Nyingma—and also in the Theravada tradition, too.

With that as a basis, I have taken a comprehensive and long term approach to the work of translation. For any language, one first must have the lettering needed to write the language. Therefore, as a member of the Nalanda Translation Committee, I spent some years in the 1980's making Tibetan word-processing software and high-quality Tibetan fonts. After that, reliable lexical works are needed. Therefore, during the 1990's I spent some years writing the *Illuminator Tibetan-English Dictionary* and a set of treatises on Tibetan grammar, preparing a variety of key Tibetan reference works needed for the study and translation of Tibetan Buddhist texts, and giving our Tibetan software the tools needed to translate and research Tibetan texts. During this time, I also translated full-time for various Tibetan gurus and ran the Drukpa Kagyu Heritage Project—at the time the largest project in Asia for the preservation of Tibetan Buddhist texts. With the dictionaries, grammar texts, and specialized software in place, and a wealth of knowledge, I turned my attention in the year 2000 to the translation and publication of important texts of Tibetan Buddhist literature.

Padma Karpo Translation Committee (PKTC) was set up to provide a home for the translation and publication work. The committee focusses on producing books containing the best of Tibetan literature, and, especially, books that meet the needs of practitioners. At the time of writing, PKTC has published a wide range of books that, collectively, make a complete program of study for those practising Tibetan Buddhism, and especially for those interested in the higher tantras. All in all, you will find many books both free and for sale on the PKTC web-site. Most are available both as paper editions and e-books.

It would take up too much space here to present an extensive guide to our books and how they can be used as the basis for a study program. However, a guide of that sort is available on the PKTC web-site, whose address is on the copyright page of this book and we recommend that you read it to see how this book fits into the overall scheme of PKTC publications.

The commentary here is by Padma Karpo, one of Tibet greatest authors, for more about him and for other texts of his which we have published, see:

- *Drukchen Padma Karpo's Collected Works on Mahāmudrā*, the entire writings on Mahāmudrā of Padma Karpo;
- *Gampopa's Mahāmudrā, The Five-Part Mahāmudrā of the Kagyus*, includes a text of Padma Karpo on Mahāmudrā and a long explanation of Padma Karpo's place in Tibetan literature
- *The Bodyless Dakini Dharma: The Dakini Hearing Lineage of the Kagyus*, with several very early teachings on the view.

Other sūtra publications of interest would be:

- *The Noble One Called "Point of Passage Wisdom", A Great Vehicle Sutra*, the root sūtra of the ten profound essence sūtras of Other Emptiness of the third turning of the wheel;
- *The Noble One Petitioned by the Householder Uncouth, A Great Vehicle Sutra*, another sūtra of the ten profound essence sūtras of Other Emptiness of the third turning of the wheel;
- *Samantabhadra's Prayer with Commentaries By Noble Nāgārjuna Tenpa'i Wangchuk, and Tony Duff.*

We make a point of including, where possible, the relevant Tibetan texts in Tibetan script in our books. We also make them available in electronic editions that can be downloaded free from our web-site, as discussed below. The Tibetan texts for this book are included at the back of the book and are available for download from the PKTC web-site.

Electronic Resources

PKTC has developed a complete range of electronic tools to facilitate the study and translation of Tibetan texts. For many years now, this software has been a prime resource for Tibetan Buddhist centres throughout the world, including in Tibet itself. It is available through the PKTC web-site.

The wordprocessor TibetDoc has the only complete set of tools for creating, correcting, and formatting Tibetan text according to the norms of the Tibetan language. It can also be used to make texts with mixed Tibetan and English or other languages. Extremely high quality Tibetan fonts, based on the forms of Tibetan calligraphy learned from old masters from pre-Communist Chinese Tibet, are also available. Because of their excellence, these typefaces have achieved a legendary status amongst Tibetans.

TibetDoc is used to prepare electronic editions of Tibetan texts in the PKTC text input office in Asia. Tibetan texts are often corrupt so the input texts are carefully corrected prior to distribution. After that, they are made available through the PKTC web-site. These electronic texts are not careless productions like so many of the Tibetan texts found on the web, but are highly reliable editions useful to non-scholars and scholars alike. Some of the larger collections of these texts are for purchase, but most are available for free download.

The electronic texts can be read, searched, and even made into an electronic library using either TibetDoc or our other software, TibetD Reader. Like TibetDoc, TibetD Reader is advanced software with many capabilities made specifically to meet the needs of reading and researching Tibetan texts. PKTC software is for purchase but we make a free version of TibetD Reader available for free download on the PKTC web-site.

A key feature of TibetDoc and Tibet Reader is that Tibetan terms in texts can be looked up on the spot using PKTC's electronic dictionaries. PKTC also has several electronic dictionaries—some Tibetan-Tibetan and some Tibetan-English—and a number of other reference works. The *Illuminator Tibetan-English Dictionary* is renowned for its completeness and accuracy.

This combination of software, texts, reference works, and dictionaries that work together seamlessly has become famous over the years. It has been the basis of many, large publishing projects within the Tibetan Buddhist community around the world for over thirty years and is popular amongst all those needing to work with Tibetan language or deepen their understanding of Buddhism through Tibetan texts.

TIBETAN TEXTS

༄༅། །འཕགས་པ་དཀོན་མཆོག་བརྩེགས་པ་ཆེན་པོའི་ཆོས་ཀྱི་རྣམ་གྲངས་ལེའུ་སྟོང་ཕྲག་བརྒྱ་པ་ལས་ལེའུ་བཞི་བཅུ་རྩ་གཅིག་པ་སྟེ། འཕགས་པ་བྱམས་པས་ཞུས་པ་ལུང་བསྟན་པ། བམ་པོ་གཅིག་པ། རྒྱ་གར་སྐད་དུ། ཨཱརྱ་མཻ་ཏྲི་ཡ་པ་རི་པྲྀ་ཙྪཱ་ནཱ་མ་མ་ཧཱ་ཡཱ་ན་སཱུ་ཏྲ། བོད་སྐད་དུ། འཕགས་པ་བྱམས་པས་ཞུས་པ་ཞེས་བྱ་བ་ཐེག་པ་ཆེན་པོའི་མདོ། སངས་རྒྱས་དང་། བྱང་ཆུབ་སེམས་དཔའ་ཐམས་ཅད་ལ་ཕྱག་འཚལ་ལོ། །འདི་སྐད་བདག་གིས་ཐོས་པ་དུས་གཅིག་ན། བཅོམ་ལྡན་འདས་ཡུལ་བཀྲ་ན་ཚུ་སྐྱིན་བྱིས་པ་གསོད་ལྷ་བུའི་རི་འཇིགས་སུ་རུང་བའི་ནགས་རི་དྭགས་ཀྱི་གནས་ན་དགེ་སློང་ལྔ་བརྒྱ་ཙམ་གྱི་དགེ་སློང་གི་དགེ་འདུན་ཆེན་པོ་མངོན་པར་ཤེས་པ་མངོན་པར་ཤེས་པ་གནས་བརྟན་ཉན་ཐོས་ཆེན་པོ་ཤ་སྟག་ལ། འདི་ལྟ་སྟེ། ཚེ་དང་ལྡན་པ་ཀུན་ཤེས་ཀཽ་ཎྜི་ནྱ་དང་། ཚེ་དང་ལྡན་པ་རྟ་ཐུལ་དང་། ཚེ་དང་ལྡན་པ་རླངས་པ་དང་། ཚེ་དང་ལྡན་པ་མིང་ཆེན་དང་། ཚེ་དང་ལྡན་པ་བཟང་ལྡན་དང་། ཚེ་དང་ལྡན་པ་དྲི་མ་མེད་དང་། ཚེ་དང་ལྡན་པ་གང་པོ་དང་། ཚེ་དང་ལྡན་པ་བ་ལང་བདག་དང་། ཚེ་དང་ལྡན་པ་རི་དྭགས་མགོ་དང་། ཚེ་དང་ལྡན་པ་ལྟེང་རྒྱས་འོད་སྲུང་དང་། ཚེ་དང་ལྡན་པ་ཆུ་ཀླུང་འོད་སྲུང་དང་། ཚེ་དང་ལྡན་པ་ག་ཡ་འོད་སྲུང་དང་། ཚེ་དང་ལྡན་པ་བྱིན་པ་འོད་སྲུང་དང་། ཚེ་དང་ལྡན་པ་འོད་སྲུང་ཆེན་པོ་དང་། ཚེ་དང་ལྡན་པ་དོན་ཡོད་རྒྱལ་པོ་དང་། ཚེ་དང་ལྡན་པ་བློ་གྲོས་བཟང་

དང་། ཚེ་དང་ལྡན་པ་ཤཱ་རིའི་བུ་དང་། ཚེ་དང་ལྡན་པ་མཽད་གལ་གྱི་བུ་ཆེན་པོ་དང་། ཚེ་དང་ལྡན་པ་རི་རྒྱལ་དང་། ཚེ་དང་ལྡན་པ་དགའ་བོ་དང་། ཚེ་དང་ལྡན་པ་ཉེ་དགའ་དང་། ཚེ་དང་ལྡན་པ་ཀུན་དགའ་བོ་དང་། ཚེ་དང་ལྡན་པ་སྒྲ་གཅན་ཟིན་དང་། དེ་དག་ལ་སོགས་པ་དགེ་སློང་ལྔ་བརྒྱ་ཙམ་དང་ཐབས་ཅིག་ཏུ་བཞུགས་སོ། །བྱམས་པ་ལ་སོགས་པ་བྱང་ཆུབ་སེམས་དཔའ་སེམས་དཔའ་ཆེན་པོ་མངོན་པར་ཤེས་པ་མངོན་པར་ཤེས་པ་ཁྲི་དང་ཡང་ཐབས་ཅིག་ལ་འདི་ལྟ་སྟེ། བྱང་ཆུབ་སེམས་དཔའ་བློ་གྲོས་འཕེལ་དང་། བྱང་ཆུབ་སེམས་དཔའ་བློ་གྲོས་བཟང་དང་། བྱང་ཆུབ་སེམས་དཔའ་བློ་གྲོས་བརྟན་དང་། བློ་གྲོས་ཡངས་པ་དང་། སྤོབས་པ་བརྩེགས་དང་། སྤྱན་རས་གཟིགས་དབང་ཕྱུག་དང་། མཐུ་ཆེན་ཐོབ་དང་། ཏོག་དཔལ་དང་། འཇམ་དཔལ་དང་། མངོན་པར་ཤེས་པའི་མེ་ཏོག་ཤིན་ཏུ་རྒྱས་པ་དང་། དམིགས་པ་མེད་པ་ཡིད་ལ་བྱེད་པ་དང་། དད་ལྡན་དང་། རིན་པོ་ཆེའི་ཏོག་དང་། དབང་པོའི་ལྷ་དང་། ཆུ་ལྷ་དང་། སྒྲ་དབྱངས་སྙན་དང་། ཞིང་རྣམ་པར་སྦྱོང་དང་། ལྷུན་པོ་བརྩེགས་དང་། སྤོབས་པ་ཕུན་སུམ་ཚོགས་དང་། དབང་པོའི་དཔལ་དང་། ས་འཛིན་དང་། སེམས་ཅན་དམྱུལ་བ་སྐེམས་དང་། ངན་སོང་སྦྱོང་དང་། རིན་ཆེན་ཟླ་བ་ཅན་དང་དེ་དག་ལ་སོགས་པ་བྱང་ཆུབ་སེམས་དཔའ་ཁྲི་དང་ཐབས་ཅིག་སྟེ། དེ་ནས་བཅོམ་ལྡན་འདས་འཁོར་བརྒྱ་སྟོང་དུ་མས་ཡོངས་སུ་བསྐོར་ཅིང་མདུན་གྱིས་བལྟས་ནས་ཆོས་སྟོན་ཏོ། །དེའི་ཚེ་བྱང་ཆུབ་སེམས་དཔའ་བྱམས་པ་འཁོར་དེ་ཉིད་དུ་འདུས་པར་གྱུར་ཏེ་འདུག་གོ །དེ་ནས་བྱང་ཆུབ་སེམས་དཔའ་བྱམས་པས་བྱང་ཆུབ་སེམས་དཔའི་འཁོར་ཆེན་པོ་དེ་འདུས་པར་རིག་ནས་སྟན་ལས་ལངས་ཏེ། བླ་གོས་ཕྲག་པ་གཅིག་ཏུ་གཟར་ནས་པུས་མོ་གཡས་པའི་ལྷ་ང་ས་ལ་བཙུགས་ཏེ། བཅོམ་ལྡན་འདས་ག་ལ་བ་དེ་ལོགས་སུ་ཐལ་མོ་སྦྱར་བ་བཏུད་ནས། བཅོམ་ལྡན་འདས་ལ་འདི་སྐད་ཅེས་གསོལ་ཏོ། །གལ་ཏེ་ཞུས་ནས་ཞུ་བ་ལུང་བསྟན་པའི་སླད་དུ་བཅོམ་ལྡན་འདས་ཀྱིས་བདག་ལ་སྐབས་ཕྱེ་ན་དེ་བཞིན་གཤེགས་པ་དགྲ་བཅོམ་པ་ཡང་དག་པར་རྫོགས་པའི་སངས་

རྒྱས་ལ་བདག་ཕྱོགས་འགའ་ཞིག་ཞུའོ། །དེ་སྐད་ཅེས་གསོལ་བ་དང་། བཅོམ་ལྡན་འདས་ཀྱིས་བྱང་ཆུབ་སེམས་དཔའ་སེམས་དཔའ་ཆེན་པོ་བྱམས་པ་ལ་འདི་སྐད་ཅེས་བཀའ་སྩལ་ཏོ། །བྱམས་པ་དྲི་བ་ལུང་བསྟན་པའི་ཕྱིར། དེ་བཞིན་གཤེགས་པས་རྟག་ཏུ་སྐབས་ཕྱེས། བྱམས་པ་ཁྱོད་ཅི་དང་ཅི་འདོད་པ་དྲིས་ཤིག་དང་། དྲིས་པ་དེ་དང་དེའི་ལུང་བསྟན་པས། སེམས་རངས་པར་བྱའོ། །དེ་ནས་བཅོམ་ལྡན་འདས་ལ་བྱང་ཆུབ་སེམས་དཔའ་སེམས་དཔའ་ཆེན་པོ་བྱམས་པས་འདི་སྐད་ཅེས་གསོལ་ཏོ། །བཅོམ་ལྡན་འདས་བྱང་ཆུབ་སེམས་དཔའ་ཆོས་དུ་དང་ལྡན་ན་ངན་སོང་ཐམས་ཅད་སྤོང་ཞིང་སྡིག་པའི་གྲོགས་པོའི་སུག་པར་མཆི་བར་མི་འགྱུར་ལ། མྱུར་དུ་བླ་ན་མེད་པ་ཡང་དག་པར་རྫོགས་པའི་བྱང་ཆུབ་མངོན་པར་རྫོགས་པར་འཚང་རྒྱ་བར་འགྱུར་བ་ལགས། དེ་སྐད་ཅེས་གསོལ་བ་དང་། བཅོམ་ལྡན་འདས་ཀྱིས་བྱང་ཆུབ་སེམས་དཔའ་སེམས་དཔའ་ཆེན་པོ་བྱམས་པ་ལ་འདི་སྐད་ཅེས་བཀའ་སྩལ་ཏོ། །བྱམས་པ་ཁྱོད་ནི་འདི་ལྟར་སྔོན་གྱི་རྒྱལ་བ་ལ་ལྷག་པར་བྱ་བ་བྱས་པ། དགེ་བའི་རྩ་བ་བསྐྱེད་པ། ཆོ་རབས་དྲན་པ། སྤྱོབས་པ་ཐོབ་པ། ཡུན་རིང་པོ་ནས་ཚངས་པར་སྤྱོད་པ་སྤྱད་པ་སྟེ། བྱམས་པ་ཁྱོད་སྐྱེ་བོ་མང་པོ་ལ་ཕན་པ་དང་། སྐྱེ་བོ་མང་པོ་ལ་བདེ་བ་དང་། འཇིག་རྟེན་ལ་སྙིང་བརྩེ་བ་དང་། སྐྱེ་བོ་ཕལ་པོ་ཆེ་དང་། ལྷ་དང་མི་རྣམས་ཀྱི་དོན་དང་། ཕན་པ་དང་། བདེ་བ་དང་། བྱང་ཆུབ་སེམས་དཔའི་ཐེག་པ་རིགས་ཀྱི་བུ་དང་། རིགས་ཀྱི་བུ་མོ་ད་ལྟར་གྱི་དང་། མ་འོངས་པ་རྣམས་ཡོངས་སུ་གཟུང་བའི་ཕྱིར་ཞུགས་ནས་ཁྱོད་དེ་བཞིན་གཤེགས་པ་ལ་དོན་འདི་འདྲི་བར་སེམས་པ་ལེགས་སོ་ལེགས་སོ། །བྱམས་པ་དེའི་ཕྱིར་ལེགས་པར་རབ་ཏུ་ཉོན་ལ་ཡིད་ལ་ཟུང་ཤིག་དང་བཤད་དོ། །བྱང་ཆུབ་སེམས་དཔའ་སེམས་དཔའ་ཆེན་པོ་བྱམས་པས་བཅོམ་ལྡན་འདས་ལ་ལེགས་སོ་ཞེས་གསོལ་ཏེ་བཅོམ་ལྡན་འདས་ཀྱི་ལྟར་ཉན་པ་དང་། བཅོམ་ལྡན་འདས་ཀྱིས་འདི་སྐད་ཅེས་བཀའ་སྩལ་ཏོ། །བྱམས་པ་བྱང་ཆུབ་སེམས་དཔའ་ཆོས་གཅིག་དང་ལྡན་ན་ངན་སོང་ཐམས་ཅད་སྤོང་ཞིང་སྡིག་པའི་གྲོགས་པོའི་ལག་ཏུ་མི་འགྲོ་ལ་མྱུར་དུ་བླ་ན་མེད་པ་ཡང་དག་པར་

རྫོགས་པའི་བྱང་ཆུབ་མངོན་པར་རྫོགས་པར་འཚང་རྒྱ་སྟེ། ཆོས་གཅིག་གང་ཞེ་ན། འདི་ལྟ་སྟེ། ལྷག་པའི་བསམ་པ་ཕུན་སུམ་ཚོགས་པའི་བྱང་ཆུབ་ཀྱི་སེམས་ཏེ། བྱམས་པ་བྱང་ཆུབ་སེམས་དཔའ་ཆོས་གཅིག་པོ་དེ་དང་ལྡན་ན་ངན་སོང་ཐམས་ཅད་སྤོང་ཞིང་སྡིག་པའི་གྲོགས་པོའི་ལག་ཏུ་མི་འགྲོ་ལ་མྱུར་དུ་བླ་ན་མེད་པར་ཡང་དག་པར་རྫོགས་པའི་བྱང་ཆུབ་མངོན་པར་རྫོགས་པར་འཚང་རྒྱའོ། །བྱམས་པ་གཞན་ཡང་བྱང་ཆུབ་སེམས་དཔའ་ཆོས་གཉིས་དང་ལྡན་ན་ངན་སོང་ཐམས་ཅད་སྤོང་ཞིང་སྡིག་པའི་གྲོགས་པོའི་ལག་ཏུ་མི་འགྲོ་ལ་མྱུར་དུ་བླ་ན་མེད་པ་ཡང་དག་པར་རྫོགས་པའི་བྱང་ཆུབ་མངོན་པར་རྫོགས་པར་འཚང་རྒྱ་སྟེ། གཉིས་གང་ཞེ་ན། འདི་ལྟ་སྟེ། ཞི་གནས་ཡོངས་སུ་ཚོལ་བ་དང་། ལྷག་མཐོང་ལ་མཁས་པ་སྟེ། བྱང་ཆུབ་སེམས་དཔའ་ཆོས་གཉིས་པོ་དེ་དག་དང་ལྡན་ན་ངན་སོང་ཐམས་ཅད་སྤོང་ཞིང་སྡིག་པའི་གྲོགས་པོའི་ལག་ཏུ་མི་འགྲོ་ལ་མྱུར་དུ་བླ་ན་མེད་པར་ཡང་དག་པར་རྫོགས་པའི་བྱང་ཆུབ་མངོན་པར་རྫོགས་པར་ཚང་རྒྱའོ། །བྱམས་པ་གཞན་ཡང་བྱང་ཆུབ་སེམས་དཔའ་ཆོས་གསུམ་དང་ལྡན་ན་ངན་སོང་ཐམས་ཅད་སྤོང་ཞིང་སྡིག་པའི་གྲོགས་པོའི་ལག་ཏུ་མི་འགྲོ་ལ་མྱུར་དུ་བླ་ན་མེད་པ་ཡང་དག་པར་རྫོགས་པའི་བྱང་ཆུབ་མངོན་པར་རྫོགས་པར་འཚང་རྒྱ་སྟེ། གསུམ་གང་ཞེ་ན། འདི་ལྟ་སྟེ། སྙིང་རྗེ་ཆེན་པོ་ཐོབ་པ་དང་། སྟོང་པ་ཉིད་ཀྱི་ཆོས་ངེས་པར་སེམས་པ་དང་། དེས་ཀྱང་རློམ་སེམས་མི་བྱེད་པ་སྟེ། བྱམས་པ་བྱང་ཆུབ་སེམས་དཔའ་ཆོས་གསུམ་པོ་དེ་དག་དང་ལྡན་ན་ངན་སོང་ཐམས་ཅད་སྤོང་ཞིང་སྡིག་པའི་གྲོགས་པོའི་ལག་ཏུ་མི་འགྲོ་ལ། མྱུར་དུ་བླ་ན་མེད་པ་ཡང་དག་པར་རྫོགས་པའི་བྱང་ཆུབ་མངོན་པར་རྫོགས་པར་འཚང་རྒྱའོ། །བྱམས་པ་གཞན་ཡང་བྱང་ཆུབ་སེམས་དཔའ་ཆོས་བཞི་དང་ལྡན་ན་ངན་སོང་ཐམས་ཅད་སྤོང་ཞིང་སྡིག་པའི་གྲོགས་པོའི་ལག་ཏུ་མི་འགྲོ་ལ་མྱུར་དུ་བླ་ན་མེད་པ་ཡང་དག་པར་རྫོགས་པའི་བྱང་ཆུབ་མངོན་པར་རྫོགས་པར་འཚང་རྒྱ་སྟེ། བཞི་གང་ཞེ་ན། འདི་ལྟ་སྟེ། ཚུལ་ཁྲིམས་ལ་གནས་པ་ཡིན། ཆོས་ཐམས་ཅད་ལ་སོམ་ཉི་མེད་པ་ཡིན། དགོན་པ་ལ་མངོན་པར་དགའ་བ་ཡིན། ཡང་དག་པར་ཞུགས་ཤིང་ཡང་

དག་པར་བླངས་པ་ལས་མི་གཡོ་བ་ཡིན་ཏེ། བྱམས་པ་བྱང་ཆུབ་སེམས་དཔའ་ཆོས་བཞི་པོ་དེ་དག་དང་ལྡན་ན་ངན་སོང་ཐམས་ཅད་སྤོང་ཞིང་སྡིག་པའི་གྲོགས་པོའི་ལག་ཏུ་མི་འགྲོ་ལ་མྱུར་དུ་བླ་ན་མེད་པར་ཡང་དག་པར་རྫོགས་པའི་བྱང་ཆུབ་མངོན་པར་རྫོགས་པར་འཚང་རྒྱའོ། །བྱམས་པ་གཞན་ཡང་བྱང་ཆུབ་སེམས་དཔའ་ཆོས་ལྔ་དང་ལྡན་ན་ངན་སོང་ཐམས་ཅད་སྤོང་ཞིང་སྡིག་པའི་གྲོགས་པོའི་ལག་ཏུ་མི་འགྲོ་ལ་མྱུར་དུ་བླ་ན་མེད་པ་ཡང་དག་པར་རྫོགས་པའི་བྱང་ཆུབ་མངོན་པར་རྫོགས་པར་འཚང་རྒྱ་སྟེ། ལྔ་གང་ཞེ་ན། འདི་ལྟ་སྟེ། སྟོང་པ་ཉིད་ལ་གནས་པ་དང་། གཞན་དག་གི་འཁྲུལ་པ་མི་ཚོལ་བ་དང་། བདག་ལ་རྟོག་པ་དང་། ཆོས་ལ་མངོན་པར་དགའ་བ་དང་། གཞན་ལ་ཕན་འདོགས་པར་ཞུགས་པ་ཡིན་ཏེ། བྱམས་པ་བྱང་ཆུབ་སེམས་དཔའ་ཆོས་ལྔ་པོ་དེ་དག་དང་ལྡན་ན་ངན་སོང་ཐམས་ཅད་སྤོང་ཞིང་སྡིག་པའི་གྲོགས་པོའི་ལག་ཏུ་མི་འགྲོ་ལ་མྱུར་དུ་བླ་ན་མེད་པར་ཡང་དག་པར་རྫོགས་པའི་བྱང་ཆུབ་མངོན་པར་རྫོགས་པར་འཚང་རྒྱའོ། །བྱམས་པ་གཞན་ཡང་བྱང་ཆུབ་སེམས་དཔའ་ཆོས་དྲུག་དང་ལྡན་ན་ངན་སོང་ཐམས་ཅད་སྤོང་ཞིང་སྡིག་པའི་གྲོགས་པོའི་ལག་ཏུ་མི་འགྲོ་ལ་མྱུར་དུ་བླ་ན་མེད་པ་ཡང་དག་པར་རྫོགས་པའི་བྱང་ཆུབ་མངོན་པར་རྫོགས་པར་འཚང་རྒྱ་སྟེ། དྲུག་གང་ཞེ་ན། འདི་ལྟ་སྟེ། བརྐམ་པ་མེད་པ་ཡིན། སྡང་བ་མེད་པ་ཡིན། རྨོངས་པ་མེད་པ་ཡིན། དྲིས་མ་ཐག་ཏུ་ཡང་དག་པ་ཇི་ལྟ་བ་བཞིན་དུ་ལན་ལྡོན་པ་ཡིན། བསྙེན་པར་དཀའ་བ་མེད་པ་ཡིན། སྟོང་པ་ཉིད་སྤྱོད་ཡུལ་བ་ཡིན་ཏེ། བྱམས་པ་བྱང་ཆུབ་སེམས་དཔའ་ཆོས་དྲུག་པོ་དེ་དག་དང་ལྡན་ན་ངན་སོང་ཐམས་ཅད་སྤོང་ཞིང་སྡིག་པའི་གྲོགས་པོའི་ལག་ཏུ་མི་འགྲོ་ལ་མྱུར་དུ་བླ་ན་མེད་པར་ཡང་དག་པར་རྫོགས་པའི་བྱང་ཆུབ་མངོན་པར་རྫོགས་པར་འཚང་རྒྱའོ། །བྱམས་པ་གཞན་ཡང་བྱང་ཆུབ་སེམས་དཔའ་ཆོས་བདུན་དང་ལྡན་ན་ངན་སོང་ཐམས་ཅད་སྤོང་ཞིང་སྡིག་པའི་གྲོགས་པོའི་ལག་ཏུ་མི་འགྲོ་ལ་མྱུར་དུ་བླ་ན་མེད་པ་ཡང་དག་པར་རྫོགས་པའི་བྱང་ཆུབ་མངོན་པར་རྫོགས་པར་འཚང་རྒྱ་སྟེ། བདུན་གང་ཞེ་ན། འདི་ལྟ་སྟེ། དྲན་པ་མཁས་པ་ཡིན། ཆོས་ལ་མཁས་པ་ཡིན།

བརྩོན་འགྲུས་བརྩམས་པ་ཡིན། དགའ་བ་ཐོབ་པ་ཡིན། ཤིན་ཏུ་སྦྱངས་པ་དང་
ལྡན་པ་ཡིན། ཏིང་ངེ་འཛིན་ལ་མཁས་པ་ཡིན། ཤེས་རབ་ཀྱིས་རབ་ཏུ་དབྱེ་བ་ལ་
མཁས་པ་ཡིན་ཏེ། བྱམས་པ་བྱང་ཆུབ་སེམས་དཔའ་ཆོས་བདུན་པོ་དེ་དག་དང་ལྡན་
ན་ངན་སོང་ཐམས་ཅད་སྤོང་ཞིང་སྡིག་པའི་གྲོགས་པོའི་ལག་ཏུ་མི་འགྲོ་ལ་མྱུར་དུ་བླ་ན་
མེད་པར་ཡང་དག་པར་རྫོགས་པའི་བྱང་ཆུབ་མངོན་པར་རྫོགས་པར་འཚང་རྒྱའོ། །
བྱམས་པ་གཞན་ཡང་བྱང་ཆུབ་སེམས་དཔའ་ཆོས་བརྒྱད་དང་ལྡན་ན་ངན་སོང་ཐམས་
ཅད་སྤོང་ཞིང་སྡིག་པའི་གྲོགས་པོའི་ལག་ཏུ་མི་འགྲོ་ལ་མྱུར་དུ་བླ་ན་མེད་པ་ཡང་དག་
པར་རྫོགས་པའི་བྱང་ཆུབ་མངོན་པར་རྫོགས་པར་འཚང་རྒྱ་སྟེ། བརྒྱད་གང་ཞེ་ན།
འདི་ལྟ་སྟེ། ཡང་དག་པའི་ལྟ་བ་ཅན་ཡིན། ཡང་དག་པའི་རྟོག་པ་ཅན་ཡིན།
ཡང་དག་པའི་ངག་ཅན་ཡིན། ཡང་དག་པའི་ལས་ཀྱི་མཐའ་ཅན་ཡིན། ཡང་
དག་པའི་འཚོ་བ་ཅན་ཡིན། ཡང་དག་པའི་རྩོལ་བ་ཅན་ཡིན། ཡང་དག་པའི་དྲན་
པ་ཅན་ཡིན། ཡང་དག་པའི་ཏིང་ངེ་འཛིན་ཅན་ཡིན་ཏེ། བྱམས་པ་ཆོས་བརྒྱད་པོ་
དེ་དག་ལྡན་ན་ངན་སོང་ཐམས་ཅད་སྤོང་ཞིང་སྡིག་པའི་གྲོགས་པོའི་ལག་ཏུ་མི་འགྲོ་ལ་
མྱུར་དུ་བླ་ན་མེད་པ་ཡང་དག་པར་རྫོགས་པའི་བྱང་ཆུབ་མངོན་པར་རྫོགས་པར་འཚང་
རྒྱའོ། །བྱམས་པ་གཞན་ཡང་བྱང་ཆུབ་སེམས་དཔའ་ཆོས་དགུ་དང་ལྡན་ན་ངན་སོང་
ཐམས་ཅད་སྤོང་ཞིང་སྡིག་པའི་གྲོགས་པོའི་ལག་ཏུ་མི་འགྲོ་ལ་མྱུར་དུ་བླ་ན་མེད་པ་ཡང་
དག་པར་རྫོགས་པའི་བྱང་ཆུབ་མངོན་པར་རྫོགས་པར་འཚང་རྒྱ་སྟེ། དགུ་གང་ཞེ་ན།
འདི་ལྟ་སྟེ། བྱམས་པ་འདི་ལ་བྱང་ཆུབ་སེམས་དཔའ་ནི་འདོད་པ་དག་ལས་དབེན་པ།
སྡིག་པ་མི་དགེ་བའི་ཆོས་རྣམས་ལས་དབེན་པ། རྟོག་པ་དང་བཅས་པ། དཔྱོད་
པ་དང་བཅས་པ། དབེན་པ་ལས་སྐྱེས་པའི་དགའ་བ་དང་བདེ་བ་ཅན་བསམ་གཏན་
དང་པོ་བསྒྲུབས་ཏེ་གནས་སོ། །རྟོག་པ་དང་དཔྱོད་པ་དང་བྲལ་ཞིང་ནང་རབ་ཏུ་དང་
སྟེ། སེམས་ཀྱི་རྒྱུད་གཅིག་ཏུ་གྱུར་པས་རྟོག་པ་མེད་པ། དཔྱོད་པ་མེད་པ།
ཏིང་ངེ་འཛིན་ལས་སྐྱེས་པའི་དགའ་བ་དང་བདེ་བ་ཅན་བསམ་གཏན་གཉིས་པ་བསྒྲུབས་
ཏེ་གནས་སོ། །དགའ་བའི་འདོད་ཆགས་དང་བྲལ་བས། བཏང་སྙོམས་ལ་

གནས་ཤིང་དྲན་པ་དང་ཤེས་བཞིན་ཅན་ཡིན་ཏེ། བདེ་བ་ལུས་ཀྱིས་མྱོང་ལ།
འཕགས་པ་རྣམས་ཀྱིས་གང་དེ་དྲན་པ་དང་ལྡན་པ་བདེ་བ་ལ་གནས་པ་བཏང་སྙོམས་
པའོ། །ཞེས་བརྗོད་པ་སྟེ། དགའ་བ་མེད་པ་བསམ་གཏན་གསུམ་པ་བསྒྲུབས་ཏེ་
གནས་སོ། །བདེ་བ་ཡང་སྤངས་ཏེ། སྔ་ནས་སྡུག་བསྔལ་ཡང་སྤངས་ཤིང་ཡིད་
བདེ་བ་དང་ཡིད་མི་བདེ་བ་ཡང་ནུབ་པས་བདེ་བ་ཡང་མ་ཡིན། སྡུག་བསྔལ་བ་ཡང་
མ་ཡིན་པ། བཏང་སྙོམས་དང་དྲན་པ་ཡོངས་སུ་དག་པ་བསམ་གཏན་བཞི་པ་
བསྒྲུབས་ཏེ་གནས་སོ། །རྣམ་པར་ཐམས་ཅད་དུ་གཟུགས་ཀྱི་འདུ་ཤེས་རྣམས་ལས་
ཡང་དག་པར་འདས་ཏེ། ཐོགས་པའི་འདུ་ཤེས་རྣམས་ནུབ་པར་གྱུར་ཅིང་སྣ་ཚོགས་
ཀྱི་འདུ་ཤེས་རྣམས་ཡིད་ལ་མི་བྱེད་པས་ནམ་མཁའ་མཐའ་ཡས་སོ་སྙམ་ནས་ནམ་
མཁའ་མཐའ་ཡས་སྐྱེ་མཆེད་བསྒྲུབས་ཏེ་གནས་སོ། །རྣམ་པ་ཐམས་ཅད་དུ་ནམ་
མཁའ་མཐའ་ཡས་སྐྱེ་མཆེད་ལས་ཡང་དག་པར་འདས་ཏེ། རྣམ་པར་ཤེས་པ་མཐའ་
ཡས་སོ་སྙམ་ནས་རྣམ་ཤེས་མཐའ་ཡས་སྐྱེ་མཆེད་བསྒྲུབས་ཏེ་གནས་སོ། །རྣམ་
པར་ཐམས་ཅད་དུ་རྣམ་ཤེས་མཐའ་ཡས་སྐྱེ་མཆེད་ལས་ཡང་དག་པར་འདས་ཏེ། ཅི་
ཡང་མེད་དོ་སྙམ་ནས་ཅི་ཡང་མེད་པའི་སྐྱེ་མཆེད་བསྒྲུབས་ཏེ་གནས་སོ། །རྣམ་པ་
ཐམས་ཅད་དུ་ཅི་ཡང་མེད་པའི་སྐྱེ་མཆེད་ལས་ཡང་དག་པར་འདས་ནས་འདུ་ཤེས་མེད་
འདུ་ཤེས་མེད་མིན་སྐྱེ་མཆེད་བསྒྲུབས་ཏེ་གནས་སོ། །རྣམ་པ་ཐམས་ཅད་དུ་འདུ་
ཤེས་མེད་འདུ་ཤེས་མེད་མིན་སྐྱེ་མཆེད་ལས་ཡང་དག་པར་འདས་ནས་འདུ་ཤེས་དང་
ཚོར་བ་འགོག་པ་བསྒྲུབས་ནས་གནས་པ་སྟེ། བྱམས་པ་བྱང་ཆུབ་སེམས་དཔའ་
ཆོས་དགུ་པོ་དེ་དག་དང་ལྡན་ན་ངན་སོང་ཐམས་ཅད་སྤོང་ཞིང་སྡིག་པའི་གྲོགས་པོའི་
ལག་ཏུ་མི་འགྲོ་ལ་མྱུར་དུ་བླ་ན་མེད་པར་ཡང་དག་པར་རྫོགས་པའི་བྱང་ཆུབ་མངོན་
པར་རྫོགས་པར་འཚང་རྒྱའོ། །བྱམས་པ་གཞན་ཡང་བྱང་ཆུབ་སེམས་དཔའ་ཆོས་
བཅུ་དང་ལྡན་ན་ངན་སོང་ཐམས་ཅད་སྤོང་ཞིང་སྡིག་པའི་གྲོགས་པོའི་ལག་ཏུ་མི་འགྲོ་ལ་
མྱུར་དུ་བླ་ན་མེད་པ་ཡང་དག་པར་རྫོགས་པའི་བྱང་ཆུབ་མངོན་པར་རྫོགས་པར་འཚང་
རྒྱ་སྟེ། བཅུ་གང་ཞེ་ན། འདི་ལྟ་སྟེ། རྡོ་རྗེ་ལྟ་བུའི་ཏིང་ངེ་འཛིན་དང་ལྡན་པ་

ཡིན། གནས་དང་གནས་མ་ཡིན་པ་ལ་མངོན་པར་བརྩོན་པའི་ཏིང་ངེ་འཛིན་དང་ལྡན་
པ་ཡིན། ཐབས་ཀྱིས་འགྲོ་བའི་ཏིང་ངེ་འཛིན་དང་ལྡན་པ་ཡིན། རྣམ་པར་སྣང་
བྱེད་ཀྱི་ཏིང་ངེ་འཛིན་དང་ལྡན་པ་ཡིན། ཀུན་ནས་སྣང་བའི་ཏིང་ངེ་འཛིན་དང་ལྡན་པ་
ཡིན། ཀུན་དུ་གསལ་བའི་ཏིང་ངེ་འཛིན་དང་ལྡན་པ་ཡིན། རིན་ཆེན་ཟླ་བའི་ཏིང་
ངེ་འཛིན་དང་ལྡན་པ་ཡིན། ཟླ་བ་སྒྲོན་མའི་ཏིང་ངེ་འཛིན་དང་ལྡན་པ་ཡིན། ཉོན་
མོངས་པ་མེད་པའི་ཏིང་ངེ་འཛིན་དང་ལྡན་པ་ཡིན། རྒྱལ་མཚན་གྱི་རྩེ་མོའི་དཔུང་
རྒྱན་གྱི་ཏིང་ངེ་འཛིན་དང་ལྡན་པ་ཡིན་ཏེ། བྱམས་པ་བྱང་ཆུབ་སེམས་དཔའ་ཆོས་
བཅུ་པོ་དེ་དག་དང་ལྡན་ན་ངན་སོང་ཐམས་ཅད་སྤོང་ཞིང་སྡིག་པའི་གྲོགས་པོའི་ལག་ཏུ་
མི་འགྲོ་ལ་མྱུར་དུ་བླ་ན་མེད་པ་ཡང་དག་པར་རྫོགས་པའི་བྱང་ཆུབ་མངོན་པར་རྫོགས་
པ་འཚང་རྒྱའོ། །དེ་ནས་བྱང་ཆུབ་སེམས་དཔའ་སེམས་དཔའ་ཆེན་པོ་བྱམས་པ་
ཚིམ་ཞིང་མགུ་ལ་ཡི་རངས་ཏེ་རབ་ཏུ་དགའ་ནས་དགའ་བ་དང་ཡིད་བདེ་བ་སྐྱེས་ཏེ།
སྟན་ལས་ལངས་ནས་བླ་གོས་ཕྲག་པ་གཅིག་ཏུ་གཟར་ཏེ་པུས་མོ་གཡས་པའི་ལྷ་ང་ས་
ལ་བཙུགས་ནས། བཅོམ་ལྡན་འདས་ག་ལ་བ་དེ་ལོགས་སུ་ཐལ་མོ་སྦྱར་བ་བཏུད་དེ།
བཅོམ་ལྡན་འདས་ལ་ཚུལ་དང་འདྲ་བའི་ཚིགས་སུ་བཅད་པ་འདི་དག་གིས་མངོན་པར་
བསྟོད་དོ། །སྔོན་ཆད་སྦྱིན་པ་སྦྱིན་མཛད་པ། །སྡུག་པའི་བུ་དང་ཟས་དང་
སྐོམ། །མགོ་དང་མིག་ཀྱང་བཏང་མཛད་དེ། །སངས་རྒྱས་སྦྱིན་ཀུན་ཕ་རོལ་
ཕྱིན། །གཡག་ཟ་བཞིན་དུ་ཡུན་རིང་ནས། །ཁྱོད་ཀྱིས་ཚུལ་ཁྲིམས་མ་ཉམས་
བསྲུངས། །ཁྲིམས་ཀྱིས་ཁྱོད་འདྲ་མ་མཆིས་ཏེ། །སངས་རྒྱས་ཁྲིམས་ལེགས་ཕ་
རོལ་ཕྱིན། །བཟོད་པའི་སྟོབས་ནི་བསྐྱེད་མཛད་ནས། །བྱིས་པ་ནོངས་པ་བཟྲིས་པ་
བཟོད། །བཟོད་པའི་སྟོབས་རྣམས་ཀུན་དང་ལྡན། །སངས་རྒྱས་བཟོད་ལེགས་ཕ་
རོལ་ཕྱིན། །བརྩོན་འགྲུས་སྟོབས་ནི་བསྐྱེད་མཛད་ནས། །ཞི་བདེ་བླ་ན་མེད་པ་
བརྙེས། །བརྩོན་འགྲུས་སྟོབས་ཀྱིས་སྟོབས་དང་ལྡན། །སངས་རྒྱས་བརྩོན་
ལེགས་ཕ་རོལ་ཕྱིན། །སྡིག་པ་ཐམས་ཅད་བསྲེག་མཛད་ནས། །འདྲེན་པ་སྐྱེས་
ཆེན་བསམ་གཏན་དགྱེས། །བསམ་གཏན་སྟོབས་ཀྱིས་སྟོབས་དང་ལྡན། །

སངས་རྒྱས་བསམ་ལེགས་ཕ་རོལ་ཕྱིན། །ཆོས་རྣམས་དེ་དག་རང་བཞིན་སྟོང་། །ངོ་བོ་ཉིད་ཀྱིས་གང་མི་སྐྱེ། །ཤེས་རབ་ཀྱིས་ནི་ཕ་རོལ་གཤེགས། །སངས་རྒྱས་ཤེས་ལེགས་ཕ་རོལ་ཕྱིན། །མཁྱེན་ཆེན་བྱང་ཆུབ་ཤིང་དྲུང་དུ། །སྡེར་བཅས་བདུད་ནི་ཁྱོད་ཀྱིས་བཏུལ། །དོན་གྱི་མཆོག་ཀྱང་བརྙེས་པར་གྱུར། །སངས་རྒྱས་བདུད་ཀྱི་ཚོགས་ངན་འཇོམས། །སྐྱེས་ཆེན་བླ་ར་ཎ་སིར་ནི། ཆོས་ཀྱི་འཁོར་ལོ་རབ་ཏུ་བསྐོར། །མུ་སྟེགས་ཚོགས་ངན་སྐྲག་པར་མཛད། །སངས་རྒྱས་མུ་སྟེགས་ཅན་ཚོགས་འཇོམས། །ཤེས་རབ་ཆེན་པོ་བླ་ན་མེད། །ཀུན་ནས་བླ་དཔེ་ཡོང་མ་མཆིས། །དཀོན་མཆོག་ཆོས་དེ་སྟོན་པར་མཛད། །འདྲེན་པ་སངས་རྒྱས་འོད་མཛད་ལགས། །སྦྱིན་པ་དང་ནི་ཁྲིམས་སྟོབས་དང་། །བཟོད་བརྩོན་ཁྱོད་དང་འདྲ་མ་མཆིས། །ཀུན་གྱི་ཕ་རོལ་ཕྱིན་པར་གྱུར། །སངས་རྒྱས་ཡོན་ཏན་མང་པོས་འཕགས། །དེ་ནས་བྱང་ཆུབ་སེམས་དཔའ་སེམས་དཔའ་ཆེན་པོ་བྱམས་པས་བཅོམ་ལྡན་འདས་ལ་ཚུལ་དང་འདྲ་བའི་ཚིགས་སུ་བཅད་པ་འདི་དག་གིས་མངོན་པར་བསྟོད་ནས་ཕྱོགས་གཅིག་ཏུ་འདུག་གོ །དེ་ནས་བཅོམ་ལྡན་འདས་ལ་ཚེ་དང་ལྡན་པ་ཀུན་དགའ་བོས་འདི་སྐད་ཅེས་གསོལ་ཏོ། །བཙུན་པ་བཅོམ་ལྡན་འདས་བྱང་ཆུབ་སེམས་དཔའ་ཆེན་པོ་བྱམས་པ་འདི་འདི་ལྟར་སྤྱོབས་པ་ཕུན་སུམ་ཚོགས་པ་དང་། འདི་ལྟར་ཤིན་ཏུ་རྣམ་པར་ངེས་པའི་ཚིག་གིས་ཆོས་སྟོན་པ་དང་། འདི་ལྟར་ཚིག་དང་ཡི་གེ་མཚུངས་པའི་ཆོས་སྟོན་པ་དང་། འདི་ལྟར་ཟབ་མོའི་ཚིག་གིས་ཆོས་སྟོན་པ་དང་། འདི་ལྟར་ལེགས་པར་འབྲེལ་བའི་ཚིག་གིས་ཆོས་སྟོན་པ་དང་། དྲན་པའི་ཚིག་གིས་ཆོས་སྟོན་པ་ནི་ངོ་མཚར་ལགས་སོ། །བཅོམ་ལྡན་འདས་ཀྱིས་བཀའ་སྩལ་པ། ཀུན་དགའ་བོ་དེ་དེ་བཞིན་ནོ། །ཇི་སྐད་སྨྲས་པ་བཞིན་ཏེ། བྱང་ཆུབ་སེམས་དཔའ་བྱམས་པ་སྤྱོབས་པ་ཕུན་སུམ་ཚོགས་པ་དང་ལྡན་ཞིང་བྱང་ཆུབ་སེམས་དཔའ་བྱམས་པ་ཤིན་ཏུ་རྣམ་པར་ངེས་པའི་ཚིག་གིས་ཆོས་སྟོན་པ་ནས་རྗེས་སུ་དྲན་པའི་ཚིག་གི་བར་གྱིས་ཆོས་སྟོན་པ་ནི་ངོ་མཚར་ཏོ། །ཀུན་དགའ་བོ་བྱང་ཆུབ་སེམས་དཔའ་བྱམས་པ་ནི་ད་ལྟ་ང་ལ་ཚུལ་དང་འདྲ་བའི་ཚིགས་སུ་བཅད་པ་དག་གིས

བསྐྱོད་པར་ཡང་མ་ཟད་དེ། དེ་ཅིའི་ཕྱིར་ཞེ་ན། ཀུན་དགའ་བོ་སྔོན་བྱུང་བ་འདས་པའི་དུས་ན་བསྐལ་པ་གྲངས་མེད་པ་བཅུར་ཚང་བར་གྱུར་པ་དེའི་ཚེ་དེའི་དུས་ན་དེ་བཞིན་གཤེགས་པ་དགྲ་བཅོམ་པ་ཡང་དག་པར་རྫོགས་པའི་སངས་རྒྱས། རིག་པ་དང་ཞབས་སུ་ལྡན་པ། བདེ་བར་གཤེགས་པ། འཇིག་རྟེན་མཁྱེན་པ། སྐྱེས་བུ་འདུལ་བའི་ཁ་ལོ་སྒྱུར་བ་བླ་ན་མེད་པ། ལྷ་དང་མི་རྣམས་ཀྱི་སྟོན་པ། སངས་རྒྱས་བཅོམ་ལྡན་འདས་སྣང་བས་རྣམ་པར་རོལ་པའི་མངོན་པར་ཤེས་པ་ཞེས་བྱ་བ་འཇིག་རྟེན་དུ་བྱུང་སྟེ། དེའི་ཚེ་བྲམ་ཟེའི་ཁྱེའུ་བཟང་དག་ཅེས་བྱ་བ་གཟུགས་བཟང་བ། མཛེས་པ། བལྟ་ན་སྡུག་པ། ཁ་དོག་བཟང་པོ་རྒྱས་པ་མཆོག་དང་ལྡན་པ་ཞིག་ཡོད་པ་དེ་སྐྱེད་མོས་ཚལ་དུ་འགྲོ་སྟེ། གྲོང་བར་དུ་ཕྱིན་པ་དང་། དེ་བཞིན་གཤེགས་པ་དགྲ་བཅོམ་པ་ཡང་དག་པར་རྫོགས་པའི་སངས་རྒྱས་སྣང་བས་རྣམ་པར་རོལ་པའི་མངོན་པར་ཤེས་པ་མཛེས་པ། དད་པར་བྱ་བ། དབང་པོ་ཞི་བ། ཐུགས་ཞི་བ། དུལ་བ་དང་ཞི་གནས་ཀྱི་མཆོག་བརྙེས་པ། དུལ་བ་དང་ཞི་གནས་ཀྱི་དམ་པ་བརྙེས་པ། དབང་པོ་བསྲུངས་པ། གླང་པོ་ཆེ་དབང་པོ་ཐུལ་བ་ལྟ་བུ། མཚོ་ལྟར་དང་ཞིང་རྙོག་པ་མེད་ལ་གསལ་བ། སྐྱེས་བུ་ཆེན་པོའི་མཚན་སུམ་ཅུ་རྩ་གཉིས་པོ་དག་གིས་སྐུ་ལེགས་པར་བརྒྱན་པ། དཔེ་བྱད་བཟང་པོ་བརྒྱད་ཅུ་པོ་དག་གིས་སྐུ་རྣམ་པར་སྤྲས་པ། ཤིང་སཱ་ལའི་རྒྱལ་པོ་མེ་ཏོག་ཤིན་ཏུ་རྒྱས་པ་འདྲ་བ། རིའི་རྒྱལ་པོ་རི་རབ་ལྟར་མངོན་པར་འཕགས་པ། ཞལ་ཟླ་བའི་དཀྱིལ་འཁོར་ལྟར་ཞི་བ། ཉི་མའི་དཀྱིལ་འཁོར་ལྟར་ལྷམ་མེ་ལྷན་ནེ་ལྷང་ངེ་བ། ཤིང་ནྱ་གྲོ་དྷ་ལྟར་ཆུ་ཞེང་གབ་པ་འོད་འབར་བའི་སྐུ་དཔལ་ཆེན་པོས་འབར་བ་མཐོང་ངོ་། །མཐོང་ནས་ཀྱང་དེ་བཅོམ་ལྡན་འདས་ལ་སེམས་དད་པར་གྱུར་ཏོ། །དེ་སེམས་དད་ནས་འདི་སྙམ་དུ་སེམས་ཏེ། ཨ་ལ་ལ་དེ་བཞིན་གཤེགས་པའི་སྐུ་འདི་རྣམ་པར་སྤྲས་ཤིང་ཁ་དོག་དང་གཟི་བརྗིད་དང་། དཔལ་དང་མཚན་རྣམས་ཀྱིས་འབར་ཞིང་ལྷམ་མེ་ལྷན་ནེ་ལྷང་ངེ་བ་ངོ་མཚར་ཏོ། །སྙམ་མོ་དེ་ནས་བྲམ་ཟེའི་ཁྱེའུ་བཟང་དག་གིས་འདི་སྐད་ཅེས་སྨྲས་ཏེ། ཨ་ལ་ལ་བདག་ཀྱང་མ་འོངས་པའི་དུས་ན་ལུས་འདི་འདྲ་བ་དང་ལྡན་

པར་གྱུར་ཅིག །ཁ་དོག་དང་། གཟི་བརྗིད་དང་། དཔལ་དང་། མཚན་རྣམས་ཀྱིས་འདི་ལྟར་འབར་ཞིང་ལྷམ་མེ་ལྷན་ནེ་ལྷང་ངེ་བར་གྱུར་ཅིག་ཅེས་དེས་སྨོན་ལམ་དེ་སྐད་བཏབ་ནས་ས་ལ་ཉལ་ཏེ་འདི་སྙམ་དུ་བསམས་སོ། །གལ་ཏེ་བདག་ཀྱང་མ་འོངས་པའི་དུས་ན་འདི་ལྟ་བུའི་ལུས་དང་ལྡན་པར་གྱུར་ཏེ། ཁ་དོག་དང་། གཟི་བརྗིད་དང་། དཔལ་དང་། མཚན་རྣམས་ཀྱིས་འབར་ཞིང་ལྷམ་མེ་ལྷན་ནེ་ལྷང་ངེ་བར་འགྱུར་ཞེ་ན། དེ་བཞིན་གཤེགས་པའི་ཞབས་བདག་གི་ལུས་ལ་རེག་པ་གྱུར་ཅིག་སྙམ་མོ། །ཀུན་དགའ་བོ་དེ་ནས་དེ་བཞིན་གཤེགས་པ་དགྲ་བཅོམ་པ་ཡང་དག་པར་རྫོགས་པའི་སངས་རྒྱས་སྣང་བས་རྣམ་པར་རོལ་པའི་མངོན་པར་ཤེས་པ་དེས་བྲམ་ཟེའི་ཁྱེའུ་བཟང་དག་གི་ལྷག་པའི་བསམ་པ་མཁྱེན་ནས་བྲམ་ཟེའི་ཁྱེའུ་བཟང་དག་ག་ལ་བ་དེར་གཤེགས་ཏེ། བྲམ་ཟེའི་ཁྱེའུ་བཟང་དག་ལ་ཞབས་ཀྱིས་རེག་པར་མཛད་དོ། །དེ་བཞིན་གཤེགས་པ་སྣང་བས་རྣམ་པར་རོལ་པའི་མངོན་པར་ཤེས་པ་དེས་བྲམ་ཟེའི་ཁྱེའུ་བཟང་དག་ལ་ཞབས་ཀྱིས་རེག་པར་མཛད་མ་ཐག་ཏུ། དེ་ནས་དེའི་ཚེ་མི་སྐྱེ་བའི་ཆོས་ལ་བཟོད་པ་ཐོབ་པར་གྱུར་ཏོ། །ཀུན་དགའ་བོ་དེ་ནས་དེ་བཞིན་གཤེགས་པ་སྣང་བས་རྣམ་པར་རོལ་པའི་མངོན་པར་ཤེས་པ་དེས་སྐུམ་ལོགས་སུ་གཟིགས་ནས་དགེ་སློང་རྣམས་ལ་བཀའ་སྩལ་པ། དགེ་སློང་དག་ཁྱེད་གང་གིས་ཀྱང་བྲམ་ཟེའི་ཁྱེའུ་བཟང་དག་དེའི་ལུས་ལ་ཆང་པས་མ་རྫེ་ཤིག །དེ་ཅིའི་ཕྱིར་ཞེ་ན། བྱང་ཆུབ་སེམས་དཔའ་སེམས་དཔའ་ཆེན་པོ་འདི་མི་སྐྱེ་བའི་ཆོས་ལ་བཟོད་པ་ཐོབ་པའི་ཕྱིར་རོ། །དེ་ནས་དེ་ཉིད་ཀྱི་ཚེ་བྲམ་ཟེའི་ཁྱེའུ་བཟང་དག་གིས་ལྷའི་མིག་དང་། ལྷའི་རྣ་བ་དང་། ཕ་རོལ་གྱི་སེམས་ཤེས་པ་དང་། སྔོན་གྱི་གནས་རྗེས་སུ་དྲན་པ་མངོན་སུམ་དུ་བྱ་བའི་ཤེས་པ་ཐོབ་བོ། །རྫུ་འཕྲུལ་ཡང་མངོན་པར་བསྒྲུབས་སོ། །དེས་དེ་བཞིན་གཤེགས་པ་སྣང་བས་རྣམ་པར་རོལ་པའི་མངོན་པར་ཤེས་པའི་སྤྱན་སྔར་ཚུལ་དང་འདྲ་བའི་ཚིགས་སུ་བཅད་པ་དག་གིས་ཀྱང་མངོན་པར་བསྟོད་དོ། །ཕྱོགས་དང་ཕྱོགས་མཚམས་རྣམས་སུ་བསྒྲེར་ཏེ་བཅོལ་བཀྲིས་ཀྱང་། །འཇིག་རྟེན་དག་ན་མི་དབང་ཁྱོད་འདྲ་ཡོད་མ་མཆིས། །འགྲོ་བ་ཀུན་ན་རྫོགས་པའི་

སངས་རྒྱས་མངོན་པར་འཕགས། །རྣམ་པར་འདྲེན་པ་རང་བྱུང་ཁྱོད་ལ་བདག་ཕྱག་འཚལ། །དཔེར་ན་བར་སྣང་ན་ནི་ཉི་མ་ལྷན་ནེ་ལྟར། ཕྱོགས་དང་ཕྱོགས་མཚམས་ཀུན་གྱི་འཇིག་རྟེན་ཁམས་རྣམས་ན། །འཇིག་རྟེན་འདི་དག་ཐམས་ཅད་འོད་ཀྱིས་ལྷམ་མེར་གྱུར། །སངས་རྒྱས་ཡོན་ཏན་གཟི་མདངའ་ཁྱོད་ལ་བདག་ཕྱག་འཚལ། །ཇི་ལྟར་སེང་གེ་ནགས་ཁྲོད་དག་ན་སྒྲ་སྒྲོགས་པ། ལྷ་ཚོགས་ཕལ་ཆེན་ཐམས་ཅད་ཟིལ་གྱིས་གནོན་པར་བགྱིད། །དེ་ལྟར་མི་ཡི་དམ་པ་མཐུ་ཆེན་མངའ་བ་ཡང་། །མུ་སྟེགས་ཅན་མང་འདུས་པ་ཐམས་ཅད་ཟིལ་གྱིས་གནོན། །བདེ་བར་གཤེགས་པ་སྨིན་མཚམས་བར་གྱི་མཛོད་སྤུ་དཀར། །དངུལ་དང་ཁ་བའི་ཚོགས་བཞིན་མཐའ་ཡས་གཟི་བརྗིད་ཅན། །དེས་ནི་འཇིག་རྟེན་འདི་དག་ཐམས་ཅད་སྣང་བར་བགྱིས། །འཇིག་རྟེན་ཀུན་ན་སངས་རྒྱས་ཁྱོད་ནི་མི་མཉམ་མཉམ། །སྐྱེས་བུ་ཁྱུ་མཆོག་ཞབས་ལ་ལྷ་ཡི་འཁོར་ལོ་མངའ། །གསལ་ཞིང་མཛེས་ལ་རྩིབས་སྟོང་ཚང་ཞིང་མུ་ཁྱུད་འཁོར། །དེ་དག་གིས་ནི་རི་དང་ནགས་བཅས་ས་འདི་རྣམས། །རབ་ཏུ་གཡོ་བགྱིད་ཐུབ་པ་གང་ཟག་མཚུངས་མེད་པ། །ཉོན་མོངས་ཤས་ཆེན་དོར་བར་བགྱི་པ་ཐམས་ཅད་བོར། །འཕགས་པ་ངེས་པར་འབྱིན་པའི་ལམ་ནི་རབ་ཏུ་བརྙེས། ནོར་རྣམས་ཀུན་དང་ལྡན་ཞིང་ཡོན་ཏན་རྣམས་ཀྱིས་ཕྱུག །བསམ་པ་བཞིན་དུ་འཕགས་པའི་ནོར་རྣམས་བགོད་པ་མཛད། །ས་དང་མཚུངས་ཤིང་སྤྲིན་པའི་གནས་གྱུར་མཚུངས་མ་མཆིས། །ཡོན་ཏན་ཀུན་ལ་མངའ་བརྙེས་ཚུལ་ཁྲིམས་རྣམ་དག་པ། ཇི་ལྟར་ནམ་མཁར་ལག་པ་མི་ཐོགས་མི་ཆགས་ལྟར། །འཇིག་རྟེན་དག་ན་ཁྱོད་ལ་རྗེས་ཆགས་ཁྲོ་མི་མངའ། །བཟོད་པ་ཟད་ཀྱིས་གཏུགས་པ་དོན་དང་ཆོས་རྣམས་ཀུན། །སྙིང་པོས་མ་མཆིས་པ་དང་གསོ་བ་དང་གསོག་ཏུ་མཁྱེན། །སྲིད་པའི་འགྲོ་བ་ཐམས་ཅད་དག་ན་གང་རྣམས་ལ། །ཧློམ་སེམས་འགྱུར་བའི་སེམས་ཅན་སྲོག་དང་དངོས་མ་བརྙེས། །ཁམས་དང་སྐྱེད་པ་དག་དང་སྐྱེར་དང་བསམ་པ་མཁྱེན། །རྨད་དུ་བྱུང་དང་རྣམ་པར་འབྱེད་མཛད་སྒྲོན་མར་གྱུར། །རྒྱུ་བོ་ཆེན་པོས་དེད་པའི་འགྲོ་བ་གཟིགས་གྱུར་ནས། །སྟོན་ཆད་བརྩོན་འགྲུས་སྟོབས

བརྟན་མཐུ་ནི་བསྐྱེད་པ་མཛད། །སྐྱེ་བ་སྤྱངས་ཤིང་ཉོན་མོངས་ཞི་བའི་ཐུགས་དང་
ལྡན། །ཐུགས་རྒྱ་ཆེན་པོ་སྐྱེ་དང་རྒ་ཤི་མཐའ་མར་འབྱིན། །ནམ་མཁའི་དཀྱིལ་
དང་མཚུངས་པར་ཆགས་པ་མི་མངའ་རྒྱུ། །འཇིག་རྟེན་ཆོས་ཀྱིས་མི་གོས་འཇིག་
རྟེན་གསུམ་ན་རྒྱུ། །བདག་ཉིད་ཆེན་པོ་ཤེས་རབ་ཀྱིས་ནི་སྣང་བར་མཛད། །སྨན་
པ་སྨན་གནག་གྱུར་པ་ཐམས་ཅད་རྣམ་པར་སེལ། །འདོད་ཆགས་རྟུལ་ཞི་མཛད་ཅིང་
ཞེ་སྡང་གཏི་མུག་གི །དྲི་མ་སྣ་ཚོགས་མུན་བསལ་ཁྱོད་ལ་ཕྱག་འཚལ་ལོ། །
ཀུན་དགའ་བོ་དེ་ཚུན་ཆད་བྲམ་ཟེའི་ཁྱེའུ་བཟང་དག་དེའི་རྫུ་འཕྲུལ་རྣམས་སམ།
མངོན་པར་ཤེས་པ་རྣམས་ཡོངས་སུ་ཉམས་པར་མ་གྱུར་ཏོ། །ཀུན་དགའ་བོ་དེའི་ཚེ་
དེའི་དུས་ན་བྲམ་ཟེའི་ཁྱེའུ་བཟང་དག་ཅེས་བྱ་བར་གྱུར་པ་དེ་གཞན་ཞིག་ཡིན་སྙམ་དུ་
ཁྱོད་དོགས་ཤིང་ཡིད་གཉིས་ཟའམ། ཐེ་ཚོམ་ཟ་ན་དེ་ལྟར་མི་བལྟའོ། །དེ་ཅིའི་
ཕྱིར་ཞེ་ན། བྱང་ཆུབ་སེམས་དཔའ་སེམས་དཔའ་ཆེན་པོ་བྱམས་པ་འདི་ཉིད་དེའི་ཚེ་
དེའི་དུས་ན་བྲམ་ཟེའི་ཁྱེའུ་བཟང་དག་ཅེས་བྱ་བར་གྱུར་ཏེ། དེ་བཞིན་གཤེགས་པ་
དགྲ་བཅོམ་པ་ཡང་དག་པར་རྫོགས་པའི་སངས་རྒྱས་སྣང་བས་རྣམ་པར་རོལ་པའི་
མངོན་པར་ཤེས་པ་དེ་ལ་སོགས་སུ་བཅད་པ་འདི་དག་གིས་མངོན་པར་བསྟོད་དོ། །
དེ་སྐད་ཅེས་བཀའ་སྩལ་པ་དང་། བཅོམ་ལྡན་འདས་ལ་ཚེ་དང་ལྡན་པ་ཀུན་དགའ་
བོས་འདི་སྐད་ཅེས་གསོལ་ཏོ། །བཅོམ་ལྡན་འདས་བྱང་ཆུབ་སེམས་དཔའ་སེམས་
དཔའ་ཆེན་པོ་བྱམས་པ་འདི་གལ་ཏེ་ཡུན་རིང་པོ་དེ་སྲིད་ནས་མི་སྐྱེ་བའི་ཆོས་ལ་བཟོད་པ་
ཐོབ་པ་ལགས་ན། ཅིའི་སླད་དུ་མྱུར་དུ་བླ་ན་མེད་པ་ཡང་དག་པར་རྫོགས་པའི་བྱང་
ཆུབ་མངོན་པར་རྫོགས་པར་སངས་མ་རྒྱས། དེ་སྐད་ཅེས་གསོལ་བ་དང་།
བཅོམ་ལྡན་འདས་ཀྱིས་ཚེ་དང་ལྡན་པ་ཀུན་དགའ་བོ་ལ་འདི་སྐད་ཅེས་བཀའ་སྩལ་
ཏོ། །ཀུན་དགའ་བོ་བྱང་ཆུབ་སེམས་དཔའ་རྣམས་ཀྱི་བཀོད་པ་དང་ཡོངས་སུ་གཟུང་
བ་ནི་གཉིས་པོ་འདི་དག་སྟེ། གཉིས་གང་ཞེ་ན། སེམས་ཅན་བཀོད་པ་དང་
སེམས་ཅན་ཡོངས་སུ་གཟུང་བ་དང་། ཞིང་བཀོད་པ་དང་ཞིང་ཡོངས་སུ་གཟུང་བ་
དང་། གཉིས་པོ་འདི་དག་ཡིན་ན་བྱང་ཆུབ་སེམས་དཔའ་སེམས་དཔའ་ཆེན་པོ་

བྱམས་པས་ནི་སྔོན་བྱང་ཆུབ་སེམས་དཔའི་སྤྱོད་པ་སྤྱོད་པའི་ཚེ་ཞིང་བཀོད་པ་རྣམ་པར་སྦྱངས་ཤིང་ཡོངས་སུ་གཟུང་བ་ཡོངས་སུ་བཟུང་ངོ་། །ཀུན་དགའ་བོ་ང་སྔོན་བྱང་ཆུབ་སེམས་དཔའི་སྤྱོད་པ་སྤྱོད་པའི་ཚེ། ངས་ནི་སེམས་ཅན་བཀོད་པ་རྣམ་པར་སྦྱངས། སེམས་ཅན་ཡོངས་སུ་གཟུང་བ་ཡོངས་སུ་བཟུང་། ཞིང་བཀོད་པ་ཡང་རྣམ་པར་སྦྱངས། ཞིང་ཡོངས་སུ་གཟུང་བ་ཡང་ཡོངས་སུ་བཟུང་ངོ་། །ཀུན་དགའ་བོ་ངས་མངོན་པར་ཤེས་ཏེ། བྱང་ཆུབ་སེམས་དཔའ་སེམས་དཔའ་ཆེན་པོ་བྱམས་པ་ཡང་དག་པར་ཞུགས་ནས་བསྐལ་པ་བཞི་བཅུ་རྩ་གཉིས་ལོན་པའི་འོག་ཏུ་གདོད་བླ་ན་མེད་པ་ཡང་དག་པར་རྫོགས་པའི་བྱང་ཆུབ་ཏུ་སེམས་བསྐྱེད་དེ། ཀུན་དགའ་བོ་བསྐལ་པ་བཟང་པོ་འདི་འདས་ནས་བསྐལ་པ་དགུ་བཅུ་རྩ་བཞི་ན་བླ་ན་མེད་པ་ཡང་དག་པར་རྫོགས་པའི་བྱང་ཆུབ་མངོན་པར་རྫོགས་པར་འཚང་རྒྱ་བ་རིགས་པ་ལས། ཀུན་དགའ་བོ་ངས་བརྩོན་འགྲུས་འབར་བར་བྱས་པས་མྱུར་དུ་བླ་ན་མེད་པ་ཡང་དག་པར་རྫོགས་པའི་བྱང་ཆུབ་མངོན་པར་རྫོགས་པར་སངས་རྒྱས་ཏེ། ཀུན་དགའ་བོ་ངས་བརྩོན་འགྲུས་རླབས་པོ་ཆེས་མྱུར་དུ་བླ་ན་མེད་པ་ཡང་དག་པར་རྫོགས་པའི་བྱང་ཆུབ་ཏུ་མངོན་པར་རྫོགས་པར་སངས་རྒྱས་སོ། །ཀུན་དགའ་བོ་ཆོས་བཅུ་པོ་འདི་དག་གིས་ང་མྱུར་དུ་བླ་ན་མེད་པ་ཡང་དག་པར་རྫོགས་པའི་བྱང་ཆུབ་མངོན་པར་རྫོགས་པར་སངས་རྒྱས་ཏེ། བཅུ་གང་ཞེ་ན། བདོག་པ་ཕངས་པ་ཐམས་ཅད་ཡོངས་སུ་བཏང་བ་དང་། ཆུང་མ་ཕངས་པ་ཡོངས་སུ་བཏང་བ་དང་། བུ་ཕངས་པ་ཡོངས་སུ་བཏང་བ་དང་། མགོ་ཕངས་པ་ཡོངས་སུ་བཏང་བ་དང་། མིག་ཕངས་པ་ཡོངས་སུ་བཏང་པ་དང་། རྒྱལ་སྲིད་ཕངས་པ་ཡོངས་སུ་བཏང་བ་དང་། ལོངས་སྤྱོད་ཕངས་པ་ཡོངས་སུ་བཏང་བ་དང་། ཁྲག་ཕངས་པ་ཡོངས་སུ་བཏང་བ་དང་། རུས་པ་དང་རྐང་ཕངས་པ་ཡོངས་སུ་བཏང་བ་དང་། ཡན་ལག་ཕངས་པ་ཐམས་ཅད་ཡོངས་སུ་བཏང་བས་ང་མྱུར་དུ་བླ་ན་མེད་པ་ཡང་དག་པར་རྫོགས་པའི་བྱང་ཆུབ་མངོན་པར་རྫོགས་པར་སངས་རྒྱས་ཏེ། ཀུན་དགའ་བོ་ཆོས་བཅུ་པོ་དེ་དག་གིས་ང་མྱུར་དུ་བླ་ན་མེད་པ་ཡང་དག་པར་རྫོགས་པའི་བྱང་ཆུབ་མངོན་པར་རྫོགས་པར་སངས་རྒྱས་

ཏེ། །ཀུན་དགའ་བོ་གཞན་ཡང་ང་ཆོས་བཅུས་མྱུར་དུ་བླ་ན་མེད་པ་ཡང་དག་པར་
རྫོགས་པའི་བྱང་ཆུབ་མངོན་པར་རྫོགས་པར་སངས་རྒྱས་ཏེ། བཅུ་གང་ཞེ་ན།
ཀུན་དགའ་བོ་ང་ཚུལ་ཁྲིམས་ཀྱི་ཡོན་ཏན་གྱི་ཆོས་ལ་གནས་ཏེ་མྱུར་དུ་བླ་ན་མེད་པ་ཡང་
དག་པར་རྫོགས་པའི་བྱང་ཆུབ་མངོན་པར་རྫོགས་པར་སངས་རྒྱས་སོ། །ཀུན་དགའ་
བོ་ང་བཟོད་པའི་སྟོབས་དང་ལྡན་པས་མྱུར་དུ་བླ་ན་མེད་པ་ཡང་དག་པར་རྫོགས་པའི་
བྱང་ཆུབ་མངོན་པར་རྫོགས་པར་སངས་རྒྱས་སོ། །ཀུན་དགའ་བོ་ང་བརྩོན་འགྲུས་
འབར་བ་བརྩམས་པས་མྱུར་དུ་བླ་ན་མེད་པ་ཡང་དག་པར་རྫོགས་པའི་བྱང་ཆུབ་མངོན་
པར་རྫོགས་པར་སངས་རྒྱས་སོ། །ཀུན་དགའ་བོ་ང་བསམ་གཏན་གྱི་ཡོན་ཏན་ལ་
གནས་ཏེ་མྱུར་དུ་བླ་ན་མེད་པ་ཡང་དག་པར་རྫོགས་པའི་བྱང་ཆུབ་མངོན་པར་རྫོགས་
པར་སངས་རྒྱས་སོ། །ཀུན་དགའ་བོ་ང་ཤེས་རབ་ཀྱི་ཕ་རོལ་ཏུ་ཕྱིན་པ་ལ་གནས་ཏེ་
མྱུར་དུ་བླ་ན་མེད་པ་ཡང་དག་པར་རྫོགས་པའི་བྱང་ཆུབ་མངོན་པར་རྫོགས་པར་སངས་
རྒྱས་སོ། །ཀུན་དགའ་བོ་ངས་སེམས་ཅན་ཐམས་ཅད་ཡོངས་སུ་མ་བཏང་བས་མྱུར་
དུ་བླ་ན་མེད་པ་ཡང་དག་པར་རྫོགས་པའི་བྱང་ཆུབ་མངོན་པར་རྫོགས་པར་སངས་རྒྱས་
སོ། །ཀུན་དགའ་བོ་ང་ཐབས་ལ་མཁས་པ་ལ་གནས་ཏེ་མྱུར་དུ་བླ་ན་མེད་པ་ཡང་
དག་པར་རྫོགས་པའི་བྱང་ཆུབ་མངོན་པར་རྫོགས་པར་སངས་རྒྱས་སོ། །ཀུན་དགའ་
བོ་ང་སེམས་ཅན་ཐམས་ཅད་ལ་སེམས་སྙོམས་པས་མྱུར་དུ་བླ་ན་མེད་པ་ཡང་དག་པར་
རྫོགས་པའི་བྱང་ཆུབ་མངོན་པར་རྫོགས་པར་སངས་རྒྱས་སོ། །ཀུན་དགའ་བོ་ངས་
སྟོང་པ་ཉིད་ཀྱི་ཆོས་རྟོགས་པས་མྱུར་དུ་བླ་ན་མེད་པ་ཡང་དག་པར་རྫོགས་པའི་བྱང་ཆུབ་
མངོན་པར་རྫོགས་པར་སངས་རྒྱས་སོ། །ཀུན་དགའ་བོ་ངས་མཚན་མ་མེད་པ་དང་།
སྨོན་པ་མེད་པའི་ཆོས་རྟོགས་པས་མྱུར་དུ་བླ་ན་མེད་པ་ཡང་དག་པར་རྫོགས་པའི་བྱང་
ཆུབ་མངོན་པར་རྫོགས་པར་སངས་རྒྱས་ཏེ། །ཀུན་དགའ་བོ་ཆོས་བཅུ་པོ་དེ་དག་
གིས་ང་མྱུར་དུ་བླ་ན་མེད་པ་ཡང་དག་པར་རྫོགས་པའི་བྱང་ཆུབ་མངོན་པར་རྫོགས་པར་
སངས་རྒྱས་སོ། །ཀུན་དགའ་བོ་ངས་ཚོར་བ་སྡུག་བསྔལ་བ་དྲག་པ་རྩུབ་པ་ཟི་ལྷ་བུ་
དག་གིས་བླ་ན་མེད་པ་ཡང་དག་པར་རྫོགས་པའི་བྱང་ཆུབ་མངོན་པར་རྫོགས་པར་

སངས་རྒྱས་པ་དེ།   གལ་ཏེ་ཁྱོད་ཀྱིས་ཞེས་སུ་ཟིན་ན་ཀུན་དགའ་བོ་ཁྱོད་སྐྱོབས་པར་
མི་འགྱུར་རོ།   །དེ་ཅིའི་ཕྱིར་ཞེ་ན།   ཀུན་དཀའ་བོ་སྔོན་བྱུང་བ་འདས་པའི་དུས་ན་
རྒྱལ་བུ་གཞོན་ནུ་ནོར་ཐམས་ཅད་སྦྱིན་པ་ཞེས་བྱ་བ་གཟུགས་བཟང་བ།   མཛེས་པ།
བལྟ་ན་སྡུག་པ།   ཁ་དོག་བཟང་པོ།   །རྒྱས་པ་མཆོག་དང་ལྡན་པ།   རྒྱལ་པོའི་
འཁོར་པ་ཆེན་པོ་དང་རྒྱལ་པོའི་མཐུ་ཆེན་པོ་དང་ལྡན་པ་ཞིག་ཡོད་པ་དེ་སྐྱིད་མོས་ཚལ་དུ་
འགྲོ་སྟེ།   གྲོང་བར་དུ་ཕྱིན་པ་དང་གནོད་པས་ཉེན་ཅིང་སྡུག་བསྔལ་ལ་ནད་ཚབས་
ཆེན་པོས་བཏབ་པའི་མི་ཞིག་མཐོང་ངོ་།   །མཐོང་ནས་ཀྱང་དེ་སྙིང་རྗེ་བར་གྱུར་ཏེ།
དེ་མི་དེ་ག་ལ་བ་དེར་སོང་སྟེ་ཕྱིན་ནས་འདི་སྐད་ཅེས་སྨྲས་སོ།   །ཀྱེ་མི་ཁྱོད་ཅི་སྡུག་
བསྔལ་ལམ།   དེས་སྨྲས་པ།   ལྷ་བདག་ནི་ནད་ཀྱིས་བཏབ་པོ།   །དེས་སྨྲས་
པ།   །ཀྱེ་མི་ཁྱོད་ཀྱི་ནད་ཅིས་ཞི་བར་འགྱུར།   ཁྱོད་ལ་ཅི་སྦྱིན།   དེས་འདི་སྐད་
ཅེས་སྨྲས་སོ།   །གལ་ཏེ་བདག་གིས་ལྷ་ཁྱོད་ཀྱི་ལུས་ལས་ཇི་ཙམ་གྱིས་ཆོམ་པར་
འགྱུར་བའི་ཁྲག་ཅིག་བཏུང་དུ་ཐོབ་པ་ལྟ་ན་བདག་གི་ནད་ཞི་བར་འགྱུར་རོ།   །ཀུན་
དགའ་བོ་དེ་ནས་རྒྱལ་བུ་གཞོན་ནུ་ནོར་ཐམས་ཅད་སྦྱིན་པ་དེས་མཚོན་རྣོན་པོ་བླངས་ཏེ།
རང་གིས་ལུས་ཕུག་ནས་ཁྲག་གཟགས་ཏེ་མི་དེ་ལ་བཏུང་བར་བྱིན་ནོ།   །ཀུན་དགའ་
བོ་མི་དེས་དེ་འཐུངས་མ་ཐག་ཏུ་མི་དེའི་ནད་སོས་པར་གྱུར་ཏོ།   །ཀུན་དགའ་བོ་རྒྱལ་
བུ་གཞོན་ནུ་ནོར་ཐམས་ཅད་སྦྱིན་པས་རང་གི་ལུས་ཕུག་སྟེ་ཁྲག་ཐམས་ཅད་གཟགས་
ཀྱང་འགྱོད་པའི་སེམས་གཅིག་ཀྱང་མེད་དོ།   །ཀུན་དགའ་བོ་དེའི་ཚེ་དེའི་དུས་ན་
རྒྱལ་བུ་གཞོན་ནུ་ནོར་ཐམས་ཅད་སྦྱིན་པར་གྱུར་པ་དེ་གཞན་ཞིག་ཡིན་པ་སྙམ་དུ་ཁྱོད་
དོགས་ཤིང་ཡིད་གཉིས་སམ།   ཐེ་ཚོམ་ཟ་ན་དེ་ལྟར་མི་བལྟའོ།   །དེ་ཅིའི་ཕྱིར་ཞེ་
ན།   ང་ཉིད་དེའི་ཚེ་དེའི་དུས་ན་རྒྱལ་བུ་གཞོན་ནུ་ནོར་ཐམས་ཅད་སྦྱིན་པ་ཞེས་བྱ་བར་
གྱུར་རོ།   །ཀུན་དགའ་བོ་རྒྱ་མཚོ་ཆེན་པོ་བཞིའི་ཆུའི་ཕུང་པོ་ནི་ཚད་གཟུང་དུ་ཡོད་ཀྱི་
བླ་ན་མེད་པ་ཡང་དག་པར་རྫོགས་པའི་བྱང་ཆུབ་འདི་ཡོངས་སུ་ཚོལ་ཞིང་ངས་སྔོན་
སེམས་ཅན་རྣམས་ལ་ཁྲག་བྱིན་པ་ནི་ཚད་མེད་དོ།   །ཀུན་དགའ་བོ་སྔོན་བྱུང་བ་
འདས་པའི་དུས་ན་རྒྱལ་བུ་གཞོན་ནུ་མེ་ཏོག་ཅེས་བྱ་བ་གཟུགས་བཟང་བ།   མཛེས་པ།

བལྟ་ན་སྡུག་པ། །ཁ་དོག་བཟང་པོ་རྒྱས་པ་མཆོག་དང་ལྡན་པ། རྒྱལ་པོའི་འཁོར་པ་ཆེན་པོ་དང་། རྒྱལ་པོའི་མཐུ་ཆེན་པོ་དང་ལྡན་པ་ཞིག་ཡོད་པ་དེ་སྐྱིད་མོས་ཚལ་གྱི་སར་འགྲོ་སྟེ། གྲོང་བར་དུ་ཕྱིན་པ་དང་སྐྲ་ཐབ་ཀྱི་ནད་ཀྱིས་བཏབ་པའི་མི་གནོད་པས་ཉེན་པ། སྡུག་བསྔལ་བ། ནད་ཚབས་ཆེན་པོ་ཞིག་མཐོང་ངོ་། །དེས་དེ་མཐོང་ནས་ཀྱང་སྙིང་རྗེ་བར་གྱུར་ཏེ། དེ་མི་དེ་ག་ལ་བ་དེར་སོང་སྟེ། འདི་སྐད་ཅེས་སྨྲས་སོ། །ཀྱེ་ཅི་ཞིག་གིས་མི་ཁྱོད་ཀྱི་ནད་འདི་ཞི་བར་འགྱུར། ཁྱོད་ལ་ཅི་ཞིག་སྨིན། དེས་འདི་སྐད་ཅེས་སྨྲས་སོ། །གལ་ཏེ་བདག་གིས་ལྷ་ཁྱོད་ཀྱི་ལུས་ལས་ཇི་ཙམ་གྱིས་ཆོམ་པར་འགྱུར་བའི་ཁྲག་ཞིག་ཐོབ་པ་ལྟ་ན་བདག་གི་ནད་ཞི་བར་འགྱུར་རོ། །དེ་ནས་རྒྱལ་བུ་གཞོན་ནུ་མེ་ཏོག་དེ་ཆོམ་ཞིང་མགུ་ལ་ཡི་རངས་ཏེ་རབ་ཏུ་དགའ་ནས་བདེ་བ་དང་ཡིད་བདེ་བ་སྐྱེས་ཏེ། རང་གི་ལུས་བརྟུངས་ནས་ཁྲག་བྲུས་ཏེ་མི་དེའི་ལུས་ལ་བསྐུས་སོ། །ཀུན་དགའ་བོ་བསྐུས་མ་ཐག་ཏུ་མི་དེའི་ནད་སོས་པར་གྱུར་ཏོ། །ཀུན་དགའ་བོ་རྒྱལ་བུ་གཞོན་ནུ་མེ་ཏོག་གིས་རང་གི་ལུས་བརྟུངས་ཏེ། ཁྲག་གཟུགས་ཀྱང་སེམས་ལ་འགྱོད་པ་མེད་པར་གྱུར་ཏོ། །ཀུན་དགའ་བོ་དེའི་ཚེ་དེའི་དུས་ན་རྒྱལ་བུ་གཞོན་ནུ་མེ་ཏོག་ཅེས་བྱ་བར་གྱུར་པ་དེ་གཞན་ཞིག་ཡིན་པ་སྙམ་དུ་ཁྱོད་དོགས་ཤིང་ཡིད་གཉིས་སམ་ཐེ་ཚོམ་ཟ་ན་དེ་ལྟར་མི་བལྟའོ། །དེ་ཅིའི་ཕྱིར་ཞེ་ན། ང་ཉིད་དེའི་ཚེ་དེའི་དུས་ན་རྒྱལ་བུ་གཞོན་ནུ་མེ་ཏོག་ཅེས་བྱ་བར་གྱུར་ཏོ། །ཀུན་དགའ་བོ་རྒྱ་མཚོ་ཆེན་པོ་བཞིའི་ཆུའི་ཕུང་པོ་ནི་ཚད་བཟུང་དུ་ཡོད་ཀྱི་བླ་ན་མེད་པ་ཡང་དག་པར་རྫོགས་པའི་བྱང་ཆུབ་འདི་ཡོངས་སུ་ཚོལ་ཞིང་ངས་སྔོན་སེམས་ཅན་རྣམས་ལ་ཁྲག་བྱིན་པ་ནི་ཚད་མེད་དོ། །ཀུན་དགའ་བོ་སྔོན་བྱུང་བ་འདས་པའི་དུས་ན་རྒྱལ་པོ་ཟླ་འོད་ཅེས་བྱ་བ་གཟུགས་བཟང་བ། མཛེས་པ། བལྟ་ན་སྡུག་པ། ཁ་དོག་བཟང་པོ་རྒྱས་པ་མཆོག་དང་ལྡན་པ། རྒྱལ་པོའི་འཁོར་བ་ཆེན་པོ་དང་རྒྱལ་པོའི་མཐུ་ཆེན་པོ་དང་ལྡན་པ་ཞིག་ཡོད་པ་དེ་སྐྱིད་མོས་ཚལ་དུ་འགྲོ་སྟེ། གྲོང་བར་དུ་ཕྱིན་པ་དང་། མི་མིག་མེད་པ་ལོང་བ། དབུལ་པོ། བཀྲེན་པ། སློང་མོ་བྱེད་པ་ཞིག་མཐོང་ངོ་། །མཐོང་ནས་ཀྱང་དེ་སྙིང་རྗེ་བར་གྱུར་ཏོ། །དེ་ནས་མི་དེ་རྒྱལ་པོ་

ཟླ་འོད་ག་ལ་བ་དེར་སོང་སྟེ་ཕྱིན་ནས་འདི་སྐད་ཅེས་སྨྲས་སོ། །ལྷ་ཁྱོད་ནི་སྐྱིད་དོ། །ལྷ་ཁྱོད་ནི་དགྱེས་སོ། །བདག་ནི་སྡུག་བསྔལ་ལོ། །ལོང་ངོ་། མིག་མ་མཆིས་སོ། །དབུལ་ལོ་བཀྲེན་ནོ། །སྙིངས་མོ་པའོ། །མགོན་མ་མཆིས་པའོ། །ཀུན་དགའ་བོ་དེ་ནས་རྒྱལ་པོ་ཟླ་འོད་ཀྱིས་མི་དེ་ཡང་མཐོང་། ཚིག་ཀྱང་ཐོས་ནས་ངུས་ཏེ་མཆི་མ་ཟག་བཞིན་དུ་དེ་ལ་འདི་སྐད་ཅེས་སྨྲས་སོ། །ཀྱེ་མི་ཁྱོད་ལ་ཅི་དགོས། ཁྱོད་ལ་བཟའ་བ་དང་། བཏུང་བ་དང་། བཞོན་པ་དང་། རྒྱན་དང་། གསེར་དང་། ནོར་བུ་དང་། མུ་ཏིག་དང་། རིན་པོ་ཆེ་སྣ་ཚོགས་སྦྱིན་པར་བྱའམ། ཁྱོད་ལ་གང་དགོས་པ་དེ་སྨྲོས་ཤིག །མི་དེས་སྨྲས་པ། བདག་ལ་མིག་འཚལ་ན་བདག་ལ་མིག་སྩལ་དུ་གསོལ། ཀུན་དགའ་བོ་དེ་ནས་རྒྱལ་པོ་ཟླ་འོད་དེས་རང་གི་མིག་ཕྱུང་སྟེ་མི་དེ་ལ་བྱིན་ནོ། །ཀུན་དགའ་བོ་དེ་ནས་རྒྱལ་པོ་ཟླ་འོད་ཀྱིས་རང་གི་མིག་ཕྱུང་སྟེ་མི་དེ་ལ་བྱིན་ཡང་དེའི་སེམས་ལ་འགྱོད་པ་མེད་པར་གྱུར་ཏོ། །ཀུན་དགའ་བོ་ཆེ་དེའི་དུས་ན་རྒྱལ་པོ་ཟླ་འོད་ཅེས་བྱ་བར་གྱུར་པ་དེ་གཞན་ཞིག་ཡིན་པ་སྙམ་དུ་ཁྱོད་དོགས་ཤིང་ཡིད་གཉིས་སམ་ཐེ་ཚོམ་ཟ་ན་དེ་ལྟར་མི་བལྟའོ། །དེ་ཅིའི་ཕྱིར་ཞེ་ན། ང་ཉིད་དེའི་ཚེ་དེའི་དུས་ན་རྒྱལ་པོ་ཟླ་འོད་ཅེས་བྱ་བར་གྱུར་ཏོ། །ཀུན་དགའ་བོ་རིའི་རྒྱལ་པོ་རི་རབ་ལ་ནི་ཚད་གཟུང་དུ་ཡོད་ཀྱི་བླ་ན་མེད་པ་ཡང་དག་པར་རྫོགས་པའི་བྱང་ཆུབ་འདི་ཡོངས་སུ་ཚོལ་ཞིང་ངས་སེམས་ཅན་རྣམས་ལ་མིག་བྱིན་པ་ནི་ཆེས་མང་སྟེ་ཚད་མེད་དོ། །ཀུན་དགའ་བོ་བྱང་ཆུབ་སེམས་དཔའ་སེམས་དཔའ་ཆེན་པོ་བྱམས་པས་ནི་སྔོན་བྱང་ཆུབ་སེམས་དཔའི་སྤྱོད་པ་སྤྱོད་པ་ན་ཐེག་པ་བདེ་བ། འཇུག་པ་བདེ་བ། ལམ་བདེ་བས་བླ་ན་མེད་པ་ཡང་དག་པར་རྫོགས་པའི་བྱང་ཆུབ་ཡང་དག་པར་བསྒྲུབས་སོ། །ཀུན་དགའ་བོ་བྱང་ཆུབ་སེམས་དཔའ་སེམས་དཔའ་ཆེན་པོ་བྱམས་པས་ནི་སྔོན་བྱང་ཆུབ་སེམས་དཔའི་སྤྱོད་པ་སྤྱོད་པའི་ཚེ་ལག་པ་ཡོངས་སུ་བཏང་བ་མ་བྱས། རྐང་པ་ཡོངས་སུ་བཏང་བ་མ་བྱས། རྐང་ཡོངས་སུ་བཏང་བ་མ་བྱས། ཆུང་མ་ཕངས་པ་ཡོངས་སུ་བཏང་བ་མ་བྱས། བུ་ཕངས་པ་ཡོངས་སུ་བཏང་བ་མ་བྱས། གྲོང་དང་། གྲོང་རྡལ་དང་། གྲོང་

ཁྱེར་དང་། ལྗོངས་དང་། ཡུལ་འཁོར་དང་། རྒྱལ་པོའི་ཕོ་བྲང་འཁོར་ཕངས་པ་ཡོངས་སུ་བཏང་བ་མ་བྱུས་ཏེ། ཀུན་དགའ་བོ་བྱང་ཆུབ་སེམས་དཔའ་སེམས་དཔའ་ཆེན་པོ་བྱམས་པས་ནི་སྔོན་བྱང་ཆུབ་སེམས་དཔའི་སྤྱོད་པ་སྤྱོད་པ་ན་ཐབས་མཁས་པས་ཡོངས་སུ་ཟིན་པས་ཐེག་པ་བདེ་བ། འཇུག་པ་བདེ་བ། ལམ་བདེ་བས་བླ་ན་མེད་པ་ཡང་དག་པར་རྫོགས་པའི་བྱང་ཆུབ་ཡང་དག་པར་བསྒྲུབས་སོ། །དེ་ནས་བཅོམ་ལྡན་འདས་ལ་ཚེ་དང་ལྡན་པ་ཀུན་དགའ་བོས་འདི་སྐད་ཅེས་གསོལ་ཏོ། །བཅོམ་ལྡན་འདས་བྱང་ཆུབ་སེམས་དཔའ་སེམས་དཔའ་ཆེན་པོ་བྱམས་པས་ཐབས་ལ་མཁས་པ་གང་ལ་གནས་ནས་བླ་ན་མེད་པ་ཡང་དག་པར་རྫོགས་པའི་བྱང་ཆུབ་ཡང་དག་པར་བསྒྲུབས་པའི་ཐབས་ལ་མཁས་པ་དེ་གང་ལགས། དེ་སྐད་ཅེས་གསོལ་བ་དང་། བཅོམ་ལྡན་འདས་ཀྱིས་ཚེ་དང་ལྡན་པ་ཀུན་དགའ་བོ་ལ་འདི་སྐད་ཅེས་བཀའ་སྩལ་ཏོ། །ཀུན་དགའ་བོ་འདི་ལ་བྱང་ཆུབ་སེམས་དཔའ་སེམས་དཔའ་ཆེན་པོ་བྱམས་པས་སྔོན་བྱང་ཆུབ་སེམས་དཔའི་སྤྱོད་པ་སྤྱོད་པའི་ཚེ། ཉིན་ལན་གསུམ་མཚན་ལན་གསུམ་དུ་བླ་གོས་ཕྲག་པ་གཅིག་ཏུ་གཟར་ནས་པུས་མོ་གཡས་པའི་ལྷ་ང་ས་ལ་བཙུགས་ཏེ་ཐལ་མོ་སྦྱར་ནས་སངས་རྒྱས་ཐམས་ཅད་མངོན་སུམ་དུ་བྱས་ཏེ་ཚིག་འདི་སྐད་ཅེས་སྨྲས་སོ། །སངས་རྒྱས་ཀུན་ལ་ཕྱག་འཚལ་ལོ། །དྲང་སྲོང་ལྷ་མིག་ལྡན་པ་ཡི། །བྱང་ཆུབ་སེམས་དཔའ་རྣམས་དང་ཡང་། །ཉན་ཐོས་རྣམས་ལ་ཕྱག་འཚལ་ལོ། །ངན་འགྲོ་ཐམས་ཅད་ཟློག་བགྱིད་ཅིང་། །མཐོ་རིས་ལམ་རི་རབ་སྟོན་ལ། །རྒ་ཤི་མེད་པར་འདྲེན་བགྱིད་པ། །བྱང་ཆུབ་སེམས་ལ་ཕྱག་འཚལ་ལོ། །སེམས་ཀྱི་དབང་དུ་གྱུར་པས་ན། །བདག་གིས་སྡིག་པ་ཅི་བགྱིས་པ། །སངས་རྒྱས་སྤྱན་སྔར་མཆིས་ནས་སུ། །བདག་གིས་དེ་དག་བཤགས་པར་བགྱི། །བདག་ལས་རྣམ་པ་གསུམ་གང་གིས། །བསོད་ནམས་ཚོགས་ནི་སྐྱེད་པ་དེ། །བདག་གི་ཀུན་མཁྱེན་ས་བོན་ཏེ། །བདག་གི་བྱང་ཆུབ་མི་ཟད་ཤོག །ཕྱོགས་བཅུ་དག་གི་ཞིང་རྣམས་སུ། །སངས་རྒྱས་མཆོད་པ་གང་བྱུང་བ། །སངས་རྒྱས་མཁྱེན་པ་ཡི་རང་བས། །དེ་ལ་བདག་ནི་ཡི་རང་ངོ་། །

སྡིག་པ་ཐམས་ཅད་བཤགས་པར་བགྱི། །བསོད་ནམས་ཀུན་ལ་ཡི་རང་ངོ་། །
སངས་རྒྱས་ཀུན་ལ་ཕྱག་འཚལ་ལོ། །བདག་ནི་ཡེ་ཤེས་མཆོག་ཐོབ་
ཤོག །ཕྱོགས་བཅུ་དག་གི་ཕྱོགས་རྣམས་ན། །ས་བཅུ་དག་ལ་གནས་པ་ཡི། །
བྱང་ཆུབ་སེམས་དཔའ་བྱང་ཆུབ་མཆོག །འཚང་རྒྱ་བགྱིད་པར་སྐུལ་མ་
འདེབས། །བྱང་ཆུབ་དམ་པར་སངས་རྒྱས་ཤིང་། །སྡེ་དང་བཅས་པའི་བདུད་
བཏུལ་ནས། གྲོག་ཆགས་ཀུན་ལ་སྨན་སླད་དུ། །ཆོས་ཀྱི་འཁོར་ལོ་སྐོར་གྱུར་
ཅིག །ཆོས་རྔ་ཆེན་པོའི་སྒྲ་ཡིས་ནི། །སྡུག་བསྔལ་སེམས་ཅན་ཐར་བགྱིད་
ཤོག །བསྐལ་པ་བྱེ་བ་བསམ་ཡས་སུ། །ཆོས་སྟོན་མཛད་ཅིང་བཞུགས་གྱུར་
ཅིག །འདོད་པའི་འདམ་དུ་བྱིང་གྱུར་ཅིང་། །སྲེད་པའི་སྲད་བུས་དམ་བཅིངས་
པ། །འཆིང་བ་ཀུན་གྱིས་བཅིངས་བདག་ལ། །རྐང་གཉིས་མཆོག་རྣམས་
གཟིགས་སུ་གསོལ། །སེམས་ཀྱི་དྲི་མར་བགྱིས་པ་ལ། །སངས་རྒྱས་རྣམས་ནི་
སྨོད་མི་མཛད། །སེམས་ཅན་རྣམས་ལ་བྱམས་ཐུགས་ལྡན། །སྲིད་པའི་མཚོ་
ལས་སྒྲོལ་བར་ཤོག །རྫོགས་པའི་སངས་རྒྱས་གང་བཞུགས་དང་། །གང་དག་
འདས་དང་མ་བྱོན་པ། །དེ་དག་རྗེས་སུ་བདག་སློབ་ཅིང་། །བྱང་ཆུབ་སྤྱོད་པ་སྤྱོད་
གྱུར་ཅིག །ཕ་རོལ་ཕྱིན་དྲུག་རྫོགས་བགྱིས་ནས། །འགྲོ་དྲུག་སེམས་ཅན་ཐར་
བགྱིད་ཤོག །མངོན་ཤེས་དྲུག་པོ་མངོན་བགྱིས་ནས། བླ་མེད་བྱང་ཆུབ་རེག་
གྱུར་ཅིག །མ་སྐྱེས་པ་དང་མི་འབྱུང་དང་། རང་བཞིན་མ་མཆིས་གནས་མ་
མཆིས། རྣམ་རིག་མ་མཆིས་དངོས་མ་མཆིས། །སྟོང་པའི་ཆོས་ནི་རྟོགས་པར་
ཤོག །སངས་རྒྱས་དྲང་སྲོང་ཆེན་པོ་ལྟར། །སེམས་ཅན་མ་མཆིས་སྲོག་མ་
མཆིས། །གང་ཟག་མ་མཆིས་གསོ་མ་མཆིས། །བདག་མ་མཆིས་པའི་ཆོས་
རྟོགས་ཤོག །བདག་འཛིན་བདག་གིར་འཛིན་པར་ནི། །དངོས་པོ་ཀུན་ལ་མི་
གནས་པར། །སེམས་ཅན་ཀུན་ལ་བདེ་སླད་དུ། །སེར་སྣ་མ་མཆིས་སྦྱིན་གཏོང་
ཤོག །དངོས་པོ་དངོས་པོ་མ་མཆིས་པས། །བདག་གི་ལོངས་སྤྱོད་ལྷུན་གྲུབ་
ཤོག །དངོས་པོ་ཐམས་ཅད་རྣམ་འཇིག་པས། །སྦྱིན་པའི་ཕ་རོལ་ཕྱིན་རྫོགས་

ཤོག །ཁྲིམས་ཀྱི་ཚུལ་ཁྲིམས་སྐྱོན་མེད་ཅིང་། །ཚུལ་ཁྲིམས་རྣམ་པར་དག་དང་
ལྡན། །ཚོམ་སེམས་མེད་པའི་ཚུལ་ཁྲིམས་ཀྱིས། ཚུལ་ཁྲིམས་ཕ་རོལ་ཕྱིན་
རྫོགས་ཤོག །སའམ་ཡང་ན་ཆུའམ་མེ། །རླུང་གི་ཁམས་ལྟར་མི་གནས་
ཤིང་། །བཟོད་པའམ་ཁྲོ་བ་མ་མཆིས་པར། །བཟོད་པའི་ཕ་རོལ་ཕྱིན་རྫོགས་
ཤོག །བརྩོན་འགྲུས་བརྩམས་པའི་བརྩོན་འགྲུས་ཀྱིས། །བརྟན་སྤྲོ་ལེ་ལོ་མ་
མཆིས་ཤིང་། །སྟོབས་དང་ལྡན་པའི་ལུས་སེམས་ཀྱིས། །བརྩོན་འགྲུས་ཕ་རོལ་
ཕྱིན་རྫོགས་ཤོག །སྒྱུ་མ་ལྟ་བུའི་ཏིང་འཛིན་དང་། དཔའ་བར་འགྲོ་བའི་ཏིང་
འཛིན་དང་། །རྡོ་རྗེ་ལྟ་བུའི་ཏིང་འཛིན་གྱིས། །བསམ་གཏན་ཕ་རོལ་ཕྱིན་རྫོགས་
ཤོག །རྣམ་པར་ཐར་པའི་སྒོ་གསུམ་དང་། །དུས་གསུམ་མཉམ་པ་ཉིད་དང་
ཡང་། །རིག་གསུམ་མངོན་སུམ་བགྱིས་པ་ཡིས། །ཤེས་རབ་ཕ་རོལ་ཕྱིན་
རྫོགས་ཤོག །སངས་རྒྱས་ཀུན་གྱིས་བསྔགས་པ་དང་། །འོད་དང་གཟི་བརྗིད་
འབར་བ་དང་། །བྱང་ཆུབ་སེམས་དཔའི་བརྩོན་འགྲུས་ཀྱིས། །བདག་གི་བསམ་
པ་རྫོགས་གྱུར་ཅིག །དེ་ལྟར་སྤྱད་པ་སྤྱོད་བྱེད་ཅིང་། །བྱམས་པ་གྲགས་དང་ལྡན་
པ་ཡིས། །ཕ་རོལ་ཕྱིན་དྲུག་རྫོགས་བྱས་ནས། །ས་བཅུ་པོ་ལ་རབ་ཏུ་
གནས། །ཀུན་དགའ་བོ་བྱང་ཆུབ་སེམས་དཔའ་ཆེན་པོ་བྱམས་པས་གང་ལ་གནས་
ནས་ཐབས་ལ་མཁས་པས་ཐེག་པ་བདེ་བ། འཇུག་པ་བདེ་བ། ལམ་བདེ་བས་བླ་
ན་མེད་པ་ཡང་དག་པར་རྫོགས་པའི་བྱང་ཆུབ་ཡང་དག་པར་བསྒྲུབས་པའི་ཐབས་ལ་
མཁས་པ་ནི་དེ་ཡིན་ནོ། །ཀུན་དགའ་བོ་བྱང་ཆུབ་སེམས་དཔའ་སེམས་དཔའ་ཆེན་
པོ་བྱམས་པས་སྔོན་བྱང་ཆུབ་སེམས་དཔའི་སྤྱད་པ་སྤྱོད་པའི་ཚེ་སེམས་ཅན་རྣམས་
འདོད་ཆགས་ཆུང་བ་དང་། ཞེ་སྡང་ཆུང་བ་དང་། གཏི་མུག་ཆུང་བ་དང་།
དགེ་བ་བཅུའི་ལས་ཀྱི་ལམ་དང་ལྡན་པར་གྱུར་ལ། ཕྱིས་བདག་བླ་ན་མེད་པ་ཡང་
དག་པར་རྫོགས་པའི་བྱང་ཆུབ་མངོན་པར་རྫོགས་པར་སངས་རྒྱས་ན་ཅི་མ་རུང་ཞེས་དེ་
ལྟར་ཞིང་རྣམ་པར་སྦྱངས་སོ། །ཀུན་དགའ་བོ་དུས་དེ་དང་ཚེ་དེ་འབྱུང་བ་ཡོད་དེ།
དེའི་ཚེ་དེའི་དུས་ན་སེམས་ཅན་དག་འདོད་ཆགས་ཆུང་བ་དང་། ཞེ་སྡང་ཆུང་བ

དང་། གཏི་མུག་ཆུང་བ་དང་། དགེ་བ་བཅུའི་ལས་ཀྱི་ལམ་དང་ལྡན་པ་དག་འབྱུང་བར་འགྱུར་ཏེ། དེའི་འོག་ཏུ་བྱང་ཆུབ་སེམས་དཔའ་སེམས་དཔའ་ཆེན་པོ་བྱམས་པ་སྨོན་ལམ་གྱི་དབང་གིས་བླ་ན་མེད་པ་ཡང་དག་པར་རྫོགས་པའི་བྱང་ཆུབ་མངོན་པར་རྫོགས་པར་འཚང་རྒྱ་བར་འགྱུར་རོ། །ཀུན་དགའ་བོ་ངས་ནི་སྔོན་བྱང་ཆུབ་སེམས་དཔའི་སྤྱད་པ་སྤྱོད་པ་ན་སྙིགས་མ་ལྔ་དང་ལྡན་པའི་འཇིག་རྟེན་གནས་པའི་ཚེ་སེམས་ཅན་འདོད་ཆགས་ཀྱི་ཤས་ཆེ་བ་དང་། ཞེ་སྡང་གི་ཤས་ཆེ་བ་དང་། གཏི་མུག་གི་ཤས་ཆེ་བ་དང་། འདོད་ཆགས་བདོ་བ་དང་། ཞེ་སྡང་བདོ་བ་དང་། གཏི་མུག་བདོ་བ་དང་། ཆོས་མ་ཡིན་པ་ལ་ཆགས་ཤིང་ཞེན་པ་དང་། ཆགས་པའི་ཡང་བས་ཟིལ་གྱིས་ནོན་པ་དང་། ཆོས་ལོག་པས་ཡོངས་སུ་ཟིན་པ་དང་། ཕ་ལ་འཁྲུ་བ་དང་། མ་ལ་འཁྲུ་བ་དང་། སྤུན་ལ་འཁྲུ་བ་དང་། མིང་སྲིང་ལ་འཁྲུ་བ་དང་། ཇོ་ཤུག་ལ་འཁྲུ་བ་དང་། ཉེ་དུ་ལ་འཁྲུ་བ་དང་། འཕགས་པ་ལ་འཁྲུ་བ་དང་། མཁན་པོ་དང་། སློབ་དཔོན་ལ་འཁྲུ་བ་དང་། བདག་ལ་འཁྲུ་བ་དང་། མི་གཞན་ལ་འཁྲུ་བ་དང་། མི་དྲི་མ་ཅན་དང་། མི་དམུ་རྒོད་དང་། མི་ཅང་ཤེས་མ་ཡིན་པ་རྣམས་ཀྱི་ནང་དུ་བདག་བླ་ན་མེད་པ་ཡང་དག་པར་རྫོགས་པའི་བྱང་ཆུབ་མངོན་པར་རྫོགས་པར་སངས་རྒྱས་ན་ཅི་མ་རུང་ཞེས་དེ་ལྟར་སྨོན་ལམ་ཡོངས་སུ་སྦྱོངས་ཏེ། དུས་ཡ་ང་བ་འདི་ལྟ་བུ་ལ་གནས་ནས་ཀུན་དགའ་བོ་ངས་སྙིང་རྗེ་ཆེན་པོ་མདུན་དུ་བྱས་ཏེ། སྙིང་རྗེ་ཆེན་པོ་དང་ལྡན་པས་ང་ད་ལྟར་གྲོང་དང་། གྲོང་ཁྱེར་དང་། གྲོང་རྡལ་དང་། ལྗོངས་དང་། ཡུལ་འཁོར་དང་། རྒྱལ་པོའི་ཕོ་བྲང་འཁོར་རྣམས་སུ་ཞུགས་ཏེ་ཆོས་སྟོན་པ་ན། ང་ལ་ཁ་ངན་ཟེར་ཞིང་གཤེ་རྒྱ་སྟེ་ཚོགས་པར་མི་དབྱུང་བ་རྩུབ་པ་བརླང་པོས་སྨྲ་བར་བྱེད་དོ། །ཀུན་དགའ་བོ་ང་ལ་ཆད་པར་སྨྲ་བ་ཡིན་ནོ་ཞེས་ཀྱང་ཟེར་རོ། །རྟག་པར་སྨྲ་བ་ཡིན་ནོ་ཞེས་ཀྱང་ཟེར་རོ། །འཁོར་འདོད་པ་མང་ངོ་ཞེས་ཀྱང་གླེང་ངོ་། །འདོད་པ་ཆེའོ་ཞེས་ཀྱང་གླེང་ངོ་། །ཁྱིམ་གྱི་ནང་དུ་ཞུགས་ན་ཡང་ང་ལ་སེམས་ཀྱང་འཕྱར་རོ། །དུག་དང་བསྲེས་པའི་ཟས་ཀྱང་བྱིན་ནོ། །མེའི་ཕུང་པོ་ཡང་ཉེ་བར་བསྒྲུབས་སོ། །འདི་ལྟ

སྟེ། སངས་རྒྱས་སུ་གྱུར་ཀྱང་མཛེས་ལྡན་མ་དང་ཞེས་བྱ་བ་ལྷ་བུ་འཁྲིག་པའི་ཆོས་དང་ལྡན་པས་ང་ལ་སྐྱུར་པ་ཡང་བཏབ་བོ། །ཀུན་དགའ་བོ་ང་ནི་སྙིང་རྗེ་ཆེན་པོ་མདུན་དུ་བྱས་ཏེ། སྙིང་རྗེ་ཆེན་པོ་དང་ལྡན་པས་ད་ལྟར་སེམས་ཅན་དེ་ལྟ་བུ་དེ་དག་ལ་ཆོས་སྟོན་ཏོ། །དེ་སྐད་ཅེས་བཀའ་སྩལ་པ་དང་། བཅོམ་ལྡན་འདས་ལ་ཚེ་དང་ལྡན་པ་ཀུན་དགའ་བོས་འདི་སྐད་ཅེས་གསོལ་ཏོ། །བཅོམ་ལྡན་འདས་སེམས་ཅན་དེ་ལྟ་བུ་དེ་དག་ལ་ཆོས་སྟོན་པར་མཛད་པ་ནི་དེ་བཞིན་གཤེགས་པ་དགྲ་བཅོམ་པ་ཡང་དག་པར་རྫོགས་པའི་སངས་རྒྱས་མ་དུལ་བ་འདུལ་བ། ཁུར་ཆེན་པོ་བསྣམས་པ། དཀའ་བ་མཛད་པ་ལགས་སོ། །དེ་སྐད་ཅེས་གསོལ་པ་དང་། བཅོམ་ལྡན་འདས་ཀྱིས་ཚེ་དང་ལྡན་པ་ཀུན་དགའ་བོ་ལ་འདི་སྐད་ཅེས་བཀའ་སྩལ་ཏོ། །ཀུན་དགའ་བོ་དེ་དེ་བཞིན་ནོ། །ཇི་སྐད་སྨྲས་པ་དེ་བཞིན་ཏེ། ཀུན་དགའ་བོ་དེ་བཞིན་གཤེགས་པ་དགྲ་བཅོམ་པ་ཡང་དག་པར་རྫོགས་པའི་སངས་རྒྱས་མ་དུལ་བ་འདུལ་བ། ཁུར་ཆེན་པོ་བསྣམས་པ། དགེ་བའི་ཆོས་ཐམས་ཅད་དང་ལྡན་པ་གང་དག་སེམས་ཅན་དེ་ལྟ་བུ་དག་ལ་ཆོས་སྟོན་པ་ནི་དཀའ་བ་མཛད་པའོ། །དེ་ཅིའི་ཕྱིར་ཞེ་ན། །འདི་ལྟར་སྙིང་རྗེ་ཆེན་པོས་ཡོངས་སུ་ཟིན་པའི་ཕྱིར་རོ། །དེ་སྐད་ཅེས་བཀའ་སྩལ་པ་དང་། བཅོམ་ལྡན་འདས་ལ་ཚེ་དང་ལྡན་པ་ཀུན་དགའ་བོས་འདི་སྐད་ཅེས་གསོལ་ཏོ། །བཅོམ་ལྡན་འདས་འདི་ལྟར་ཆོས་ཀྱི་རྣམ་གྲངས་འདི་མཛེས་པ་དང་། བདག་གིས་ཆོས་ཀྱི་རྣམ་གྲངས་འདི་ཐོས་ཤིང་བཅོམ་ལྡན་འདས་ཀྱི་ཁྱུ་མཆོག་གི་གནས་འདི་ཐོས་ནས་སྤྲུ་ཟིང་ཞེས་བགྱིད་པ་ནི་ངོ་མཚར་ལགས་སོ། །བཅོམ་ལྡན་འདས་ཆོས་ཀྱི་རྣམ་གྲངས་འདིའི་མིང་ཅི་ལགས། འདི་ཇི་ལྟར་གཟུང་བར་བགྱི། བཅོམ་ལྡན་འདས་ཀྱིས་བཀའ་སྩལ་པ། ཀུན་དགའ་བོ་དེའི་ཕྱིར་ཆོས་ཀྱི་རྣམ་གྲངས་འདི་སྟོན་གྱི་སྨོན་ལམ་ཡང་དག་པར་འཕགས་པ་ཞེས་བྱ་བ་ཟུང་ཤིག །དེ་བཞིན་གཤེགས་པ་ཡང་དག་པར་འབྱུང་བ་ཞེས་བྱ་བར་ཡང་ཟུང་ཤིག །བྱང་ཆུབ་ཀྱི་དགོངས་པ་འབྱུང་བ་ཞེས་བྱ་བར་ཡང་ཟུང་ཤིག །བྱམས་པས་ཞུས་པ་ཞེས་བྱ་བར་ཡང་ཟུང་ཤིག །བཅོམ་ལྡན་འདས་ཀྱིས་དེ་སྐད་ཅེས་བཀའ་

སྨྲས་ནས། ཚེ་དང་ལྡན་པ་ཀུན་དགའ་བོ་དང་། བྱང་ཆུབ་སེམས་དཔའ་བྱམས་པ་དང་། དགེ་སློང་ལྔ་བརྒྱ་པོ་དེ་དག་དང་། ཐམས་ཅད་དང་ལྡན་པའི་འཁོར་དེ་དང་། ལྷ་དང་མི་དང་། ལྷ་མ་ཡིན་དང་། དྲི་ཟར་བཅས་པའི་འཇིག་རྟེན་ཡི་རངས་ཏེ་བཅོམ་ལྡན་འདས་ཀྱིས་གསུངས་པ་ལ་མངོན་པར་བསྟོད་དོ། །འཕགས་པ་དཀོན་མཆོག་བརྩེགས་པ་ཆེན་པོའི་ཆོས་ཀྱི་རྣམ་གྲངས་ལེའུ་སྟོང་ཕྲག་བརྒྱ་པ་ལས་བྱམས་པས་ཞུས་པའི་ལེའུ་ཞེས་བྱ་སྟེ་བཞི་བཅུ་རྩ་གཅིག་པ་རྫོགས་སོ།། །།རྒྱ་གར་གྱི་མཁན་པོ་ཛི་ན་མི་ཏྲ་དང་། སུ་རེན་དྲ་བོ་དྷི་དང་། ཞུ་ཆེན་གྱི་ལོ་ཙ་བ་བན་དེ་ཡེ་ཤེས་སྡེས་བསྒྱུར་ཅིང་ཞུས་ཏེ་གཏན་ལ་ཕབ་པ།། །།

༄༅། །འཕགས་པ་དཀོན་མཆོག་བརྩེགས་པ་ཆེན་པོའི་ཆོས་ཀྱི་རྣམ་གྲངས་ལེའུ་སྟོང་ཕྲག་བརྒྱ་པ་ལས་ལེའུ་བཞི་བཅུ་རྩ་གཉིས་པ་སྟེ་འཕགས་པ་བྱམས་པས་ཆོས་བརྒྱད་ཞུས་པ་ལུང་བསྟན་པ། བམ་པོ་ཕྱེད་པ། རྒྱ་གར་སྐད་དུ། ཨཱརྱ་མཻ་ཏྲི་ཡ་པ་རི་པྲྀཙྪཱ་ནཱ་མ་མ་ཧཱ་ཡཱ་ན་སཱུ་ཏྲ། བོད་སྐད་དུ། འཕགས་པ་བྱམས་པས་ཞུས་པ་ཞེས་བྱ་བ་ཐེག་པ་ཆེན་པོའི་མདོ། སངས་རྒྱས་དང་བྱང་ཆུབ་སེམས་དཔའ་ཐམས་ཅད་ལ་ཕྱག་འཚལ་ལོ། །འདི་སྐད་བདག་གིས་ཐོས་པའི་དུས་གཅིག་ན། བཅོམ་ལྡན་འདས་རྒྱལ་པོའི་ཁབ་ན་བྱ་རྒོད་ཕུང་པོའི་རི་ལ་དགེ་སློང་སྟོང་ཉིས་བརྒྱ་ལྔ་བཅུའི་དགེ་སློང་གི་དགེ་འདུན་ཆེན་པོ་དང་། བྱང་ཆུབ་སེམས་དཔའ་ཁྲི་དང་ཐབས་ཅིག་ཏུ་བཞུགས་ཏེ། དེ་ནས་བཅོམ་ལྡན་འདས་འཁོར་བརྒྱ་སྟོང་དུ་མས་ཡོངས་སུ་བསྐོར་ཅིང་མདུན་གྱིས་བལྟས་ནས་ཆོས་སྟོན་ཏོ། །དེའི་ཚེ་བྱང་ཆུབ་སེམས་དཔའ་ཆེན་པོ་བྱམས་པ་ཞེས་བྱ་བ་འཁོར་དེ་ཉིད་དུ་འདུས་པར་གྱུར་ཏེ་འདུག་གོ །དེ་ནས་བྱང་ཆུབ་སེམས་དཔའ་སེམས་དཔའ་ཆེན་པོ་བྱམས་པ་སྟན་ལས་ལངས་ཏེ་བླ་གོས་ཕྲག་པ་གཅིག་ཏུ་གཟར་ནས་པུས་མོ་གཡས་པའི་ལྷ་ང་ས་ལ་བཙུགས་ཏེ། བཅོམ་ལྡན་འདས་ག་ལ་བ་དེར་ལོགས་སུ་ཐལ་མོ་སྦྱར་བ་བཏུད་ནས་བཅོམ་ལྡན་འདས་ལ་འདི་སྐད་ཅེས་གསོལ་ཏོ། །གལ་

ཏེ་ཞུས་ནས་ཞུ་བ་ལུང་བསྟན་པའི་སླད་དུ་བཅོམ་ལྡན་འདས་ཀྱིས་བདག་ལ་སྐབས་ཕྱེ་ན། དེ་བཞིན་གཤེགས་པ་དགྲ་བཅོམ་པ་ཡང་དག་པར་རྫོགས་པའི་སངས་རྒྱས་ལ་བདག་ཕྱོགས་འགའ་ཞིག་ཞུ་ལགས་སོ། །དེ་སྐད་ཅེས་གསོལ་བ་དང་། བཅོམ་ལྡན་འདས་ཀྱིས་བྱང་ཆུབ་སེམས་དཔའ་ཆེན་པོ་བྱམས་པ་ལ་འདི་སྐད་ཅེས་བཀའ་སྩལ་ཏོ། །བྱམས་པ་ཁྱོད་དེ་བཞིན་གཤེགས་པ་དགྲ་བཅོམ་པ་ཡང་དག་པར་རྫོགས་པའི་སངས་རྒྱས་ལ་ཅི་དང་ཅི་འདོད་པ་དྲིས་ཤིག་དང་། དྲིས་པ་དེ་དང་དེའི་ལུང་བསྟན་པས་ངས་ཁྱོད་ཀྱི་སེམས་རངས་པར་བྱའོ། །དེ་ནས་བཅོམ་ལྡན་འདས་ཀྱིས་སྐབས་ཕྱེ་བས་བྱང་ཆུབ་སེམས་དཔའ་སེམས་དཔའ་ཆེན་པོ་བྱམས་པས་བཅོམ་ལྡན་འདས་ལ་འདི་སྐད་ཅེས་གསོལ་ཏོ། །བཅོམ་ལྡན་འདས་བྱང་ཆུབ་སེམས་དཔའ་སེམས་དཔའ་ཆེན་པོ་ཆོས་དུ་དང་ལྡན་ན་བླ་ན་མེད་པ་ཡང་དག་པར་རྫོགས་པའི་བྱང་ཆུབ་ལས་ཕྱིར་མི་ལྡོག་པའི་ཆོས་ཅན་དུ་འགྱུར་ཞིང་མི་ཉམས་ལ་ཡོངས་སུ་མི་ཉམས་ཏེ། ཁྱད་པར་ཐོབ་པར་འགྱུར་བ་དང་། བདུད་ཕྱིར་རྒོལ་བ་བཅོམ་པར་འགྱུར་བ་དང་། བྱང་ཆུབ་སེམས་དཔའི་སྤྱད་པ་སྤྱོད་པ་ན་ཆོས་ཐམས་ཅད་ཀྱི་ངོ་བོ་ཉིད་ཀྱི་མཚན་ཉིད་ཇི་ལྟ་བ་བཞིན་དུ་རྟོགས་ནས་འཁོར་བ་ན་ཡོངས་སུ་མི་སྐྱོ་བ་དང་། ཡོངས་སུ་མི་སྐྱོ་བའི་ཡིད་དང་ལྡན་པར་གྱུར་ནས་ཀྱང་གཞན་གྱི་ཁ་ན་མ་ལས་པའི་ཡེ་ཤེས་ཀྱི་མྱུར་དུ་བླ་ན་མེད་པ་ཡང་དག་པར་རྫོགས་པའི་བྱང་ཆུབ་མངོན་པར་རྫོགས་པར་འཚང་རྒྱ་བར་འགྱུར་ལགས། དེ་སྐད་ཅེས་གསོལ་པ་དང་། བཅོམ་ལྡན་འདས་ཀྱིས་བྱང་ཆུབ་སེམས་དཔའ་སེམས་དཔའ་ཆེན་པོ་བྱམས་པ་ལ་འདི་སྐད་ཅེས་བཀའ་སྩལ་ཏོ། །བྱམས་པ་ལེགས་སོ། །བྱམས་པ་ཁྱོད་དེ་བཞིན་གཤེགས་པ་ལ་དོན་འདི་འདྲི་བར་སེམས་པ་ཁྱོད་ཡང་ལེགས་སོ། །བྱམས་པ་དེའི་ཕྱིར་ལེགས་པར་རབ་ཏུ་ཉོན་ལ་ཡིད་ལ་ཟུང་ཤིག་དང་ངས་ཁྱོད་ལ་བཤད་དོ། །བཅོམ་ལྡན་འདས་དེ་ལྟར་འཚལ་ལོ་ཞེས་གསོལ་ཏོ། །བྱང་ཆུབ་སེམས་དཔའ་སེམས་དཔའ་ཆེན་པོ་བྱམས་པ་བཅོམ་ལྡན་འདས་ཀྱི་ལྟར་ཉན་པ་དང་། བཅོམ་ལྡན་འདས་ཀྱིས་དེ་ལ་འདི་སྐད་ཅེས་བཀའ་སྩལ་ཏོ། །བྱམས་པ་བྱང་ཆུབ་སེམས་དཔའ་སེམས་དཔའ་ཆེན་པོ་ཆོས་བརྒྱད་དང་

ལྡན་ན་བླ་ན་མེད་པ་ཡང་དག་པར་རྫོགས་པའི་བྱང་ཆུབ་ལས་ཕྱིར་མི་ལྡོག་པའི་ཆོས་ཅན་དུ་འགྱུར་ཞིང་མི་ཉམས་ལ་ཡོངས་སུ་མི་ཉམས་ཏེ། ཁྱད་པར་ཐོབ་པར་འགྱུར། བདུད་ཕྱིར་རྒོལ་བ་བཅོམ་པར་འགྱུར། བྱང་ཆུབ་སེམས་དཔའི་སྤྱོད་པ་སྤྱོད་པ་ན་ཆོས་ཐམས་ཅད་ཀྱི་ངོ་བོ་ཉིད་ཀྱི་མཚན་ཉིད་ཇི་ལྟ་བ་བཞིན་དུ་རྟོགས་ནས་འཁོར་བ་ན་ཡོངས་སུ་མི་སྐྱོ་བར་འགྱུར། ཡོངས་སུ་མི་སྐྱོ་བའི་ཡིད་དང་ལྡན་པར་གྱུར་ནས་ཀྱང་གཞན་གྱི་ཁ་ན་མ་ལས་པའི་ཡེ་ཤེས་ཀྱིས་མྱུར་དུ་བླ་ན་མེད་པ་ཡང་དག་པར་རྫོགས་པའི་བྱང་ཆུབ་མངོན་པར་རྫོགས་པར་འཚང་རྒྱའོ། །བརྒྱད་གང་ཞེ་ན། འདི་ལྟ་སྟེ། བྱམས་པ་འདི་ལ་བྱང་ཆུབ་སེམས་དཔའ་སེམས་དཔའ་ཆེན་པོ་ནི་བསམ་པ་ཕུན་སུམ་ཚོགས་པ་ཡིན། སྦྱོར་བ་ཕུན་སུམ་ཚོགས་པ་ཡིན། གཏོང་བ་ཕུན་སུམ་ཚོགས་པ་ཡིན། ཡོངས་སུ་བསྔོ་བ་ལ་མཁས་པ་ཡིན། བྱམས་པ་ཕུན་སུམ་ཚོགས་པ་ཡིན། སྙིང་རྗེ་ཕུན་སུམ་ཚོགས་པ་ཡིན། ཐབས་ལ་མཁས་པ་ཡིན། ཤེས་རབ་ཀྱི་ཕ་རོལ་ཏུ་ཕྱིན་པ་ལ་ངེས་པར་སྦྱང་བ་ཡིན་ནོ། །བྱམས་པ་ཇི་ལྟར་ན་བྱང་ཆུབ་སེམས་དཔའ་སེམས་དཔའ་ཆེན་པོ་བསམ་པ་ཕུན་སུམ་ཚོགས་པ་ཡིན་ཞེ་ན། བྱམས་པ་འདི་ལ་བྱང་ཆུབ་སེམས་དཔའ་སེམས་དཔའ་ཆེན་པོ་ནི་སངས་རྒྱས་ཀྱི་བསྔགས་པའམ། བསྔགས་པ་མ་ཡིན་པ་ཐོས་ཀྱང་བླ་ན་མེད་པ་ཡང་དག་པར་རྫོགས་པའི་བྱང་ཆུབ་ལ་བསམ་པ་ངེས་པ་ཡིན། ཆོས་ཀྱི་བསྔགས་པའམ་བསྔགས་པ་མ་ཡིན་པ་ཐོས་ཀྱང་བླ་ན་མེད་པ་ཡང་དག་པར་རྫོགས་པའི་བྱང་ཆུབ་ལ་བསམ་པ་ངེས་པ་ཡིན། དགེ་འདུན་གྱི་བསྔགས་པའམ་བསྔགས་པ་མ་ཡིན་པ་ཐོས་ཀྱང་བླ་ན་མེད་པ་ཡང་དག་པར་རྫོགས་པའི་བྱང་ཆུབ་ལ་བསམ་པ་ངེས་པ་ཡིན་ཏེ། བྱམས་པ་དེ་ལྟར་ན་བྱང་ཆུབ་སེམས་དཔའ་སེམས་དཔའ་ཆེན་པོ་བསམ་པ་ཕུན་སུམ་ཚོགས་པ་ནི་ཡིན་ནོ། །བྱམས་པ་ཇི་ལྟར་ན་བྱང་ཆུབ་སེམས་དཔའ་སེམས་དཔའ་ཆེན་པོ་སྦྱོར་བ་ཕུན་སུམ་ཚོགས་པ་ཡིན་ཞེ་ན། བྱམས་པ་འདི་ལ་བྱང་ཆུབ་སེམས་དཔའ་སེམས་དཔའ་ཆེན་པོ་ནི་སྲོག་གཅོད་པ་སྤངས་པ་ཡིན། མ་བྱིན་པར་ལེན་པ་དང་། འདོད་པ་ལ་ལོག་པར་གཡེམ་པ་དང་། བརྫུན་དུ་སྨྲ་བ་དང་། ཕྲ་མའི་ཚིག་དང་།

ངག་རྩུབ་པོ་དང་། ཚིག་ཀྱལ་པ་སྤྱངས་པ་ཡིན་ཏེ། བྱམས་པ་དེ་ལྟར་ན་བྱང་ཆུབ་སེམས་དཔའ་སེམས་དཔའ་ཆེན་པོ་སྦྱོར་བ་ཕུན་སུམ་ཚོགས་པ་ཡིན་ནོ། །བྱམས་པ་ཇི་ལྟར་ན་བྱང་ཆུབ་སེམས་དཔའ་སེམས་དཔའ་ཆེན་པོ་གཏོང་བ་ཕུན་སུམ་ཚོགས་པ་ཡིན་ཞེ་ན། བྱམས་པ་འདི་ལ་བྱང་ཆུབ་སེམས་དཔའ་སེམས་དཔའ་ཆེན་པོ་ནི་དགེ་སློང་དང་། བྲམ་ཟེ་རྣམས་དང་། ཕོངས་པ་དང་སློང་བ་རྣམས་ལ་གོས་དང་། ཟས་དང་། མལ་ཆ་དང་། ན་བའི་གསོས་སྨན་དང་། ཡོ་བྱད་རྣམས་གཏོང་བ་དང་། སྦྱིན་པ་དག་ཏུ་སྒྱུར་པ་ཡིན་ཏེ། བྱམས་པ་དེ་ལྟར་ན་བྱང་ཆུབ་སེམས་དཔའ་སེམས་དཔའ་ཆེན་པོ་གཏོང་བ་ཕུན་སུམ་ཚོགས་པ་ཡིན་ནོ། །བྱམས་པ་ཇི་ལྟར་ན་བྱང་ཆུབ་སེམས་དཔའ་སེམས་དཔའ་ཆེན་པོ་ཡོངས་སུ་བསྔོ་བ་ལ་མཁས་པ་ཡིན་ཞེ་ན། བྱམས་པ་འདི་ལ་བྱང་ཆུབ་སེམས་དཔའ་སེམས་དཔའ་ཆེན་པོ་ནི་ལུས་དང་ངག་དང་། ཡིད་ཀྱིས་དགེ་བའི་རྩ་བ་མངོན་པར་འདུ་བྱེད་པ་གང་ཅི་ཡང་རུང་སྟེ། དེ་ཐམས་ཅད་བླ་ན་མེད་པ་ཡང་དག་པར་རྫོགས་པའི་བྱང་ཆུབ་ཏུ་ཡོངས་སུ་སྔོ་བར་བྱེད་དེ། བྱམས་པ་དེ་ལྟར་ན་བྱང་ཆུབ་སེམས་དཔའ་སེམས་དཔའ་ཆེན་པོ་ཡོངས་སུ་བསྔོ་བ་ལ་མཁས་པ་ཡིན་ནོ། །བྱམས་པ་ཇི་ལྟར་ན་བྱང་ཆུབ་སེམས་དཔའ་སེམས་དཔའ་ཆེན་པོ་བྱམས་པ་ཕུན་སུམ་ཚོགས་པ་ཡིན་ཞེ་ན། བྱམས་པ་འདི་ལ་བྱང་ཆུབ་སེམས་དཔའ་སེམས་དཔའ་ཆེན་པོ་ནི་བྱམས་པའི་ལུས་ཀྱི་ལས་དང་ལྡན་པ་ཡིན། བྱམས་པའི་ངག་གི་ལས་དང་ལྡན་པ་ཡིན། བྱམས་པའི་ཡིད་ཀྱི་ལས་དང་ལྡན་པ་ཡིན་ཏེ། བྱམས་པ་དེ་ལྟར་ན་བྱང་ཆུབ་སེམས་དཔའ་སེམས་དཔའ་ཆེན་པོ་བྱམས་པ་ཕུན་སུམ་ཚོགས་པ་ཡིན་ནོ། །བྱམས་པ་ཇི་ལྟར་ན་བྱང་ཆུབ་སེམས་དཔའ་སེམས་དཔའ་ཆེན་པོ་སྙིང་རྗེ་ཕུན་སུམ་ཚོགས་པ་ཡིན་ཞེ་ན། བྱམས་པ་འདི་ལ་བྱང་ཆུབ་སེམས་དཔའ་སེམས་དཔའ་ཆེན་པོ་ནི་གནོད་སེམས་མེད་པའི་ལུས་ཀྱི་ལས་དང་ལྡན་པ་ཡིན། གནོད་སེམས་མེད་པའི་ངག་གི་ལས་དང་ལྡན་པ་ཡིན། གནོད་སེམས་མེད་པའི་ཡིད་ཀྱི་ལས་དང་ལྡན་པ་ཡིན་ཏེ། བྱམས་པ་དེ་ལྟར་ན་བྱང་ཆུབ་སེམས་དཔའ་སེམས་དཔའ་ཆེན་པོ་སྙིང་རྗེ་ཕུན་སུམ་ཚོགས་པ་ཡིན་ནོ། །བྱམས་པ་

ཇི་ལྟར་ན་བྱང་ཆུབ་སེམས་དཔའ་སེམས་དཔའ་ཆེན་པོ་ཐབས་ལ་མཁས་པ་ཡིན་ཞེ་ན། བྱམས་པ་འདི་ལ་བྱང་ཆུབ་སེམས་དཔའ་སེམས་དཔའ་ཆེན་པོ་ནི་ཀུན་རྫོབ་ཀྱི་དོན་ལ་མཁས་པ་ཡིན། དམ་པའི་དོན་ལ་མཁས་པ་ཡིན། གཉི་གའི་དོན་ལ་མཁས་པ་ཡིན་ཏེ། བྱམས་པ་དེ་ལྟར་ན་བྱང་ཆུབ་སེམས་དཔའ་སེམས་དཔའ་ཆེན་པོ་ཐབས་ལ་མཁས་པ་ཡིན་ནོ། །བྱམས་པ་ཇི་ལྟར་ན་བྱང་ཆུབ་སེམས་དཔའ་སེམས་དཔའ་ཆེན་པོ་ཤེས་རབ་ཀྱི་ཕ་རོལ་ཏུ་ཕྱིན་པ་ལ་ངེས་པར་འབྱུང་བ་ཡིན་ཞེ་ན། བྱམས་པ་འདི་ལ་བྱང་ཆུབ་སེམས་དཔའ་སེམས་དཔའ་ཆེན་པོ་ནི་འདི་ལྟར་ཡང་དག་པར་སློབ་སྟེ། འདི་ཡོད་པའི་ཕྱིར་འདི་འབྱུང་། འདི་སྐྱེས་པས་འདི་སྐྱེ་བ་སྟེ། འདི་ལྟ་སྟེ། མ་རིག་པའི་རྐྱེན་གྱིས་འདུ་བྱེད་རྣམས། འདུ་བྱེད་ཀྱི་རྐྱེན་གྱིས་རྣམ་པར་ཤེས་པ། རྣམ་པར་ཤེས་པའི་རྐྱེན་གྱིས་མིང་དང་གཟུགས། མིང་དང་གཟུགས་ཀྱི་རྐྱེན་གྱིས་སྐྱེ་མཆེད་དྲུག །སྐྱེ་མཆེད་དྲུག་གི་རྐྱེན་གྱིས་རེག་པ། རེག་པའི་རྐྱེན་གྱིས་ཚོར་བ། ཚོར་བའི་རྐྱེན་གྱིས་སྲེད་པ། སྲེད་པའི་རྐྱེན་གྱིས་ལེན་པ། ལེན་པའི་རྐྱེན་གྱིས་སྲིད་པ། སྲིད་པའི་རྐྱེན་གྱིས་སྐྱེ་བ། སྐྱེ་བའི་རྐྱེན་གྱིས་རྒ་ཤི་དང་། མྱ་ངན་དང་། སྨྲེ་སྔགས་འདོན་པ་དང་། སྡུག་བསྔལ་བ་དང་། ཡིད་མི་བདེ་བ་དང་། འཁྲུག་པ་རྣམས་འབྱུང་བར་འགྱུར་ཏེ། དེ་ལྟར་ན་སྡུག་བསྔལ་གྱི་ཕུང་པོ་ཆེན་པོ་འབའ་ཞིག་པོ་འདི་འབྱུང་བར་འགྱུར་རོ། །འདི་མེད་པའི་ཕྱིར་འདི་མི་འབྱུང་། འདི་འགགས་པས་འདི་འགག་སྟེ། འདི་ལྟ་སྟེ། མ་རིག་པ་འགགས་པས་འདུ་བྱེད་འགག །འདུ་བྱེད་འགགས་པས་རྣམ་པར་ཤེས་པ་འགག །རྣམ་པར་ཤེས་པ་འགགས་པས་མིང་དང་གཟུགས་འགག །མིང་དང་གཟུགས་འགགས་པས། སྐྱེ་མཆེད་དྲུག་འགག །སྐྱེ་མཆེད་དྲུག་འགགས་པས་རེག་པ་འགག །རེག་པ་འགགས་པས་ཚོར་བ་འགག །ཚོར་བ་འགགས་པས་སྲེད་པ་འགག །སྲེད་པ་འགགས་པས་ལེན་པ་འགག །ལེན་པ་འགགས་པས་སྲིད་པ་འགག །སྲིད་པ་འགགས་པས་སྐྱེ་བ་འགག །སྐྱེ་བ་འགགས་པས་རྒ་ཤི་དང་། མྱ་ངན་དང་། སྨྲེ་སྔགས་འདོན་པ་དང་། སྡུག་བསྔལ་བ་དང་། ཡིད་མི་བདེ་བ་དང་།

འཁྲུག་པ་རྣམས་འགག་པར་འགྱུར་ཏེ། དེ་ལྟར་ན་སྡུག་བསྔལ་གྱི་ཕུང་པོ་ཆེན་པོ་འབའ་ཞིག་པོ་འདི་འགག་པར་འགྱུར་རོ། །སླམ་པ་སྟེ། བྱམས་པ་དེ་ལྟར་ན་བྱང་ཆུབ་སེམས་དཔའ་སེམས་དཔའ་ཆེན་པོ་ཤེས་རབ་ཀྱི་ཕ་རོལ་ཏུ་ཕྱིན་པ་ལ་ངེས་པར་འབྱུང་བ་ཡིན་ནོ། །བྱམས་པ་བྱང་ཆུབ་སེམས་དཔའ་སེམས་དཔའ་ཆེན་པོ་ཆོས་བརྒྱད་པོ་དེ་དག་དང་ལྡན་ན་བླ་ན་མེད་པ་ཡང་དག་པར་རྫོགས་པའི་བྱང་ཆུབ་ལས་ཕྱིར་མི་ལྡོག་པའི་ཆོས་ཅན་དུ་འགྱུར་ཞིང་མི་ཉམས་ལ་ཡོངས་སུ་མི་ཉམས་ཏེ། ཁྱད་པར་ཐོབ་པར་འགྱུར། བདུད་ཕྱིར་རྒོལ་བ་བཅོམ་པར་འགྱུར། བྱང་ཆུབ་སེམས་དཔའི་སྤྱོད་པ་སྤྱོད་པ་ན་ཆོས་ཐམས་ཅད་ཀྱི་ངོ་བོ་ཉིད་ཀྱི་མཚན་ཉིད་ཇི་ལྟ་བ་བཞིན་དུ་རྟོགས་ནས་འཁོར་བ་ན་ཡོངས་སུ་མི་སྐྱོ་བར་འགྱུར། ཡོངས་སུ་མི་སྐྱོ་བའི་ཡིད་དང་ལྡན་ནས་ཀྱང་གཞན་གྱི་ཁ་ན་མ་ལས་པའི་ཡེ་ཤེས་ཀྱིས་མྱུར་དུ་བླ་ན་མེད་པ་ཡང་དག་པར་རྫོགས་པའི་བྱང་ཆུབ་མངོན་པར་རྫོགས་པར་འཚང་རྒྱའོ། །བཅོམ་ལྡན་འདས་ཀྱིས་དེ་སྐད་ཅེས་བཀའ་སྩལ་ནས། བྱང་ཆུབ་སེམས་དཔའ་སེམས་དཔའ་ཆེན་པོ་བྱམས་པ་དང་། དགེ་སློང་དེ་དག་དང་། བྱང་ཆུབ་སེམས་དཔའ་དེ་དག་དང་། ལྷ་དང་། མི་དང་། ལྷ་མ་ཡིན་དང་། དྲི་ཟས་བཅས་པའི་འཇིག་རྟེན་ཡི་རངས་ཏེ། བཅོམ་ལྡན་འདས་ཀྱིས་གསུངས་པ་མངོན་པར་བསྟོད་དོ།། །།འཕགས་པ་དཀོན་མཆོག་བརྩེགས་པ་ཆེན་པོའི་ཆོས་ཀྱི་རྣམ་གྲངས་ལེའུ་སྟོང་ཕྲག་བརྒྱ་པ་ལས་བྱམས་པས་ཞུས་པ་ཆོས་བརྒྱད་པ་ཞེས་བྱ་བའི་ལེའུ་ལྔེ་བཞི་བཅུ་རྩ་གཉིས་པ་རྫོགས་སོ།། །།རྒྱ་གར་གྱི་མཁན་པོ་ཛཱི་ན་མི་ཏྲ་དང་། དཱ་ན་ཤཱི་ལ་དང་། ཞུ་ཆེན་གྱི་ཙ་བ་བན་དེ་ཡེ་ཤེས་སྡེས་བསྒྱུར་ཅིང་ཞུས་ཏེ་སྐད་གསར་ཅད་ཀྱིས་ཀྱང་བཅོས་ནས་གཏན་ལ་ཕབ་པ།། །།

༄༅། །སྡེ་དགེ་དཔར་མ་ལས། དཀོན་བརྩེགས་ལེའུ་ཞེ་གཅིག་པ་བྱམས་པས་ཞུས་པ་ལས་བྱུང་བའི་བྱམས་པའི་སྨོན་ལམ་ནི། །དཀོན་བརྩེགས་ལེའུ་ཞེ་གཅིག་པ་བྱམས་པས་ཞུས་པ་ལས་བྱུང་བའི་བྱམས་པའི་སྨོན་ལམ་ནི། སངས་རྒྱས་ཀུན་ལ་ཕྱག་འཚལ་

ལོ། །དྲང་སྲོང་ལྷ་མིག་ལྡན་པ་ཡི། །བྱང་ཆུབ་སེམས་དཔའ་རྣམས་དང་
ཡང་། །ཉན་ཐོས་རྣམས་ལ་ཕྱག་འཚལ་ལོ། །ངན་འགྲོ་ཐམས་ཅད་ཟློག་བགྱིད་
ཅིང་། །མཐོ་རིས་ལམ་ནི་རབ་སྟོན་ལ། །རྒ་ཤི་མེད་པར་འདྲེན་བགྱིད་པ། །
བྱང་ཆུབ་སེམས་ལ་ཕྱག་འཚལ་ལོ། །སེམས་ཀྱི་དབང་དུ་གྱུར་པས་ན། །བདག་
གིས་སྡིག་པ་ཅི་བགྱིས་པ། །སངས་རྒྱས་སྤྱན་སྔར་མཆིས་ནས་སུ། །བདག་
གིས་དེ་དག་བཤགས་པར་བགྱི། །བདག་ལས་རྣམ་པ་གསུམ་གང་གིས། །
བསོད་ནམས་ཚོགས་ནི་བསྐྱེད་པ་སྟེ། །བདག་གི་ཀུན་མཁྱེན་ས་བོན་ཏེ། །བདག་
གི་བྱང་ཆུབ་མི་ཟད་ཤོག །ཕྱོགས་བཅུ་དག་གི་ཞིང་རྣམས་སུ། །སངས་རྒྱས་
མཆོད་པ་གང་བྱུང་བ། །སངས་རྒྱས་མཁྱེན་པ་ཡི་རང་བ། །དེ་ལ་བདག་ནི་ཡི་
རང་ངོ་། །སྡིག་པ་ཐམས་ཅད་བཤགས་པར་བགྱི། །བསོད་ནམས་ཀུན་ལ་ཡི་
རང་ངོ་། །སངས་རྒྱས་ཀུན་ལ་ཕྱག་འཚལ་ལོ། །བདག་ནི་ཡེ་ཤེས་མཆོག་ཐོབ་
ཤོག །ཕྱོགས་བཅུ་དག་གི་ཕྱོགས་རྣམས་སུ། །ས་བཅུ་དག་ལ་གནས་པ་
ཡི། །བྱང་ཆུབ་སེམས་དཔའ་བྱང་ཆུབ་མཆོག །འཚང་རྒྱ་བགྱིད་པར་བསྐུལ་མ་
འདེབས། །བྱང་ཆུབ་དམ་པ་སངས་རྒྱས་ཤིང་། །སྡེ་དང་བཅས་པའི་བདུད་
བཏུལ་ནས། །སྲོག་ཆགས་ཀུན་ལ་སྨན་སླད་དུ། །ཆོས་ཀྱི་འཁོར་ལོ་བསྐོར་གྱུར་
ཅིག །ཆོས་ཛ་ཆེན་པོ་སྒྲ་ཡིས་ནི། །སྡུག་བསྔལ་སེམས་ཅན་ཐར་[174]བགྱིད་
ཤོག །བསྐལ་པ་བྱེ་བ་བསམ་ཡས་སུ། །ཆོས་སྟོན་མཛད་ཅིང་བཞུགས་གྱུར་
ཅིག །འདོད་པའི་འདམ་དུ་བྱིང་གྱུར་ཅིང་། །སྲིད་པའི་སྲད་བུས་དམ་བཅིངས་
པ། །འཆིང་བ་ཀུན་གྱིས་བཅིངས་བདག་ལ། །རྐང་གཉིས་མཆོག་རྣམས་
གཟིགས་སུ་གསོལ། །སེམས་ཀྱིས་དྲི་མར་བགྱིས་པ་ལ། །སངས་རྒྱས་རྣམས་
ནི་སྨོད་མི་མཛད། །སེམས་ཅན་རྣམས་ལ་བྱམས་ཐུགས་ལྡན། །སྲིད་པའི་མཚོ་
ལས་སྒྲོལ་བར་ཤོག །རྫོགས་པའི་སངས་རྒྱས་གང་བཞུགས་དང་། །གང་དག་

[174] Two other editions in Kangyur have "mthar".

འདས་དང་མ་བྱོན་པ། །དེ་དག་རྗེས་སུ་བདག་སློབ་ཅིང་། །བྱང་ཆུབ་སྤྱོད་པ་སྤྱོད་
གྱུར་ཅིག །ཕ་རོལ་ཕྱིན་དྲུག་རྫོགས་བགྱིས་ནས། །འགྲོ་དྲུག་སེམས་ཅན་ཐར་
བགྱིད་ཤོག །མངོན་ཤེས་དྲུག་པོ་མངོན་བགྱིས་ནས། །བླ་མེད་བྱང་ཆུབ་རེག་
གྱུར་ཅིག །མ་སྐྱེས་པ་དང་མི་འབྱུང་དང་། །རང་བཞིན་མ་མཆིས་གནས་མ་
མཆིས། །རྣམ་རིག་མ་མཆིས་དངོས་མ་མཆིས། །སྟོང་པའི་ཆོས་ནི་རྟོགས་པར་
ཤོག །སངས་རྒྱས་དྲང་སྲོང་ཆེན་པོ་ལྟར། །སེམས་ཅན་མ་མཆིས་སྲོག་མ་
མཆིས། །གང་ཟག་མ་མཆིས་གསོ་མ་མཆིས། །བདག་མ་མཆིས་པའི་ཆོས་
རྟོགས་ཤོག །བདག་འཛིན་བདག་གིར་འཛིན་པ་ཡི། །དངོས་པོ་ཀུན་ལ་མི་
གནས་པར། །སེམས་ཅན་ཀུན་ལ་བདེ་དྲུ། །སེར་སྣ་མ་མཆིས་སྦྱིན་གཏོང་
ཤོག །དངོས་པོ་དངོས་པོ་མ་མཆིས་པས། །བདག་གི་ལོངས་སྤྱོད་ལྷུན་གྲུབ་
ཤོག །དངོས་པོ་ཐམས་ཅད་རྣམ་འཇིག་པས། །སྦྱིན་པའི་ཕ་རོལ་ཕྱིན་རྫོགས་
ཤོག །ཁྲིམས་ཀྱི་ཚུལ་ཁྲིམས་སྐྱོན་མེད་ཅིང་། །ཚུལ་ཁྲིམས་རྣམ་པར་དག་དང་
ལྡན། །ཀློམ་སེམས་མེད་པའི་ཚུལ་ཁྲིམས་ཀྱིས། །ཚུལ་ཁྲིམས་ཕ་རོལ་ཕྱིན་
རྫོགས་ཤོག །ས་འམ་ཡང་ན་ཆུ་འམ་མེ། །རླུང་གི་ཁམས་ལྟར་མི་གནས་
ཞིང་། །བཟོད་པའམ་ཁྲོ་བ་མ་མཆིས་པར། །བཟོད་པའི་ཕ་རོལ་ཕྱིན་རྫོགས་
ཤོག །བརྩོན་འགྲུས་བརྩམས་པའི་བརྩོན་འགྲུས་ཀྱིས། །བརྟན་སྤྲོ་ལེ་ལོ་མ་
མཆིས་ཞིང་། །སྟོབས་དང་ལྡན་པའི་ལུས་སེམས་ཀྱིས། །བརྩོན་འགྲུས་ཕ་རོལ་
ཕྱིན་རྫོགས་ཤོག །སྒྱུ་མ་ལྟ་བུའི་ཏིང་འཛིན་དང་། །དཔའ་བར་འགྲོ་བའི་ཏིང་
འཛིན་དང་། །རྡོ་རྗེ་ལྟ་བུའི་ཏིང་འཛིན་གྱིས། །བསམ་གཏན་ཕ་རོལ་ཕྱིན་རྫོགས་
ཤོག །རྣམ་པར་ཐར་པའི་སྒོ་གསུམ་དང་། །དུས་གསུམ་མཉམ་པ་ཉིད་དང་
ཡང་། །རིག་གསུམ་མངོན་སུམ་བགྱིས་པ་ཡིས། །ཤེས་རབ་ཕ་རོལ་ཕྱིན་
རྫོགས་ཤོག །སངས་རྒྱས་ཀུན་གྱིས་བསྔགས་པ་དང་། །འོད་དང་གཟི་བརྗིད་
འབར་བ་དང་། །བྱང་ཆུབ་སེམས་དཔའི་བརྩོན་འགྲུས་ཀྱིས། །བདག་གི་བསམ་
པ་རྫོགས་གྱུར་ཅིག །དེ་ལྟར་སྤྱོད་པ་སྤྱོད་བྱེད་ཅིང་། །བྱམས་པ་གྲགས་དང་ལྡན་

པ་ཡིས། །ཕ་རོལ་ཕྱིན་དྲུག་རྫོགས་བྱས་ནས། །ས་བཅུ་པོ་ལ་རབ་ཏུ་གནས།། །།རྒྱ་གར་གྱི་མཁན་པོ་ཛི་ན་མི་ཏྲ་དང་། སུ་རེནྡྲ་བོ་དྷི་དང་། ཞུ་ཆེན་གྱི་ལོ་ཙྪ་བ་བནྡེ་ཡེ་ཤེས་སྡེས་བསྒྱུར་ཅིང་ཞུས་ཏེ་གཏན་ལ་ཕབ་པའོ།། །།

༄༅། །འཕགས་པ་བྱམས་པའི་སྨོན་ལམ་གྱི་འགྲེལ་པ་ཐོགས་མེད་ཀྱི་དགོངས་པ་གསལ་བར་བསྟན་པ་བཞུགས་སོ།།

༄༅། །བླ་མ་དམ་པའི་ཞབས་ལ་ཕྱག་འཚལ་ལོ། །བྱམས་མགོན་བདུད་རྩིའི་ཆར་ཕབ་ནས། །མ་རིག་ནད་ཀུན་དྲུངས་འབྱིན་པས། །སྨན་པ་ཆེ་མཆོག་ལྷ་ཡི་རྗེར། །ལན་བརྒྱར་བཏུད་དེ་ཕྱག་འཚལ་ལོ། །རྒྱལ་བའི་དབང་པོའི་ལྷུགས་ཉིད་ཀྱིས། །རིམ་གྲོར་བྱས་འདི་ཀུན་དགའ་བོའི། །ཐོས་པའི་ཚོགས་ནང་གྲགས་ཧེ་བཞིན། །ལྷ་བརྒྱ་པ་ལ་བཤད་པར་རིགས། །སེམས་ཅན་ཐམས་ཅད་ལ་བྱམས་པ་གཞན་ལས་ཕུལ་དུ་བྱུང་བ་ཉིད་ཀྱིས་བྱམས་པ། དེའི་སྨོན་ལམ་ཡིན་པས་དང་། འདུན་པ་ཙམ་ལའང་སྨོན་ལམ་གྱི་སྒྲ་འཇུག་པས། དེ་ལས་ལོགས་སུ་བཀར་བའི་ཕྱིར་རྒྱལ་པོ་སྟེ། བྱང་ཆུབ་སེམས་དཔའི་སྤྱོད་པ་ཡོངས་སུ་བསྔོ་བ་ཞེས་བྱ་བའི་ཐ་ཚིག་གོ །དེའི་ཕྱིར་འཕགས་པ་བྱམས་པའི་སྨོན་ལམ་རྒྱལ་པོ་ཞེས་བྱ་བ་འདི་བཤད་པ་ལ། གླེང་གཞི་དང་། སྨོན་ལམ། མཇུག་སྡུད་དང་གསུམ་ལས། དང་པོ་ནི། ཀུན་དགའ་བོ། བྱང་ཆུབ་སེམས་དཔའ་སེམས་དཔའ་ཆེན་པོ་བྱམས་པ་སྔོན་བྱང་ཆུབ་སེམས་དཔའི་སྤྱད་པ་སྤྱོད་པའི་ཚེ། ཉིན་ལན་གསུམ་མཚན་ལན་གསུམ་དུ་བླ་གོས་ཕྲག་པ་གཅིག་ཏུ་གཟར་ནས། པུས་མོ་གཡས་པའི་ལྷ་ང་ས་ལ་བཙུགས་ཏེ་ཐལ་མོ་སྦྱར་ནས་ཚིག་འདི་སྐད་ཅེས་སྨོན་ལམ་བཏབ་བོ། །དྲང་བའི་དོན་དུ་འཕགས་པ་བྱམས་པ་ནི་རྒྱལ་ཚབ་ཏུ་དབང་བསྐུར་བའི་བྱང་ཆུབ་སེམས་དཔའ་ཆེན་པོ་སྐྱེ་བ་གཅིག་གིས་ཐོབ་པ། དེའི་དབང་དུ་བྱས་ན། སྨོན་ཞེས་པ། དེ་

སེམས་བསྐྱེད་ནས་རིང་པོར་མ་ལོན་པ་ན་ཞེས་ཐོས་ལ། ངེས་པའི་དོན་དུ་འོག་མིན་དུ་སངས་རྒྱས་ནས་སྤྲུལ་པའི་སྐུ་དགའ་ལྡན་དུ་བཞུགས་ཏེ། འཛམ་བུའི་གླིང་པ་རྣམས་ལ་འཚང་རྒྱ་བར་སྟོན་པ་ལ་འབྱོན་ཁ་མ་ཞིག་གོ །དེའི་ཚེ། སྔོན་ཞེས་པ་བྱང་ཆུབ་སེམས་དཔའ་སློབ་པའི་སྐབས་ན་ཞེས་པའོ། །གཉིས་པ་ལ། ཕྱག་སྔོན་དུ་མཛད་པ་དང་། དེ་ནས་སྨོན་ལམ་གང་བཏབ་པ་གཉིས་ལས། དང་པོ་ནི། ཕྱག་གི་ཡུལ་ནི་དཀོན་མཆོག་གསུམ་ཡིན་ལ། དེ་ལས་སངས་རྒྱས་ནི། སངས་རྒྱས་ཀུན་ལ་ཕྱག་འཚལ་ལོ། །ཀུན་ཞེས་པ་བྱོན་ཟིན་པ་ད་ལྟ་བཞུགས་པ་འབྱོན་པར་འགྱུར་བ་ཐམས་ཅད་དམིགས་པའི་ཡུལ་དུ་མཛད་པའོ། །དགེ་འདུན་ནི། དྲང་སྲོང་ལྷ་མིག་ལྡན་པ་ཡི། །བྱང་ཆུབ་སེམས་དཔའ་རྣམས་དང་། དེས་ནི་མངོན་པར་ཤེས་པ་དྲུག་ཐོབ་པའི་བྱང་ཆུབ་སེམས་དཔའི་ཚོགས། ཡང་། ཉན་ཐོས་རྣམས་ལ་ཕྱག་འཚལ་ལོ། །འཕགས་པ་ཟུང་བཞི་ཡ་བརྒྱད་ཀྱི་དགེ་འདུན་ནོ། །ཕྱག་ནི་ཡིད་དང་ལུས་འདུད་པ་དང་བཅས་པའི་ངག་ཏུ་ཕྱག་འཚལ་ལོ་ཐོན་པའོ། །དམ་པའི་ཆོས་ནི་རྣམ་པ་གཉིས་ལས། དྲང་དོན་སྐྱེ་བ་བཟང་པོར་བྱེད་པ་དང་། ངེས་དོན་སྐྱེ་བ་ཟད་པར་བྱེད་པའོ། །དེ་ལས་དང་པོ་ནི། ངན་འགྲོའི་ལམ་ནི་ཟློག་བགྱིད་ཅིང་། །ངན་འགྲོ་ནི་ངན་སོང་གསུམ། དེའི་ལམ་ནི་མི་དགེ་བ། དེ་ལས་ཟློག་པ་ནི་སྡིག་པ་ཐམས་ཅད་སྤང་བ། མཐོ་རིས་ལམ་ནི་རབ་སྟོན་ལ། །མཐོ་རིས་ནི་མི་དང་ལྷ་རྣམ་པར་ཐར་པའི་སྣོད་དག དེའི་ལམ་ནི། འདུ་བྱེད་རྣམ་པ་གཉིས་ཀྱིས་དག་པ་ཕུན་སུམ་ཚོགས་པར་སྤྱོད་པ་དེ་ལ་མངོན་མཐོའི་ཐེག་པ་ཞེས་བྱ། ངེས་དོན་སྐྱེ་བ་ཟད་པར་བྱེད་པ་ནི། རྒ་ཤི་མེད་པ། རྒ་ཤི་མེད་པ་མྱ་ངན་ལས་འདས་པ་སྟེ། དེ་ཡང་ཞི་བ་མྱང་འདས་དང་། མི་གནས་པའི་མྱང་འདས་གཉིས་སོ། །འདྲེན་བགྱིད་པ། །བྱང་ཆུབ་སེམས་ལ་ཕྱག་འཚལ་ལོ། །དེར་འདྲེན་པ་ནི་དེར་བགྲོད་པའི་ལམ་གྱི་རིམ་པ་སྟེ། དེ་ཡང་ཉན་ཐོས་བྱང་ཆུབ་ཏུ་སེམས་བསྐྱེད་པ་དང་། རང་བྱང་ཆུབ་ཏུ་དང་། བླ་ན་མེད་པའི་བྱང་ཆུབ་ཏུ་སེམས་བསྐྱེད་པར་དེ་དང་དེའི་བྱང་ཆུབ་ཏུ་བགྲོད་པར་བྱེད་པ་ཐམས་ཅད་འདུ་བ་ཡིན་ནོ། །དེ་ནི་ངེས་པ་

ལེགས་པའི་ཐེག་པ་ཞེས་བྱའོ། །གཉིས་པ་ལ། རྒྱལ་བ་ཐམས་ཅད་ཀྱི་དམ་པའི་
ཆོས་འཛིན་པར་སྨོན་ལམ་བཏབ་པ་དང་། དེ་གང་གིས་སྒྲུབ་པའི་བྱང་ཆུབ་སེམས་
དཔའི་སྤྱོད་པ་ཡོངས་སུ་བསྔོ་བ་གཉིས་ལས། དང་པོ་ནི། ཐེག་པ་དང་པོ་དེ་
འཛིན་པ། སེམས་ཀྱི་དབང་དུ་བྱས་པས་ན། །དེ་ནི་ལས་ཀྱི་སྒྲིབ་པ་ཐམས་ཅད་
རྣམ་པར་དག་པའི་མདོ་ལས། དགེ་སློང་ཙི་སེམས་ཀུན་ནས་ཉོན་མོངས་པས་
སེམས་ཅན་རྣམས་ཀུན་ནས་ཉོན་མོངས་པ་ཅན་དུ་འགྱུར་ལ། སེམས་རྣམ་པར་དག་
པས་སེམས་ཅན་རྣམས་རྣམ་པར་དག་པར་འགྱུར་རོ། །ཞེས་གསུངས་པ་ཉིད་དེ།
འཁོར་བའམ་མྱ་ངན་ལས་འདས་པ་སེམས་ལ་རག་ལས་པར་བསྟན་ལ། འཁོར་
བ་དེར་སྐྱེ་བ་ངན་པ་དང་བཟང་བ་སྡིག་པ་དང་དགེ་བའི་མཐུ་དགེའམ་སྡིག་ཀྱང་བསམ་
པ་ལ་རག་ལས་པས། ཨཱརྻ་དེ་ཝས། དེ་ཕྱིར་བསམ་པའི་རྩ་བ་ལྟ། །
བསོད་ནམས་སྡིག་པ་རྣམ་པར་གནས། །ཞེས་གསུངས་ཤིང་། འདུལ་བའི་ལུང་
ལས། ཆོས་རྣམས་སྔོན་དུ་ཡིད་འགྲོ་ཡིད་གཙོ་ཡིན། །དང་། མངོན་པར།
ལས་ལས་འཇིག་རྟེན་སྣ་ཚོགས་སྐྱེས། །དེ་ནི་སེམས་པ་དང་དེས་བྱས། །ཞེས་
འབྱུང་བ་ཡིན་ནོ། །བདག་གིས་སྡིག་པ་ཅི་བགྱིས་པ། །སངས་རྒྱས་སྤྱན་སྔར་
མཆིས་ནས་སུ། །བདག་གིས་དེ་དག་བཤགས་པར་བགྱི། །དེས་ན་སྐྱེ་གནས་
ངན་པ་དེར་མི་འགྲོ་བར་འདོད་ན། སྔར་བྱས་ཀྱི་སྡིག་པ་བཤགས་ཤིང་ཕྱིས་མི་བྱེད་
པ་སྡོམ་པ་ཞིག་དགོས་པས་བཤགས་པ་བསྟན། དེ་ཡང་སྟོབས་རྣམ་པ་བཞི་ཚང་
བའི་སྒོ་ནས་ཏེ། རྟེན་གྱི་སྟོབས། རྣམ་པར་སུན་འབྱིན་པའི་སྟོབས། གཉེན་
པོ་ཀུན་ཏུ་སྤྱོད་པའི་སྟོབས། ཉེས་པ་ལས་སླར་ལྡོག་པའི་སྟོབས་སོ། །བཤགས་བྱ་
ཡང་། སྔོན་བྱས་པ། བྱེད་དུ་བཅུག་པ། གཞན་བྱེད་པ་ལ་དགའ་བ། ད་
ལྟར་བྱེད་པ། བྱེད་དུ་བཅུག་པ། གཞན་བྱེད་པ་ལ་ཡི་རང་བ་རྣམས་ཡིན་ལ།
བསྡམས་པས་མ་འོངས་པ་ན་མི་འབྱུང་བའི་ཕྱིར་དེ་བཤགས་པ་མ་གསུངས་ངོ་། །
བདག་ལ་རྣམ་པ་གསུམ་གང་གིས། །བསོད་ནམས་ཚོགས་ནི་བསྐྱེད་པ་སྟེ། །
མིར་སྐྱེ་བར་བྱེད་པའི་བསོད་ནམས་ཀྱི་ལས་དང་། ལྷར་སྐྱེ་བར་བྱེད་པའི་བསོད་

ནམས་ཀྱི་ལས་དང་། །ཁམས་གོང་མར་སྐྱེ་བར་བྱེད་པའི་མི་གཡོ་བའི་ལས་གསུམ་སྟེ། ལུགས་ལས། མིའི་ཐེག་པ་དང་། ལྷའི་ཐེག་པ་དང་། ཚངས་པའི་ཐེག་པ་ཞེས་མངོན་པར་མཐོ་བ་དེ་གསུམ་དུ་ཕྱེ་ནས་གསུངས་པའི་ཕྱིར་རོ། །འཇིག་རྟེན་པ་ལ་ཡེ་ཤེས་ཀྱི་ཚོགས་མེད་པས་ཐམས་ཅད་བསོད་ནམས་ཀྱི་ཚོགས་སུ་བགྲངས་སོ། །ངེས་ལེགས་ཀྱི་ཐེག་པ་འཛིན་པ་ནི། བདག་གི་ཀུན་མཁྱེན་ས་བོན་ཏེ། །བདག་གི་བྱང་ཆུབ་མི་ཟད་ཤོག །ཀུན་མཁྱེན། ཀུན་ཤེས། དེའི་གྲོགས་སྟོབས་ཀྱིས་ལམ་ཤེས་དང་། རྣམ་མཁྱེན་ཡང་བསྟན་པས། དེ་གསུམ་ས་བོན་དུ་བྱས་པས་འཕགས་པ་བཞི་སྨྱུ་གུ་ལྟ་བུར་འབྱུང་ལ་དེས་བྱང་ཆུབ་ས་གསུམ་དུ་འགྲུབ་པས་མི་ཟད་པ་སྟེ་མང་བ་ཡིན་ལ། དེ་བས་ན་འཕགས་པ་ཉན་རང་གཉིས་ཀུན་ཤེས་ཀྱི་འབྲས་བུའོ། །ལམ་ཤེས་ཀྱི་བྱང་སེམས་འཕགས་པའི་གནས་སྐབས། དེའི་མཐར་ཐུག་གི་འབྲས་བུ་རྣམ་མཁྱེན་ནོ། །བདག་གི་ཞེས་སྨྲར་བ་ནི། ཀུན་ཤེས་དེ་ལ་ཡང་བྱང་ཆུབ་སེམས་དཔའ་རྣམས་ཀྱི་བསླབ་པ་སྟེ། བྱང་ཆུབ་སེམས་དཔས་མི་སློབ་པའི། །དེ་ནི་གང་ཡང་ཡོད་མ་ཡིན། །ཞེས་པས་སོ། །འོན་ཀྱང་དེ་ཤེས་པར་བྱའི་ཕྱིར་ཡིན་ལ། མངོན་དུ་བྱ་བའི་ཕྱིར་ནི་མ་ཡིན་ནོ། །ངེས་པའི་དོན་དུ། ཀུན་མཁྱེན་ནི་བདེ་བར་གཤེགས་པ། ས་བོན་ནི་དྲི་མ་དགུའི་སྦུབས་ན་གནས་པའི་ཚེ་དེ་ལ་བདེ་བར་གཤེགས་པའི་སྙིང་པོ་ཞེས་བྱ་བར་བསྟན་པས་ཁམས། དེ་ཡང་། སེམས་ཅན་བྱང་ཆུབ་སེམས་དཔའ་དང་། བདེ་བར་གཤེགས་པར་སྟོན་པ་ནི། ངོ་བོ་ལ་ཁྱད་པར་འབྱེད་རྒྱུ་མ་བྱུང་བས་དང་རྣམ་པ་ལ་སྒྲིབ་པ་དང་བཅས་པའི་ཚེ་གནས་སྐབས་དང་པོ་གཉིས་སུ་བཞག སྒྲིབ་པ་དང་བྲལ་བ་ན་ཕྱི་མར་བཞག་པས། །དེ་བཞིན་ཉིད་ནི་ཐམས་ཅད་ལ། །ཁྱད་པར་མེད་ཀྱང་དག་གྱུར་པ། །དེ་བཞིན་གཤེགས་ཉིད་དེ་ཡི་ཕྱིར། །འགྲོ་ཀུན་དེ་ཡི་སྙིང་པོ་ཅན། །ཞེས་གསུངས་སོ། །ངོ་བོ་རང་གཅིག་ཡིན་པའི་གནད་དེས། སྦྱངས་པ་མཐར་ཐུག་ན་དེ་ཀ་མངོན་དུ་འགྱུར་བས་འབྲས་བུ་གཅིག དེའི་ཕྱིར། མཐར་ཐུག་ཐེག་པ་གཅིག་ཏུ་བསྟན། འདི་ལས་རང་སངས་རྒྱས་ན། ཞུལ་ན་སེམས་ཅན་གཞན་མི་ལས་ཏེ།

རང་དང་གཞན་དུ་སྣང་བ་ནི་གློ་བུར་བ་འཁྲུལ་པའི་ཆོས་ཡིན་ནོ་ཞེས་ཀྱང་ཤེས་པར་བྱའོ། །དེས་ན་ཡུལ་འཁྲུལ་པ་མེད་ལ། བློའི་འཛིན་སྟངས་ཀྱིས་གཟུང་བས་དེ་དང་བྲལ་དུ་རུང་བས། གློ་བུར་དག་གི་ཁམས་སྟོང་གི །ཞེས་ཐོབ། རང་བཞིན་གཞན་དུ་འགྱུར་མི་སྲིད་པས། བླ་མེད་ཆོས་ཀྱིས་སྟོང་མ་ཡིན། །ཞེས་བྱས། རང་བཞིན་དེ་བཤད་པ་ནའང་ནམ་མཁའ་ལྟ་བུ་ཞེས་དཔེར་མཚོན་པའི་དབང་གིས་དེ་དངོས་པོར་མི་གཟུང་ངོ་། །དེ་བས་ན་འདིར་ཆོས་ཐམས་ཅད་འཛིན་པར་སྨོན་ལམ་བཏབ། སྨོན་ལམ་དེར་བྱང་ཆུབ་སེམས་དཔའི་ཡོངས་སུ་བསྔོ་བ་ཐམས་ཅད་འདུས་པར་བཟང་སྤྱོད་འགྲེལ་པ་ལས་བཤད་པས་སྨོན་ལམ་ཐམས་ཅད་མདོར་བསྟན་པ་ཡིན་ནོ། །གཉིས་པ་ལ་འཇུག་པའི་སྤྱོད་པ། སྒྲུབ་པའི་སྤྱོད་པ། འགྲུབ་པའི་སྤྱོད་པ་གསུམ་ལས། དང་པོ་ནི། ཕྱོགས་བཅུ་དག་གི་ཞིང་ཁམས་སུ། །སངས་རྒྱས་མཆོད་པ། ཞིང་ཁམས་ཐམས་ཅད་དུ་མཆོད་པའི་སྤྲིན་ཆེན་པོ་ཡིད་ཀྱིས་སྤྲུལ་པ། དངོས་སུ་བཤམས་པ་དེ་དག་རང་དུ་ཡོད་པར་མོས་པས་གཟུང་བ་རྣམས་ནི་རྒྱ་ཆེ་བའི་མཆོད་པའོ། །གང་བྱུང་བ། སེམས་ཅན་མགུ་བྱ་མ་གཏོགས་པ། །རྒྱལ་བ་མཉེས་པའི་ཐབས་གཞན་མེད། །ཅེས་པས། བྱང་ཆུབ་ཏུ་སེམས་བསྐྱེད་པ་རང་མཆོད་པ་ཐམས་ཅད་ཀྱི་མཆོག་ཡིན་པས་དེ་སྟོན་པ་ཡིན་ནོ། །སངས་རྒྱས་མཁྱེན་པས་ཡི་རང་བ། །དེ་ལ་བདག་ནི་ཡི་རང་ངོ་། །འཁོར་གསུམ་དག་པ་ཉིད་བླ་ན་མེད་པའི་མཆོད་པ་ཡིན་པས་དེ་བཤད་པའོ། །སྡིག་པ་ཐམས་ཅད་བཤགས་པར་བགྱི། །གཞན་གྱི། བསོད་ནམས་ཀུན་ལ་ཡི་རང་ངོ་། །སངས་རྒྱས་ཀུན་ལ་ཕྱག་འཚལ་ལོ། །བདག་ནི་ཡེ་ཤེས་མཆོག་ཐོབ་ཤོག །བཞི་པ་དེ་གང་དུ་བསྔོས་པ་དེ་ལྟར་བསྒྱུར་བར་བྱས་པས་དགེ་བའི་རྩ་བ་རྣམས་ལ་གསེར་འགྱུར་གྱི་རྩི་ལྟ་བུའོ། །ཕྱོགས་བཅུ་དག་གི་ཕྱོགས་རྣམས་ན། །ས་བཅུ་དག་ལ་གནས་པ་ཡི། །བྱང་ཆུབ་སེམས་དཔའ་བྱང་ཆུབ་མཆོག །འཚང་རྒྱ་བགྱི་བ་བསྐུལ་མ་འདེབས། །སྡེ་དང་བཅས་པའི་བདུད་བཏུལ་ནས། །བྱང་ཆུབ་དམ་པར་སངས་རྒྱས་ཏེ། །སྲོག་ཆགས་ཀུན་ལ་སྨན་སླད་དུ། །ཆོས་ཀྱི་

འཁོར་ལོ་བསྐོར་གྱུར་ཅིག །ཅེས་བསྒྱུར་བ་ལྟར་འཐད་དོ། །འདི་ནི་བྱང་ཆུབ་སེམས་དཔའ་སེམས་དཔའ་ཆེན་པོ་རྣམས་ལ་བསྐུལ་མ་འདེབས་པའོ། །ཆོས་རྔ་ཆེན་པོ་སྒྲ་ཡིས་ནི། །སྡུག་བསྔལ་སེམས་ཅན་མཐར་བགྱིད་ཤོག །སངས་རྒྱས་རྣམས་ལ་ཆོས་ཀྱི་འཁོར་ལོ་བསྐོར་བ་བསྐུལ་བའོ། །བསྐལ་པ་བྱེ་བ་བསམ་ཡས་སུ། །ཆོས་སྟོན་མཛད་ཅིང་བཞུགས་གྱུར་ཅིག །མྱ་ངན་ལས་མི་འདའ་བ་གསོལ་བ་འདེབས་པ་སྟེ་ཡན་ལག་བདུན་པ་སྟོན་དུ་འགྲོ་བའི་ཆོས་སོ། །འདོད་པའི་འདམ་དུ་བྱིང་གྱུར་ཅིང་། །སྲིད་པའི་སྲད་བུས་དམ་བཅིངས་པ། །འཆིང་བ་ཀུན་གྱིས་བཅིངས་བདག་ལ། །གང་བསྐྱབ་པའི་སེམས་ཅན། རྐང་གཉིས་མཆོག་རྣམས་གཟིགས་སུ་གསོལ། །གང་གིས་སྐྱོབ་པ། མཐར་ཐུག་པའི་སྐྱབས་དེ་ཁོ་ན་ཡིན་ལ། དེ་ལ་ཆོས་དང་དགེ་འདུན་ཡང་འདུ་བ་ཡིན་ན། སེམས་ཀྱི་དྲི་མ་གྱུར་པ་ལ། །སངས་རྒྱས་རྣམས་ནི་སྨོད་མི་མཛད། །སེམས་ཅན་རྣམས་ལ་བྱམས་ཐུགས་ལྡན། །སྐྱོབ་པའི་རྒྱ་མཚན། བུ་མ་རུང་ཀྱང་མ་དེ་ལ་བརྩེ་བ་ལྟ་བུ་ཡིན་པས་སོ། །ཇི་ལྟར་བསྐྱབ་པ། སྲིད་པའི་མཚོ་ལས་སྒྲོལ་བར་ཤོག །རྫོགས་པའི་སངས་རྒྱས་གང་བཞུགས་དང་། །གང་དག་འདས་དང་མ་བྱོན་པ། །དེ་དག་རྗེས་སུ་བདག་སློབ་ཅིང་། །བྱང་ཆུབ་སྤྱད་པ་སྤྱོད་གྱུར་ཅིག །ཕ་རོལ་ཕྱིན་དྲུག་རྫོགས་བགྱིས་ནས། །འགྲོ་དྲུག་སེམས་ཅན་མཐར་བགྱིད་ཤོག །སེམས་བསྐྱེད་པ་ཁྱད་པར་ཅན་གྱི་ཚིག་དེ་དངོས་གཞིའོ། །ཁྱད་པར་ཅན་མ་ཡིན་པ་ནི་ཉན་ཐོས་ཀྱི་གཞུང་ལས་ཀྱང་བཤད་པ་དང་། འདི་དེར་མ་བཤད་པས་འཕགས་པ་ཀླུ་སྒྲུབ་ཀྱིས། ཉན་ཐོས་སྡེ་སྣོད་དེ་ལས་ནི། །སྤྱོད་པ་ཡོངས་བསྔོ་མ་བཤད་དེ། །ཞེས་གསུངས་པ་ཤེས་པར་བྱ་ཡི། དེའི་གཞུང་ལས་བསྔོ་བ་མ་བཤད་པ་ལྟ་བུར་སེམས་པ་ནི་ནོར་བ་ཡིན་ནོ། །བློ་ལྡན་སེམས་མཆོག་བསྐྱེད་མ་ཐག་ཏུ་ཡང་། །མཐའ་ཡས་ཉེས་པ་བྱེད་ལས་སེམས་རབ་བསྡམས། །ཞེས་པས་བྱང་ཆུབ་ཏུ་སེམས་བསྐྱེད་པ་དེ་ཀ་བྱང་ཆུབ་སེམས་ཀྱི་སྡོམ་པར་སོང་། སེམས་བསྐྱེད་པ་དེ་ཡང་བསྒྲུབ་པ་ཕུན་སུམ་ཚོགས་པས་རྫོགས་པར་བྱ་དགོས་པས། གཉིས་པ་བསྒྲུབ་པའི་སྤྱོད་པ་ལ། དོན་

དམ་འཛིན་པའི་ཤེས་རབ་དང་། ཀུན་རྫོབ་འཛིན་པའི་སྙིང་རྗེ་གཉིས། དང་པོ་ལ།
སྔོན་དུ་འགྲོ་བ་ཞི་གནས། དེ་ལ་གནས་པའི་ལྷག་མཐོང་གཉིས་ལས། དང་པོ་ནི།
མངོན་ཤེས་དྲུག་པོ་མངོན་བགྱིས་ནས། །ཟླ་མེད་བྱང་ཆུབ་རིག་འགྱུར་ཅིག །འདི་
ལ་ཨ་ཏི་ཤེས། བསོད་ནམས་ཡེ་ཤེས་རང་བཞིན་གྱིས། །ཚོགས་ནི་ཡོངས་སུ་
རྫོགས་པ་ཡི། །རྒྱུ་ནི་སངས་རྒྱས་ཐམས་ཅད་དག །མངོན་ཤེས་བསྐྱེད་པ་ཉིད་དུ་
བཞེད། །ཇི་ལྟར་འདབ་ཤོག་མ་ཚང་བའི། །བྱ་ནི་མཁའ་ལ་ཕུར་མི་ནུས། །དེ་
བཞིན་མངོན་ཤེས་སྟོབས་བྲལ་བས། །སེམས་ཅན་དོན་བྱེད་ནུས་མ་ཡིན། །
མངོན་ཤེས་ལྡན་པའི་ཉིན་མཚན་གྱི། །བསོད་ནམས་དག་ནི་གང་ཡིན་པ། །
མངོན་ཤེས་དག་དང་བྲལ་གྱུར་པ། །སྐྱེ་བ་བརྒྱར་ཡང་ཡོད་མ་ཡིན། །མངོན་
ཤེས་ཀྱང་ཞི་གནས་ཀྱི་ཏིང་ངེ་འཛིན་གྲུབ་པ་ལས་ཡིན་པས། ཞི་གནས་གྲུབ་པ་མ་
ཡིན་ན། །མངོན་ཤེས་འགྲུབ་པར་མི་འགྱུར་བས། །དེ་ཕྱིར་ཞི་གནས་སྒྲུབ་པའི་
ཕྱིར། །ཡང་དང་ཡང་དུ་འབད་པར་བྱ། །དེ་བཞིན། བསོད་ནམས་ཚོགས་ནི་
ཡང་དག་རྫོགས། །དེ་ནས་བློ་ལྡན་བསམ་པ་བརྟན། །དད་སོགས་དགེ་བའི་ཆོས་
རྣམས་ནི། །རྒྱུད་ནི་ཡོངས་སུ་བགོས་གྱུར་པ། །བསྐལ་པ་གྲངས་མེད་ངེས་
འབྱུང་བས། །ཡེ་ཤེས་ཚོགས་ནི་བསྒྲུབ་བྱའི་ཕྱིར། །མངོན་ཤེས་གདམས་ངག་
བསྟན་པ་ཡི། །སྤྱོད་པའི་ས་ལ་རབ་ཏུ་འཇུག །ཅེས་གསུངས་སོ། །གཉིས་པ་
ལ། ཤེས་རབ་དངོས་སུ། དེའི་བྱ་བ་ཁོངས་ནས་བསྟན་པ་གཉིས་ལས། དང་
པོ་ནི། སྤྱོད་པར། ཤེས་རབ་ཀྱིས་ནི་ཆོས་ཀྱི་རང་བཞིན་ཡོངས་ཤེས་ནས། །
ཁམས་གསུམ་མ་ལུས་པ་ལས་ཡང་དག་འདའ་བར་འགྱུར། །ཞེས་པས་སོ། །
མ་སྐྱེས་པ་དང་མི་འབྱུང་དང་། །ཤེས་རབ་ནི། ཆོས་རབ་ཏུ་རྣམ་པར་འབྱེད་པའི་
ཆ་ནས་བཞག དབྱེ་ན། ཐོས་བྱུང་དང་བསམ་བྱུང་སྒོམ་བྱུང་གི་ཤེས་རབ་
གསུམ། ཐོས་པའི་ཤེས་རབ་ལ་བརྟེན་ནས་བསམ་བྱུང་གི་ཤེས་རབ་ཀྱིས་དཔྱད་དེ།
དེ་ལ་གནས་པས་སྒོམ་བྱུང་གི་ཤེས་རབ་སྐྱེད་པ་ཡིན་ནོ། །དང་པོ་ནི། དགེ་བའི་
བཤེས་གཉེན་ལ་བརྟེན་ནས་དམ་པའི་ཆོས་ཉན་པ་ལས་འབྱུང་། དགེ་བའི་བཤེས་

གཉེན་ཀྱང་། དང་པོར་བྱང་ཆུབ་སེམས་དཔའི་སྤྱི་སྤྱོད་ལ་མཁས་པ་ལ་བརྟེན་པའམ་
ཡང་དག་པའི་གདམས་ངག་འབོགས་ནུས་པ་ཙམ་ལ་བརྟེན་ལ། ཕྱིས་སངས་རྒྱས་
དང་མངོན་སུམ་དུ་མཇལ་ཏེ། དེས་ཡང་དག་པའི་ལམ་གྱི་གདམས་ངག་བསྟན་པར་
མཛད་དོ། ཇི་ལྟར་ཐོས་པ་དེའི་ཚིག་དང་དོན་ལ་བསམ་གཞིག་ལེགས་པར་གཏོང་
བ་ནི་བསམ་པ་ཡིན་ལ། ལུང་དང་རིགས་པའི་ལམ་དང་མཐུན་པར་གོ་བའི་ཚེ་སྒྲོ་
འདོགས་ཆོད་པ་ཞེས་བྱའོ། །དེའི་ཚུལ་ཡང་དངོས་པོ་ཐམས་ཅད་རྒྱུ་རྐྱེན་ལ་རག་
ལུས་པ་ཉིད་ཀྱིས་མ་སྐྱེས་པ་དང་། མ་སྐྱེས་པ་ཉིད་ཀྱིས་གང་ན་ཡང་མ་བྱུང་བ་དང་།
རང་བཞིན་མ་མཆིས་གནས་མ་མཆིས། །སྒྱུ་མ་ཉིད་ཀྱི་རང་བཞིན་མེད་པ་དང་།
དབུས་མཐའ་མེད་པས་ཕྱོགས་དང་ཆ་གང་ལའང་མི་གནས་པ་དང་། རྣམ་རིག་མ་
མཆིས་དངོས་མ་མཆིས། །རྣམ་པར་ཤེས་པ་ལས་འདས་པས་རྣམ་རིག་མེད་པ་དང་།
གཟུང་བ་དང་འཛིན་པའི་དམིགས་པ་ཐམས་ཅད་དང་བྲལ་བས་དངོས་པོ་མ་མཆིས་པ་
དང་། སྟོང་པའི་ཆོས་ནི་རྟོགས་པར་ཤོག །དེ་ནི་སྟོང་པ་ཉིད་ཡིན་པས་དེ་ལྟར་
གཏན་ལ་འབེབས་པ་ཡིན་ནོ། །དེ་ནི་ཆོས་ལ་བདག་མེད་པ་ཞེས་བྱ། ཆོས་ཀྱི་
བདག་ནི། ཆོས་སུ་རུང་བ་སྟེ། བརྟགས་པས་དེར་རུང་བ་མི་རྙེད། དེས་
དམིགས་པ་ཐམས་ཅད་འཇིག་པའི་ཕྱིར། དེ་ལ་དངོས་པོ་ཐམས་ཅད་འཇིག་པར་བྱེད་
པ་ཞེས་ཀྱང་བྱའོ། །མུ་སྟེགས་བྱེད་རྣམས་ཀྱིས་བདག་རྟག་པ་གཅིག་པུ་རང་དབང་
ཅན་ཞེས་བྱ་བ་ཞིག་བཏགས་ནས། དེ་ལ་སེམས་ཅན། སྲོག གང་ཟག
གསོ་བ་སོགས་སུ་འདོགས་པས། དེ་ནི་དོན་དང་ཐ་སྙད་གཉིས་ཀས་སྟོང་པས།
སངས་རྒྱས་དྲང་སྲོང་ཆེན་པོ་ལྟར། །དེ་རྣམས་ཀྱིས་གསུངས་པ་ལྟར། སེམས་
ཅན་མ་མཆིས་སྲོག་མ་མཆིས། །གང་ཟག་མ་མཆིས་གསོ་མ་མཆིས། །བདག་
མ་མཆིས་པའི་ཆོས་རྟོགས་ཤོག །དེ་ལྟར་དོན་ལ་གནས་སོ་ཞེས་བསྟན་ཞིང་།
འདིས་གང་ཟག་བདག་གཉིས་ལས་ཀུན་བརྟགས་ཀྱི་བདག་བཀག་པ་ཡིན་ནོ། །
བདག་འཛིན་བདག་གིར་འཛིན་པ་ནི། །དངོས་པོ་ཀུན་ལ་མི་གནས་པ། །བདག་
ཅེས་བྱ་བ་ནི། དངོས་པོ་རང་མ་ཡིན། དེ་ལས་གཞན་པ་མ་ཡིན། དེ་དག་གི་

ངོ་བོ་མ་ཡིན། འབྲས་དང་ཐོལ་མིག་ལྟར་དེ་ལ་བརྟེན་པ་ཡང་མ་ཡིན། དངོས་པོ་རྣམས་ལ་གནས་པ་མ་ཡིན་པས་འདི་ལྟར་འཛིན་པ་ནི་ཕྱིན་ཅི་ལོག་འབའ་ཞིག་གོ །ཞེས་སྟོན་པས་འཇིག་ལྟ་ལྷན་སྐྱེས་ཀྱི་བདག །ཐ་སྙད་དུ་ལས་འབྲས་ཀྱི་རྟེན་དུ་གཟུང་བ་དེ་མེད་པར་བསྒྲུབས་སོ། །གཉིས་པ་ནི། ཤེས་རབ་དེའི་ལས་ནི་དེ་ཁ་སྒོམ་པ་ཡིན་ལ་དེས། བྱང་ཆུབ་སེམས་དཔའ་མཉམ་གཞག་པས། །ཡིད་ཀྱིས་བརྗོད་པ་མ་རྟོགས་པར། །དོན་ཀུན་རབ་ཏུ་མི་མཐོང་ངོ་། །ཞེས་ཆོས་ལ་ངེས་པར་རྟོག་པའི་བཟོད་པ་ཐོབ། དེ་ནས། ཆོས་ཀྱི་སྣང་བ་འཕེལ་བྱའི་ཕྱིར། །བརྩོན་འགྲུས་བརྟན་པ་ཀུན་ཏུ་བརྩམ། །རྒྱུ་དེས་ཆོས་ཆེན་པོ་ལ་བཟོད་པ་ཐོབ་སྟེ། དེའི་ཚེ། ཆོས་ཀྱི་སྣང་བ་འཕེལ་ནས་ནི། །སེམས་ཙམ་ལ་ནི་གནས་པར་འགྱུར། །དེ་ནས་དོན་དུ་སྣང་བ་ཀུན། །སེམས་སུ་རབ་ཏུ་སྣང་བར་འགྱུར། །དེ་ཚེ་དེ་ཡི་གཟུང་བ་ཡི། །རྣམ་པར་གཡེང་བ་དེ་སྤངས་འགྱུར། །དེ་ནས་དེ་ལ་འཛིན་པ་ཡི། །རྣམ་པར་གཡེང་བ་འབའ་ཞིག་ལུས། །ཞེས་སོ། །དེ་ནས་གཟུང་བ་དང་འཛིན་པའི་རྣམ་པ་ཞི། ཤེས་པ་རང་གི་རང་བཞིན་རང་རིག་རང་གསལ་ལ་གནས་པས་དེ་ཉིད། དེ་ཚེ་བར་ཆད་མེད་པ་ཡི། །ཏིང་ངེ་འཛིན་ལ་མྱུར་དུ་རེག །ཅེས་བྱ། དེ་ནི་གཞན་སྟོང་དབུ་མར་གཞོག་པ་དེ་ཡིན། དེ་ནས་འོད་གསལ་བ་དེ་ལ་ཞུགས་པས། ལས་དང་ཉོན་མོངས་པ་ཐམས་ཅད་ཟད་ནས་རང་རིག་ཙམ་དུའང་མི་སྣང་། དོན་དེའི་རང་རིག་སྟེ་རྣམ་པར་ཤེས་པ་ཉིད་ཡིན། ཕྱི་མ་ནི་རྣམ་པར་ཤེས་པ་ལས་འདས་པ་ཡེ་ཤེས་ཞེས་བྱ་བའི་མིང་སྙན་པོ་བཏགས་ས་དེ་ཡིན་པས། མིའམ་ཅིའི་རྒྱལ་པོ་ལྗོན་པས་ཞུས་པ་ལས། གང་འོད་གསལ་བ་དེ་སེམས་ཀྱི་རང་བཞིན་ནོ། །སེམས་ཀྱི་རང་བཞིན་གང་ཡིན་པ་དེ་འཇུག་པའོ། །གང་འཇུག་པ་དེ་མཚན་མ་ཐམས་ཅད་གནོན་པའོ། །གང་མཚན་མ་ཐམས་ཅད་གནོན་པ་དེ་སྐྱོན་མེད་པ་ལ་འཇུག་པ་ཞེས་བྱའོ། །བྱང་ཆུབ་སེམས་དཔའི་སྐྱོན་མེད་པ་ལ་འཇུག་པ་གང་ཡིན་པ་དེ་ནི་མི་སྐྱེ་བའི་ཆོས་ལ་བཟོད་པ་སྟེ། དེས་ན་སྐྱོན་མེད་པ་ལ་ཞུགས་པའི་བྱང་ཆུབ་སེམས་དཔའ་མི་སྐྱེ་བའི་ཆོས་ལ་བཟོད་པ་ཐོབ་པ་ཞེས་

བྱའོ། །གང་བཟོད་པ་ཐོབ་པ་དེས་ཐམས་ཅད་བཟོད་དོ། །དེ་སྟོང་པར་ཡང་བཟོད།
དེ་གང་ཟག་ཏུའང་བཟོད། དེ་ཅིའི་ཕྱིར་ཞེ་ན་གང་ཟག་ལས་སྟོང་པ་གཞན་མ་ཡིན་པ་
སྟེ། གང་ཟག་ཉིད་སྟོང་པའོ་ནས། རིགས་ཀྱི་བུ་དེ་ལྟར་མི་སྐྱེ་བའི་ཆོས་ལ་
བཟོད་པ་ཐོབ་པའི་བྱང་ཆུབ་སེམས་དཔའ་ནི་འགལ་བ་མེད་པ་སྟེ་ཆོས་ཐམས་ཅད་དང་
འགལ་བ་མེད་པ་ཡིན་ནོ། །ཞེས་གསུངས། དེ་ནི་ལངྐར་གཤེགས་པ་ལས།
སེམས་ཙམ་ལ་ནི་བརྟེན་ནས་སུ། །ཕྱི་རོལ་དོན་ལ་མི་རྟོག་གོ །དེ་བཞིན་ཉིད་ལ་
གནས་ནས་སུ། །སེམས་ཙམ་ལས་ཀྱང་འདའ་བར་བྱ། །སེམས་ཙམ་ལས་ནི་
འདས་ནས་སུ། །སྣང་བ་མེད་ལ་གནས་པར་བྱ། །སྣང་མེད་གནས་པའི་རྣལ་
འབྱོར་པ། །དེ་ནི་ཐེག་པ་ཆེན་པོ་མཐོང་། །ཞེས་གསུངས་པ་དེ་བཞིན། །
སེམས་ལས་གཞན་མེད་པར་ནི་བློས་རིག་ནས། །དེ་ནས་སེམས་ཀྱང་མེད་པ་ཉིད་དུ་
རྟོགས། །བློ་དང་ལྡན་པས་གཉིས་པོ་མེད་རིག་ནས། །དེ་མི་ལྡན་པའི་ཆོས་ཀྱི་
དབྱིངས་ལ་གནས། །ཞེས་བྱ་བས་ཀྱང་ཡིན་ནོ། །གཉིས་པ་ཀུན་རྫོབ་འཛིན་པའི་
སྙིང་རྗེ་ལ། སྤྱི་བཤད་དང་། གཞུང་དོན་གཉིས་ལས། དང་པོ་ནི། ཡུམ་
ལས། རྣམ་པ་ཐམས་ཅད་མཁྱེན་པ་ཉིད་དང་ལྡན་པའི་སེམས་ཀྱི་ཕ་རོལ་ཏུ་ཕྱིན་པ་
དྲུག་ལ་སྤྱད་དེ་མྱུར་དུ་མངོན་པར་རྫོགས་པར་སངས་རྒྱའོ། །ཞེས་གསུངས་ལ།
ཐབས་ནི་སེམས་ཅན་མི་གཏོང་བའི་བྱང་ཆུབ་ཀྱི་སེམས་སོ། །དེ་ནི་ཕ་རོལ་ཏུ་ཕྱིན་པ་
དྲུག་ཏུ་འདུ་བ་སྟེ། སྦྱིན་ཚུལ་བཟོད་གསུམ་གྱིས་གཞན་དོན། བརྩོན་བསམ་ཤེས་
གསུམ་གྱིས་རང་དོན་བསྒྲུབ་པ་སྟེ། སེམས་ཅན་དོན་ལ་རབ་བརྩོན་པ། གཏོང་
བ་མི་གནོད་བཟོད་པ་སྟེ། །གནས་དང་གྲོལ་བ་གཞིར་བཅས་པ། །རང་དོན་རྣམ་
པ་ཐམས་ཅད་སྤྱོད། །དང་། དང་པོ་གསུམ་གྱིས་ལྷག་པ་ཚུལ་ཁྲིམས། ལྔ་
པས་ལྷག་པ་སེམས། ཕྱི་མས་ལྷག་པ་ཤེས་རབ་ཀྱི་བསླབ་པ། བརྩོན་འགྲུས་
ཀུན་གྱི་གྲོགས་ཏེ། བསླབ་གསུམ་དབང་དུ་མཛད་ནས་ནི། །རྒྱལ་བས་ཕ་རོལ་
ཕྱིན་པ་དྲུག །ཡང་དག་བཤད་དེ་དང་པོ་གསུམ། །ཐ་མ་གཉིས་ཀྱིས་རྣམ་པ་
གཉིས། །གཅིག་ནི་གསུམ་ཀར་ལ་ཡང་གཏོགས། །དང་པོ་བཞི་ནི་མངོན་མཐོ།

ཐ་མ་གཉིས་ཀྱིས་ངེས་ལེགས་འགྲུབ་པས་ཀྱང་སྟེ། ཡོངས་སྤྱོད་དང་ལུས་ཕུན་སུམ་ཚོགས་པ་དང་། །འཁོར་བཙུན་ཕུན་སུམ་ཚོགས་པ་མངོན་མཐོང་དང་། །རྟག་ཏུ་ཉོན་མོངས་དབང་ཉིད་མི་འགྲོ་དང་། །བྱ་བ་རྣམས་ལ་ཕྱིན་ཅི་མ་ལོག་པའོ། །ཞེས་དང་། སྦྱིན་པ་ལས་ཚུལ་ཁྲིམས་འབྱུང་བ་སོགས་སྐྱེ་བའི་གོ་རིམ་དང་། དམན་མཆོག་དང་། སྦྱིན་པ་བསྒྲུབ་སླ་ཞིང་མཚན་ཉིད་ཤེས་སླ་བས། དང་པོར་བསྟན་པ་སོགས་རགས་ཕྲའི་ཕྱིར་གོ་རིམ་དེ་ལྟར་བཞག་པ་སྟེ། སྔ་མ་ལ་བརྟེན་ཕྱི་མ་སྐྱེ། །དམན་དང་མཆོག་ཏུ་གནས་ཕྱིར་དང་། །རགས་པ་དང་ནི་ཕྲ་བའི་ཕྱིར། །དེ་དག་རིམ་པར་བསྟན་པ་ཡིན། །ཞེས་སོ། །ཐབས་དེའི་བྱ་བ་ནི། ལུས་དང་ངག་དང་ཡིད་ཀྱི་སྤྱོད་པ་ཐམས་ཅད་སེམས་ཅན་གྱི་ཆེད་དུ་མ་ཡིན་པ་ཅི་ཡང་མེད་དེ་དངོས་སམ་བརྒྱུད་པའོ། །དེ་ལ་སེམས་ཅན་ལ་དམིགས་པ་དང་། དམིགས་པ་མེད་པའི་རིམ་པ་གཉིས་ལས། དང་པོ་ནི། བྱང་ཆུབ་སེམས་དཔའ་ལས་དང་པོ་པའི་གང་ཟག་གིས་བདག་ཡོད་པས་སེམས་ཅན་ཞེས་བཏགས་ཤིང་། དེས་སྡུག་བསྔལ་བ་ལ་སྙིང་རྗེ་བསྐྱེད་དོ། །སྙིང་རྗེ་དེས་སྦྱིན་པ་ལ་སོགས་པ་ལ་སློབ་བོ། །དེ་ལ་གོམས་པས་སེམས་ཅན་ཞེས་བྱ་བ་ནི་དང་པོ་ཉིད་ནས་མེད་ཀྱི། བློ་བུར་དུ་བཏགས་པ་ཟད་དོ། །གཞན་དུ་ན་ཕུང་པོ་དང་ཁམས་དང་སྐྱེ་མཆེད་ཙམ་ཞིག་ལས་འདི་ན་ཅི་ཡང་མེད་དོ་སྙམ་དུ་རྟོག་པ་དང་། ཡང་འདི་དག་ནི་རང་གི་སེམས་འབའ་ཞིག་ཏུ་ཟད་ཀྱི་གཞན་འདི་ན་ཅི་ཡང་མེད་དོ་སྙམ་རྟོག་ནས། དེས་སྡུག་བསྔལ་བ་རྣམས་ལ་སྙིང་རྗེ་སྐྱེའོ། །དེ་སྐྱེས་པས་སྦྱིན་པ་ལ་སོགས་པ་ལ་འཇུག་པ་ཡིན་ནོ། །དམིགས་པ་མེད་པའི་རིམ་པ་ནི། དོན་དམ་པ་དང་ཀུན་རྫོབ་ཀྱི་བདེན་པ་རྣམས་དེ་ཁོ་ན་ཉིད་རོ་གཅིག་ཏུ་རྟོགས་ཀྱང་ཐབས་རྣམ་པ་སྣ་ཚོགས་ཀྱིས་ཐེག་པ་གསུམ་གང་རིགས་རིགས་སུ་སེམས་ཅན་རྣམས་ཡོངས་སུ་སྨིན་པར་བྱེད་དོ། །དེ་བཞིན་བློ་གྲོས་མི་ཟད་པའི་མདོ་འགྲེལ་ལས། སྔར་བསྟན་པ་ལྟར་སྤྱོད་ལམ་ཐམས་ཅད་དུ་མཉམ་པར་གཞག་པ་ཡིན་ཡང་། སེམས་ཅན་ཡོངས་སུ་སྨིན་པར་བྱ་བའི་ཆེད་དུ་རྒྱལ་རིགས་ལ་སོགས་པ་འཇིག་རྟེན་ཐམས་ཅད་ཀྱི་རྗེས་སུ་བསླེགས་ཏེ། དེ་

དག་དང་མཐུན་པར་སྤྱོད་པའི་ཐབས་མཁས་པ་དང་ཡང་ལྡན་ལ། ཤེས་རབ་ཀྱིས་ཟིན་པས་དེ་དག་གི་ནང་ན་གནས་ཀྱང་འཇིག་རྟེན་དང་མ་འདྲེས་པ་ཡིན་ནོ། །ཇི་ལྟར་མ་འདྲེས་ཞེ་ན། འཇིག་རྟེན་གྱི་ཆོས་བརྒྱད་ལས་འདས་པ་ཉོན་མོངས་པ་ཐམས་ཅད་དང་མ་འདྲེས་པ་ཞེས་གསུངས་པ་དེ་ཡིན་ནོ། །གཉིས་པ་གཞུང་གི་དོན་ནི། སྦྱིན་པའི་ཆེད་དུ་བྱ་བ། སེམས་ཅན་ཀུན་ལ་སྨན་སླད་དུ། །མི་མཐུན་ཕྱོགས་སྤང་བ་ནི། སེར་སྣ་མ་མཆིས། མཐུན་ཕྱོགས་ལ་སློབ་པ་ནི། སྦྱིན་གཏོང་ཤོག །སྦྱིན་བྱ་ཟད་པར་མི་འགྱུར་བའི་ཕྱིར་རམ་འབྲས་བུ། དངོས་པོ་དངོས་པོ་མ་མཆིས་པས། །བདག་གི་ལོངས་སྤྱོད་ལྷུན་གྲུབ་ཤོག །ནམ་མཁའི་མཛོད་ཅེས་བྱ་བ་ཐོབ་པ། མཛོད་དེར་ཡང་གཏེར་མང་པོ་སྦྱངས་ནས་གནས་པ་ལྟ་བུ་མ་ཡིན་ཏེ། ཅི་འདོད་པ་ཐམས་ཅད་དེ་འཕྲུལ་དུ་ཕུན་སུམ་ཚོགས་པར་འབྱུང་བ་ཞིག་གོ །དེ་ནི་ལས་དང་པོ་པའི་དབང་དུ་བྱས་ལ། དངོས་པོ་ཐམས་ཅད་རྣམ་འཇིག་པའི། །སྦྱིན་པའི་ཕ་རོལ་ཕྱིན་རྫོགས་ཤོག །སྦྱིན་བྱ་སྦྱིན་པ་པོ། སྦྱིན་པའི་ཡུལ། སྦྱིན་པ་ཐམས་ཅད་ཀྱི་དམིགས་པ་ཉེ་བར་ཞི་བ་ལ་གནས་ནས། སྒྱུ་མའི་སྐྱེས་བུ་ལྟ་བུར་སྦྱིན་པ། དེ་ནི་འཇིག་རྟེན་ལས་འདས་པ་ཡིན་པས། དེ་ལྟར་ནུས་པ་ཕྱིན་ནས་སྦྱིན་པས་ཕ་རོལ་ཏུ་ཕྱིན་པའི་མིང་ཐོབ་པའོ། །དེ་ནི་དཱ་ན་དབུལ་བ་འདོར་བས་སྦྱིན་པའོ། །དེའི་མཚན་ཉིད་ཡོངས་སུ་གཏོང་བས། རྒྱས་པར་ན་དེ་ཉིད་ཀྱང་ཕ་རོལ་ཏུ་ཕྱིན་པ་དྲུག་ཏུ་ཕྱེ་སྟེ་གསུངས་པའོ། །ཁྲིམས་ཀྱི་ཚུལ་ཁྲིམས། ཁྲིམས་ཀྱི་ཞེས་པ་སངས་རྒྱས་རྣམས་ཀྱིས་བཅས་པ་སྟེ། ཉེས་སྤྱོད་སྡོམ་པ་སོ་སོ་ཐར་པ་དང་། དགེ་བ་ཆོས་སྡུད་དང་། སེམས་ཅན་དོན་བྱེད་གསུམ་ཚང་བ་བྱང་ཆུབ་སེམས་ཀྱི་སྡོམ་པའོ། །དེ་ནི་ཤཱི་ལ་སྟེ། ཉོན་མོངས་པའི་གདུང་བ་ལས་བསིལ་བ་ཐོབ་པའི་ཕྱིར་དེ་ལ་ཚུལ་ཁྲིམས་ཞེས་བྱའོ། །མི་མཐུན་ཕྱོགས་སྤོང་བ། སྐྱོན་མེད་ཅིང་། ཚུལ་ཁྲིམས་འཆལ་པའི་སྐྱོན་མེད་པའོ། །མཐུན་ཕྱོགས། ཚུལ་ཁྲིམས་རྣམ་པར་དག་དང་ལྡན། །ཚུལ་ཁྲིམས་དེ། ཡན་ལག་དྲུག་དང་ལྡན་པར་སྟེ། སོ་སོ་ཐར་པའི་ཚུལ་ཁྲིམས་དང་ལྡན་པར་གནས་པ་དང་། བཅས་པའི་སྡོམ་པས་བསྡམས་

པ་དང་། ཚིག་ཕུན་སུམ་ཚོགས་པ་དང་། སྤྱོད་ཡུལ་ཕུན་སུམ་ཚོགས་པ་དང་། ཁ་ན་མ་ཐོ་བ་ཕྲ་རབ་ཙམ་ལའང་འཇིགས་པར་ལྟ་བ་དང་། བསླབ་པའི་གཞི་རྣམས་ཡང་དག་པར་བླངས་ཤིང་སློབ་པའོ། །དེ་ལྟར་ཡན་ལག་དྲུག་དང་ལྡན་པའི་ཚུལ་ཁྲིམས་ནི་ཚུལ་ཁྲིམས་ཀྱི་ཚོགས་སམ་ཚུལ་ཁྲིམས་ཀྱི་ཕུང་པོ་ཞེས་བྱ། རློམ་སེམས་མེད་པའི་ཚུལ་ཁྲིམས་ཀྱི། །ཚུལ་ཁྲིམས་ཕ་རོལ་ཕྱིན་རྫོགས་ཤོག །དང་པོར་ཚུལ་ཁྲིམས་ཡང་དག་པར་བླངས་པ་ནས་བརྩམས་ཏེ་ཐ་མ་རྣམ་པར་གྲོལ་བའི་ཡེ་ཤེས་ལ་ཐུག་གི་བར་དུ་རྡུལ་ཙམ་ཡང་ཉམས་པ་དང་གོད་པ་མེད་པ། དེ་ལྟར་ཉམས་པ་དང་གོད་པ་མེད་པས་ཚུལ་ཁྲིམས་མཐར་ཕྱིན་ཏེ་ཟག་མེད་པའི་ཚུལ་ཁྲིམས་ཀྱི་མཚན་ཉིད་དུ་གྱུར་པའི་ཚེ་ཚུལ་ཁྲིམས་ཀྱི་ཕུང་པོ་ཡོངས་སུ་རྫོགས་པ་སྟེ། དེས་ན་རློམ་སེམས་མེད་པ་དང་འཁོར་གསུམ་དུ་མི་རྟོག་པ་གཏན་གཅིག་པས་ཚུལ་ཁྲིམས་དེས་ཕ་རོལ་ཏུ་ཕྱིན་པའི་མིང་ཐོབ་བོ། །ས་འམ་ཡང་ན་ཆུ་འམ་མེ། །རླུང་གི་ཁམས་ལྟར་མི་གནས་ཤིང་། །བཟོད་པ། འབྱུང་བ་ཆེན་པོ་བཞི་ལ་ཁྲོ་བ་མི་གནས་ཏེ་སེམས་མེད་པའི་ཕྱིར་རོ། །དེ་དང་འཁོར་གསུམ་དུ་མི་རྟོག་པའང་མཚུངས་པས། ཀྵཱནྟི་ཁྲོ་བ་ཞི་བ་དེའི་ཆ་ནས་དེ་ལ་བཟོད་པ་ཞེས་བྱའོ། །མི་མཐུན་ཕྱོགས་སྤོང་བ། ཁྲོ་བ་མ་མཆིས་པས། །མཐུན་ཕྱོགས་ལ་སློབ་པ་ནི། བཟོད་པའི་ཕ་རོལ་ཕྱིན་རྫོགས་ཤོག །ཅེས་པ། དཀོན་མཆོག་བརྩེགས་པ་བྱང་ཆུབ་སེམས་དཔའི་སྡེ་སྣོད་ཀྱི་མདོ་ལས། ཁོང་ཁྲོ་བ་ཁོང་ཁྲོ་བ་ཞེས་བྱ་བ་ནི། བསྐལ་པ་བརྒྱ་སྟོང་དུ་བསྒྲུབས་པའི་དགེ་བའི་རྩ་བ་འཇོམས་པ་སྟེ་ཞེས་དང་། འཇམ་དཔལ་རྣམ་པར་རོལ་པའི་མདོ་ནས། ཁོང་ཁྲོ་བ། ཁྲོ་བ་ཞེས་བྱ་བ་ནི་བསྐལ་པ་བརྒྱར་བསགས་པའི་དགེ་བའི་རྩ་བ་འཇོམས་པ་སྟེ། ཞེས་གསུངས་པ་རྩ་བའི་ཉོན་མོངས་པ་དང་། ཉེ་བའི་ཉོན་མོངས་ཀྱི་དང་། ཡུལ་གྱི་ཁྱད་དུའང་ཤེས་པར་བྱའོ། །བརྩོན་འགྲུས་བརྩམས་པའི་བརྩོན་འགྲུས་ཀྱིས། །བརྟན་སྤྲོ། ཐེག་མཆོག་ལ་སྦྱོར་བས་བརྩོན་འགྲུས་དང་། བརྩམས་པ་དེའི་འབད་པ་དང་། བརྟན་ཞེས་པས་རྟག་སྦྱོར། སྤྲོ་ཞེས་པ་གུས་སྦྱོར། མི་མཐུན་ཕྱོགས་སྤོང་བ། ལེ་ལོ་མ་མཆིས་ཤིང་།

མཐུན་ཕྱོགས་ལ་སློབ་པ། སྟོབས་དང་ལྡན་པའི་ལུས་སེམས་ཀྱིས། །བརྩོན་འགྲུས་ཕ་རོལ་ཕྱིན་རྫོགས་ཤོག །གོ་ཆ་ཆེན་པོ་བགོས་པས་དང་། ངོམ་པ་མེད་པའི་ཕྱིར་མི་མཐུན་ཕྱོགས་ཀྱིས་བརྫི་བ་མི་ནུས་པས་སྟོབས་ལྡན་ཅི་ཙམ་འབད་ཀྱང་ངལ་དང་སྐྱོ་བ་སྒྱིད་ལུག་པ་མེད་པའི་ཐ་ཚིག་གོ །ཕ་རོལ་ཕྱིན་ཚུལ་ནི་འདྲའོ། །ཧྲུ་ན་བསམ་པ་གཏན་པོས་བསམ་གཏན། དེ་ཡང་། སྒྱུ་མ་ལྟ་བུའི་ཏིང་འཛིན་དང་། །དེ་ནི་ལང་ཀར་གཤེགས་པ་ལས། སྙིང་རྗེ་ཆེན་པོ་དང་ཐབས་ལ་མཁས་པ་ལྡན་གྱིས་གྲུབ་པའི་སྦྱོར་བ་དང་། སེམས་ཅན་གྱི་ཁམས་ཐམས་ཅད་སྒྱུ་མ་དང་གཟུགས་བརྙན་དང་། མཉམ་པ་ཉིད་དང་། རྐྱེན་གྱིས་མ་བསྐུམས་པ་དང་། ཕྱི་ནང་གི་ཡུལ་རྣམ་པར་དབེན་པ་དང་། སེམས་ཕྱི་རོལ་དུ་བལྟ་བ་བས་མཚན་མ་མེད་པའི་བྱིན་གྱིས་བརླབས་པ་དང་ལྡན་པ་རྣམས། རིམ་གྱིས་སའི་རིམ་པའི་ཏིང་ངེ་འཛིན་ཡུལ་ལ་རྗེས་སུ་འཇུག་པ་དང་། ཁམས་གསུམ་དག་གི་སེམས་སྒྱུ་མར་ཤིན་ཏུ་མོས་པས་རབ་ཏུ་སྒོམ་པ་སྒྱུ་མ་ལྟ་བུའི་ཏིང་ངེ་འཛིན་རབ་ཏུ་ཐོབ་པར་འགྱུར་རོ། །ཞེས་གཟུགས་ནས་རྣམ་པ་ཐམས་ཅད་མཁྱེན་པའི་བར་དུ་བཞག་པའི་ཆོས་ཐམས་ཅད་རྨི་ལམ་ལྟ་བུ་སྒྱུ་མ་ལྟ་བུར་མངོན་སུམ་གྱི་ལྟ་བས་ཏིང་ངེ་འཛིན་དེ་སྒྱུ་མ་ལྟ་བུའོ། །དཔའ་བར་འགྲོ་བའི་ཏིང་འཛིན་དང་། དཔའ་བར་འགྲོ་བའི་ཏིང་ངེ་འཛིན་གྱི་མདོ་ལས། གང་གི་དཔའ་བར་འགྲོ་བའི་ཏིང་ངེ་འཛིན་འདི་ཐོབ་པའི་སྐྱེས་བུ་དམ་པ་འདི་དག་ནི། སངས་རྒྱས་ཐམས་ཅད་ཀྱི་ཡུལ་དུ་མཆིས་པ་ལགས་སོ། །རང་དབང་གི་ཡེ་ཤེས་ལ་དབང་བསྒྱིད་པ་ལགས་སོ་ཞེས་དང་། རིགས་ཀྱི་བུ་དག་དེ་ལྟ་བས་ན་ངེས་པར་འབྱུང་བའི་ལམ་ཐམས་ཅད་དུ་ངེས་པར་འབྱུང་བར་འདོད་པའི་བྱང་ཆུབ་སེམས་དཔའ་སྒོམ་སེམས་ཐམས་ཅད་མེད་པའི་ཕྱིར་དཔའ་བར་འགྲོ་བའི་ཏིང་ངེ་འཛིན་ལ་བསླབ་པར་བྱའོ། །ཞེས་གསུངས་ལ། དམག་དཔོན་དཔའ་བོ་དང་འདྲ་བར་སྤང་བྱ་ཐམས་ཅད་ཐོགས་པ་མེད་པར་འཇོམས་པའི་ཏིང་ངེ་འཛིན་ནི་དཔའ་བར་འགྲོ་བར་ཞེས་བྱའོ། །རྡོ་རྗེ་ལྟ་བུའི་ཏིང་འཛིན་གྱིས། །བསམ་གཏན་ཕ་རོལ་ཕྱིན་རྫོགས་ཤོག །ཡང་གཤེགས་ལས། བློ་གྲོས་ཆེན་པོ་དེ་ལྟ་བས་ན། བདག་གི་

སེམས་སྣང་བ་མེད་པ་ཙམ་ལ་འཇུག་པས་ཤེས་རབ་ཀྱི་ཕ་རོལ་ཏུ་ཕྱིན་པ་ལ་གནས་པ་རྗེས་སུ་ཐོབ་པ་སྐྱེ་བ་དང་། བྱ་བ་དང་བྲལ་བའི་བྱང་ཆུབ་སེམས་དཔའ་རྣམས་ཏིང་ངེ་འཛིན་རྡོ་རྗེའི་གཟུགས་ལྟ་བུ་དེ་བཞིན་གཤེགས་པའི་སྐུའི་རྗེས་སུ་སོང་བ། དེ་བཞིན་ཉིད་ཀྱི་སྤྲུལ་པ་དང་ལྡན་པའི་སྟོབས་དང་། མངོན་པར་ཤེས་པ་དང་། དབང་དང་། སྙིང་བརྩེ་བ་དང་། སྙིང་རྗེ་དང་ཐབས་ཀྱིས་བརྒྱན་པ་དང་། སངས་རྒྱས་ཐམས་ཅད་ཀྱི་ཞིང་གི་མུ་སྟེགས་ཅན་གྱི་གནས་སུ་ཉེ་བར་འགྲོ་བའི་སེམས་དང་ཡིད་དང་། ཡིད་ཀྱི་རྣམ་པར་ཤེས་པ་དང་བྲལ་ནས་རིམ་གྱིས་གནས་འཕོས་པའི་དེ་བཞིན་གཤེགས་པའི་སྐུ་ཐོབ་པར་འགྱུར་རོ། །བློ་གྲོས་ཆེན་པོ་དེ་ལྟ་བས་ན་བྱང་ཆུབ་སེམས་དཔའ་སེམས་དཔའ་ཆེན་པོ་དེ་བཞིན་གཤེགས་པའི་སྐུའི་རྗེས་སུ་འབྲང་བ་རབ་ཏུ་ཐོབ་པ་རྣམས་ཀྱི་ཕུང་པོ་ཁམས་དང་སྐྱེ་མཆེད་དང་སེམས་དང་རྒྱུ་དང་བྱ་བ་དང་ལྡན་པ་དང་། སྐྱེ་བ་དང་གནས་པ་དང་འཇིག་པའི་རྣམ་པར་རྟོག་པ་སྤྲོས་པ་དང་བྲལ་བ་སེམས་ཅན་གྱི་རྗེས་སུ་འབྲང་བར་བྱའོ། །ཞེས་གསུངས་པས་སྒྲིབ་པ་ཐམས་ཅད་འཇོམས་པའི་ཏིང་ངེ་འཛིན་དེ་ལ་རྡོ་རྗེ་ལྟ་བུའི་ཏིང་ངེ་འཛིན་ཞེས་བྱའོ། ༑ཤེས་རབ་ནི་པྲཛྙཱ་ཏེ། ཆོས་རབ་ཏུ་རྣམ་འབྱེད་པའི་བློ་དོན་དམ་པ་ཤེས་པའི་ཆ་དེ་ལ་བྱ་སྟེ། དེའི་ཆ་འགའ་ཞིག་ལ་ནི་ཐབས། སྟོབས། སྨོན་ལམ། ཡེ་ཤེས་འབྱེད་པ་ཡིན་ནོ། །རྣམ་པར་ཐར་པའི་སྒོ་གསུམ་དང་། སྟོང་ཉིད་ཀྱི་རྣམ་པར་ཐར་པ་དང་། མཚན་མ་མེད་པའི། སྨོན་པ་མེད་པའི་རྣམ་པར་ཐར་པ་དང་། དུས་གསུམ་མཉམ་པ་ཉིད་དང་། དུས་གསུམ་མཉམ་པ་ནི། དོན་ལ་དུས་མེད་དུ་གོ་བར་བྱེད་པ་ཡིན་ལ། ཡང་། རིག་གསུམ་མངོན་སུམ་བགྱིས་པ་ཡིས། ༑ཤེས་རབ་ཕ་རོལ་ཕྱིན་ཐོབ་ཤོག །ཡང་སྣང་དོར་དུས་གསུམ་ལ་བལྟོས་ནས་རིག་པ་གསུམ་འཇོག་པ་སྟེ། མི་འམ་ཅིའི་རྒྱལ་པོ་ལྗོན་པས་ཞུས་པའི་མདོ་ལས། ཡང་དག་པར་རྫོགས་པའི་སངས་རྒྱས་ནི་ཐོགས་པ་མེད་པའི་ཡེ་ཤེས་མཐོང་བ་དང་ལྡན་ནོ། །དེ་ཅིའི་ཕྱིར་ཞེས་ན། རིགས་ཀྱི་བུ་གང་སེམས་ཅན་ཐམས་ཅད་ཀྱི་འདས་པའི་སེམས་ཀྱི་རྒྱུད་ཟད་པ་དང་འགགས་པ་དང་བྲལ་བ་དང་རྣམ་པར་གྱུར་པ་ཐམས་ཅད་ནི་དེ་བཞིན་

གཤེགས་པས་རབ་ཏུ་མཁྱེན་ཏེ། རྒྱུ་གང་དག་ལས་སེམས་ཀྱི་རྒྱུད་དེ་དག་བྱུང་བ་དང་། རྒྱུ་གང་དག་མེད་པས་ཟད་ཅིང་བྲལ་བར་བསྟན་པ་དང་། དགེ་བའམ་མི་དགེ་བའམ། ལུང་དུ་བསྟན་པའམ། མ་བསྟན་པ་དེ་དག་ཐམས་ཅད་རྣམ་པ་དང་བཅས། གཞི་དང་བཅས། གཏན་ཚིག་དང་བཅས་པ་དེ་བཞིན་གཤེགས་པས་རབ་ཏུ་མཁྱེན་ཏོ། །ད་ལྟར་བྱུང་བའི་སེམས་ཅན་ཐམས་ཅད་ཀྱི་སེམས་ཀྱི་རྒྱུད་བྱུང་བ་དགེ་བའམ་མི་དགེའམ། ལུང་དུ་བསྟན་པའམ་ལུང་དུ་མ་བསྟན་པ་ཡང་རུང་སྟེ། སེམས་གང་གི་འོག་ཏུ་སེམས་གང་འབྱུང་བ་དེ་དག་ཐམས་ཅད་ཀྱང་རྣམ་པ་དང་བཅས་པ། ཡུལ་དང་ཕྱོགས་དང་བཅས། གཞི་ཅི་ལས་གྱུར་པ་དང་བཅས་པ་དེ་བཞིན་གཤེགས་པས་རབ་ཏུ་ཤེས་སོ། །གང་མ་འོངས་པའི་སེམས་ཅན་ཐམས་ཅད་ཀྱི་སེམས་ཀྱི་རྒྱུད་དང་། སེམས་ལས་བྱུང་བའི་ཚོས་དགེའམ་མི་དགེའམ་ལུང་དུ་བསྟན་པའམ་ལུང་དུ་མ་བསྟན་པ་ཡང་རུང་ཏེ། སེམས་གང་གི་འོག་ཏུ་སེམས་གང་འབྱུང་བར་གྱུར་པ་དེ་དག་ཐམས་ཅད་ཀྱང་། རྣམ་པ་དང་བཅས་ཡུལ་དང་ཕྱོགས་དང་བཅས། གཞི་ཅི་ལས་གྱུར་པ་དང་བཅས་པར་དེ་བཞིན་གཤེགས་པས་རབ་ཏུ་ཤེས་སོ། །རིགས་ཀྱི་བུ་དེ་ལྟར་ན་དེ་བཞིན་གཤེགས་པ་དགྲ་བཅོམ་པ་ཡང་དག་པ་རྫོགས་པའི་སངས་རྒྱས་ནི་ཐོགས་པ་མེད་པའི་ཡེ་ཤེས་དང་ནི་ལྡན་པ་ཡིན་ནོ་ཞེས་གསུངས་སོ། །འདིར་བསམ་གཏན་དང་ཤེས་རབ་གཉིས་ལ་མི་མཐུན་ཕྱོགས་སྤོང་བ་མ་བཤད་པ་ནི་སྲིད་ཞི་མཉམ་ཉིད་དུ་འཁྲེར་བ་ཡིན་པས་དེར་སྤང་བླང་མེད་པ་ཤེས་པར་བྱའི་ཕྱིར་རོ། །སོ་སོ་སྐྱེ་བོའི་གནས་སྐབས་ན་ནི་བསམ་གཏན་དེ་སེམས་རྩེ་གཅིག་པའི་ཏིང་ངེ་འཛིན་དེའི་མི་མཐུན་ཕྱོགས་སྤོང་རྒྱུ་རྣམ་པར་གཡེང་བ། ཤེས་རབ་ནི་དོན་བཞིན་དུ་རྣམ་པར་འབྱེད་པ་ཡིན་ལ། མི་མཐུན་ཕྱོགས་ནི་འཆལ་བའི་ཤེས་རབ་བོ། །གསུམ་པ་འགྲུབ་པའི་སྤྱོད་པ་ནི། གནས་སྐབས་དང་མཐར་ཐུག་གཉིས་ལས། དང་པོ་ནི། སངས་རྒྱས་ཀུན་གྱིས་བསྔགས་པ་དང་། །སྒོམ་པའི་ལམ་དུ་ཡིན་ལ། འོད་དང་གཟི་བརྗིད་འབར་བ་དང་། །ཕྱིར་བྱང་ཆུབ་སེམས་དཔའི་ཡོན་ཏན་མཐའ་ཡས་པ་ཐོབ་པ་དང་། ཁྱད་པར་ས་བཅུ་པར་འོད་

གསལ་ཆེན་པོའི་དབང་བསྐུར་བ་ཐོབ་པས་རྒྱལ་ཚབ་ཏུ་བཀོད་པ་ཐོན་ནོ། །མཐར་ཐུག་ནི། བྱང་ཆུབ་སེམས་དཔའི་བརྩོན་འགྲུས་ཀྱི། །གྲངས་མེད་གསུམ་མམ་སུམ་ཅུ་རྩ་གཉིས་སམ་མཐའ་ཡས་པར་གདུལ་བྱ་སྨིན་པ་དང་སྨོན་ལམ་རྫོགས་པར་བྱ་བ་དང་། ཞིང་སྦྱོང་བ་ལ་འབད་པས། བདག་གི་བསམ་པ་རྫོགས་གྱུར་ཅིག །སྐུ་གསུམ་མཛད་པ་དང་བཅས་པར་སངས་རྒྱ་བར་ཤོག་ཅིག་པའོ། །མཇུག་སྡུད་ནི། དེ་ལྟར་སྤྱོད་པ་སྤྱོད་གྱུར་ཅིང་། །སྨོན་ལམ་བཏབ་པ་དང་མཐུན་པར་སྤྱོད་པས། བྱམས་པ་གྲགས་དང་ལྡན་པ་ཡི། །ཕ་རོལ་ཕྱིན་དྲུག་རྫོགས་བགྱིས་ནས། །ས་བཅུ་པོ་ལ་རབ་ཏུ་གནས། །བྱང་ཆུབ་ཏུ་སེམས་བསྐྱེད་པ་དང་པོ་ནས་བརྩམས་ཏེ་ཕ་རོལ་ཏུ་ཕྱིན་པ་དྲུག་རིམ་བཞིན་གྱིས་ས་བཅུ་རིམ་པས་བགྲོད་པར་བསྟན་ལ། རྗེ་བཙུན་འདིས་བདག་ཅག་གི་སྟོན་པ་བཞིན་དབུ་ལ་སོགས་པ་སྦྱིན་པའི་དགའ་བ་མ་མཛད་པར་ཐབས་མཁས་པས་བདེ་བས་བྱང་ཆུབ་བསྒྲུབས་སོ་ཞེས་འབྱུང་ངོ་། །རིང་བསམས་སྙན་ངག་འགའ་ཞིག་སྦྱར་ཐུབ་པས། །བློ་གྲོས་ཅན་རློམ་སྤོབས་པའི་གོ་བགགས་འདིས། །རིག་གནས་ཀུན་ཤེས་གཞུང་བརྒྱའི་དོན་འགྲེལ་མཁན། །སྲིད་པའི་རྣ་བར་ཤོང་ཐབས་ཅང་ཡོད་དམ། །དགེ་བ་དགའ་ལྡན་བདག་པོའི་ལུང་། །འཛིག་རྟེན་ཀུན་ཏུ་བསྒྱུར་ནས་སུ། །ཐུབ་པའི་རྒྱལ་སྲིད་ཡངས་པ་ལས། །ཆེས་ཡངས་འགྱུར་བའི་ཕྱིར་བསྔོའོ། །ཅེས་པས་འཛིག་ལྷ་ལྡན་སྐྱེས་ཀྱི་བད་པདྨ་དཀར་པོས་བྱམས་པ་ཆེན་པོའི་ཆོས་གླིང་དུ་སྦྱར་བའི་ཡི་གེ་པ་རྟོགས་ལྡན་གྲོ་མོ་པའོ།། །།མངྒ་ལམ།།

INDEX

a commentary on Maitreya's prayer . . . . iii, xiv
a single bundle 3
a yak and its tail 15
abiding in emptiness 10
abiding within discipline 9
about the author of the commentary . . . . iii, xv
about the commentary . . . iii, xvi
about The Noble Great Stack of Jewels . . . . iii, vi
absence of old age and death 30, 51, 58
absorption . . . 12, 16, 26, 33, 54, 77, 86, 88, 90
absorptions 12, 13
accumulation of merit . . . 30, 51, 60, 61, 69
accumulation of wisdom 61
acting for the sake of sentient beings 82
actual meaning of "noble" vi
adventitious 62, 63, 62, 96
affliction 59, 75, 84, 96, 99
afflictions 14, 21, 23, 34, 63, 78, 84, 96, 109
āgama . . . . viii, 59, 97
aggregate of discipline 83
aggregate of formatives 58
aggression 32-34, 54, 83, 84
Akaniṣhṭha 56
alertness 12, 96, 97, 110
all-knowing . iv, vi, xv-xvii, xx, 5, 30, 49, 51, 55, 61, 62, 97
all-knowing of enlightenment 61
All-Knowing One 97
All-Knowing Padma Karpo . . iv, vi, xv-xvii, 49, 55
Ālokavikrīditābhijñāna . . . 18-20, 24
Amogharāja 5
Ānanda . . xi, 4, 5, 17, 18, 24-29, 33-36, 55
appropriation 46, 47, 97
arhat 6, 7, 18, 19, 24, 35, 42, 90, 102
armoured with the great armour 85
arousing of mind 67
arousing the mind 97
Āryadeva 59

as an illusory being 81
Asaṅga . . . . xvii, 61, 68
ascertained the dharma of emptiness 9
assembly of bodhisatvas 57
asuras 36, 47
at the time of the Buddha ix
Aśhvajit 5
authoritative statement . . . iii, iv, viii, ix, 1, 3, 6, 39, 41, 42, 71, 97
Avalokiteśhvara 5
avarice 32, 53, 80
Avataṃsaka Sūtra xiii
awareness 75, 98, 101, 118
āyatana of infinite consciousness 13
āyatana of infinite space 13
āyatana of nothing at all 13
bad māra hordes 16
bad migrations 7-14, 30, 51, 57, 58
bad tīrthika groups 16
Bande Yeshe De 37, 48
becoming . . xvi, xviii, 22, 31, 46, 47, 52, 56, 65-67, 90, 93, 94, 98, 101
beginning bodhisatva 79
best of bipeds 31, 52, 66
bhadanta 17
Bhadrau 18-20
Bhadrika 5
bhagavan . . . 4-8, 14, 17-19, 24, 29, 35, 36, 41-43, 47
Birth Tales xi
birth, aging, and death 23
blazing perseverance 25, 26
bliss 11-13, 27, 28, 98, 117
bliss of mind 13
bloated . . . . xvi, 9, 22, 93
bloated learned people . . xvi, 93
blood 25, 27
bodhichitta 8, 98, 102, 114
bodhisatva . . . v, x-xiv, xvi, 4-14, 17, 18, 20, 24, 25, 29, 33, 34, 36, 41-47, 54-56, 59, 63, 65, 67, 70, 76, 79, 81, 82, 85, 87, 88, 91, 92, 98, 99, 102, 114
bodhisatva conduct 59, 63
bodhisatva mahāsattva . . . x, 5-8, 14, 17, 20, 24, 25, 29, 33, 34, 42-47, 56, 98, 99
bodhisatva mahāsattva Maitreya . . x, 6-8, 14, 17, 24, 25, 29, 33, 34, 42, 43, 47, 56
bodhisatva mahāsattva who has skilful means 45
bodhisatva mahāsattvas . . . 5, 65, 88, 99
bodhisatva vehicle 7
bodhisatva vows 82
bodhisatvas . . . . xiii, 5, 6, 13, 30, 31, 41, 47, 51, 52, 57, 61-63, 65, 88, 91, 99
bodhi-tree 16
brahman boy called Bhadrau . 18
buddha . . vii-xiii, xvi, xvii, 4, 6, 7, 11-24, 35, 36, 41, 42, 44, 46, 55-57, 61-63, 66, 70, 78, 82, 89-93, 96, 98, 99, 101-103, 106-109, 111, 114-117
buddha in direct perception . 70
Buddha Śhākyamuni x
buddhas . . xiii, 20, 30-33, 51-54, 56-58, 60, 64-68, 73, 87, 88, 91, 94
Buddhist sūtras vi
bundles 3

calm-abiding 8, 11
Capable One . . . 21, 94, 99, 111
causes and conditions 71
child-killing crocodile 4
clinging 99, 100
community of monks 4, 41
compassion 9, 27, 28, 34, 35, 44, 45, 68, 77, 79, 86, 88
compassion apprehending fiction 68
complete discernment 23
complete emancipation . . 33, 54, 58, 89
complete purity . . 32, 53, 59, 82, 100
completed buddhas . . 31, 53, 67
concentration 11-14, 32, 33, 54, 69, 75, 86-90, 96
concept token 75, 76, 100
concept tokens 75, 87, 100
conducive side . . . 80, 82, 84, 85, 90, 91
conduct of enlightenment . . . 31, 53, 67
confession 108
confusion . . xx, 10, 62, 100, 114
confusion of others 10
conquerors 7, 55, 59, 64
consciousness 13, 46, 72, 75, 77, 87, 88, 98, 101, 105, 116
constituents, conducts, applications, and intentions 22
corrected editions of the two sūtras xix
corrected electronic editions . xix
countless great aeons 91
country of Varga 4
co-emergent self 73
cyclic existence 100, 101, 106, 111
dāna 5
Dāna Kāśhyapa 5
Dānaśhīla 48
dazzling, striking, and conspicuous 19
defeated the attacking māras 42, 44, 47
definite arising 88
definite release 88
definitive meaning 56-58, 62, 111
degrading companions 7-14
Derge edition . . . . xix, 65-67
Descent into Laṅka 76, 86, 88
Descent into Laṅka Sūtra . . 86, 88
dharma enumerations . iv, vii, 1, 3, 36, 39, 41
Dharma Sanctuary of Great Maitreya 94
dharmadhātu 77, 101
dharmakāya . . 92, 101, 105, 107
dharmas . . . iv, xvi, xvii, 7-14, 16, 25, 26, 35, 39, 41-43, 47, 59, 63, 69, 70, 80, 82, 87, 89, 90, 101, 117
dharmatā 101
dhyāna 12, 16
diacritical marks . . . . ii, xxi
dimensionality 72
discipline . . 9, 15, 17, 22, 25, 32, 53, 78, 82, 83
discipline has six aspects 82
discipline without conceit . . . 32, 53, 83
discursive thought 89, 102
disintegration of all references 72
distraction 75, 91, 97
divine doctor 55
divine wheel 21
Dromo . . . . xvi, 94

Drukchen Padma Karpo's Collected Works on Mahāmudrā 121
Drukpa Kagyu tradition xv
dualistic mind of saṃsāra ... 88
duḥkha 117
eight worldly dharmas 80
Eightfold Path of the Noble Ones 11
eighty excellent insignia 19
elaboration 102
electronic editions ..... xix, 122
electronic texts 122, 123
emptiness .... xiv, xvii, xxi, 9, 10, 26, 71, 72, 74-76, 81, 89, 102, 109, 121
emptiness of the three spheres 81
empty phenomena 32, 53, 72, 74
empty superfact 89
engaged perseverance 85
enlightenment .. vii, x-xii, xiv, 4, 7-16, 22, 24-31, 33, 34, 42-45, 47, 51-53, 55, 57, 58, 61-68, 77, 78, 88, 92, 94, 97-99, 102, 103, 105-108, 110, 114, 116, 117
enlightenment mind .. 8, 30, 51, 57, 64, 68, 77, 97, 98, 102, 103, 114
entirely ripen sentient beings 79
entity .. 16, 62, 71, 73, 103, 116
equality of becoming and peace 90
equality of the three times ... 33, 54, 89
equipoise and post-attainment 103, 111
essential character of all phenomena 42, 44, 47
evil . 12, 16, 30, 51, 52, 58-60, 64
evil deeds . 16, 30, 51, 58, 60, 64
exaggeration 103
exaggerations 71
examination and analysis 12
explanation of emptiness xiv
expressions 74, 103
extra-perceptions .... xi, 4, 5, 24, 25, 31, 53, 57, 68, 69, 88
extremes of action 11
eyes 15, 25, 28, 29
fact .. xvi, 20, 64, 72, 75, 99, 100, 104-109, 113, 115, 116
fictional 45, 79, 97, 104
fictional and superfactual ... 45, 104
fictional truth 104
field, field realm 105
fields of the ten directions ... 30, 52, 64
fifth world-leading buddha .. xiii
five aggregates 46, 94
Five Dharmas of Maitreya .. xvi, xvii
five dregs 34
five important prayers of the Great Vehicle .... iii, xii
five mental events 59
five root thoughts 59
Flower ..... xiii, 19, 27, 28, 101
Flower Ornament xiii
forbearance 20, 24, 74, 76
force of complete rejection .. 60
force of fully performing of the antidote 60
force of reliance 60
force of turning away from repeating the bad action ... 60
formatives 46, 58
forty-first chapter ... x-xii, 1, 3, 36, 51

forty-nine chapters . . . vi, vii, ix
forty-second chapter . . . iv, x-xii, 39, 47
four great elements 84
four types of force 60
fourth aggregate 58
fourth Drukchen xv
free from anger 10
free from desire 10
free from stupidity 10
function of prajñā 11
Gaṇḍavyūha Sūtra xiii
Gampopa's Mahāmudrā, The Five-Part Mahāmudrā of the Kagyus 121
gandharvas 36, 47
garbha 62, 115
gathering virtuous dharmas . . 82
Gavampati 5
Gaya Kāśhyapa 5
generosity 15, 17, 22, 32, 53, 71, 77-82, 93
Giver of All Wealth 27
gods and men 7, 18, 36, 58
gods and men, asuras, and gandharvas 36
gods who could be taught dharma 36
Going Like A Hero Concentration . . 32, 54, 87, 88
Going Like A Hero Concentration Sūtra 87
good age of one thousand and two buddhas xiii
grammar texts 120
grasped-at 72, 75, 105
grasped-at and grasping . . 72, 75, 105
great bodhisatva . . . . . v, x, 41, 56
great bodhisatvas xiii
great compassion . . 9, 34, 35, 86
great drum of dharma 31, 52, 65
great elder hearers 4
Great Kāśhyapa 5
Great Maudgalyayāna 5
great ṛiṣhis 32, 53, 73
Great Soul 23
Great Vehicle . . . iii, v, vi, xii-xiv, 3, 41, 42, 56, 67, 68, 74, 76-78, 85, 102, 103, 106, 109, 114, 121
Great Vehicle sūtra . . . vi, 3, 41, 68, 74, 77, 78
half a bundle 41
hearing, contemplating, and meditating 70
heartfelt love for the world . . . 7
higher strata 30, 51, 58, 61
highest bodhisatva levels 99
hostile to 34
Illuminator Tibetan-English Dictionary 117, 120, 123
Illusion-Like Concentration 32, 54, 86, 87
independent wisdom 87
India . . . . ix, xvii, 14, 35, 66, 99, 106, 109, 113
Indian Buddhist texts 3
Indian preceptors 37, 48, 54
Inexhaustible Intellect Sūtra . . . 79
infinite good qualities 91
insight 8, 114, 117
inspired perseverance 85
irreversibility 42
irreversible from unsurpassed, truly complete enlightenment 42, 43, 47
Jinamitra 37, 48, 54
joy 10, 12, 14, 27

Kagyu . . . . xv, 112, 119, 120
kalpa 18, 25
Kangyur . . . . xix, 153
Kauṇḍinya 5
kāya 106
kāyas 92, 107
king of mountains Sumeru 19, 29
knower of the world 18
knowledge of all . . . ix, 61, 77, 87
knowledge of superficies 61
knowledge of the path 61
knowledgeability . 7, 17, 18, 108
lax prajñā 91
lay aside . 30, 51, 52, 60, 64, 108
lay aside every evil . . . 30, 52, 64
laying aside 60, 108, 109
Lesser Vehicle . . vi, 67, 106, 109
Lesser Vehicle sūtra vi
levels . . . x, xv, 31, 36, 52, 61, 65, 78, 86, 89, 92, 99, 101, 102, 112, 120
lion roaring in the jungle . . . 21
Lotsāwa Bandhe Yeshe 54
love for sentient beings 31, 52, 66
loving kindness . . 33, 44, 45, 54, 55, 92
luminosity 75, 76, 91, 109
luminosity is the nature of mind 75
lung 71, 97
Mahāmati 88
Mahānāma 5
Mahāsthāmaprāpta 5
Maitreya . . ii-xi, xiii, xiv, xvi, xvii, xix, 5-14, 17, 18, 24, 25, 29, 33, 34, 36, 41-47, 51, 55, 56, 62, 67, 68, 91-94, 112
Maitreya the guardian 55
Maitreya's prayer . . . iii-v, xi, xii, xiv, xv, xvii, xviii, 49, 51, 55
Maitriya 1, 3, 39
major marks 21
manifest complete buddhahood 7-14, 24-26, 33, 34, 77
Mañjuśhrī . . . . xiii, xiv, 5, 84
Mañjuśhrī's Prayer xii
māra 16, 42, 109
māras 31, 42, 44, 47, 52, 65
māras with their regiments . . 31, 52, 65
marrow 25, 27-29
master of the tenth level 91
meritorious karma 60
merits 30, 52, 64, 66, 69
Meru 5
migrator 20, 31, 53, 67, 109
migrator sentient beings 31, 53, 67
migrators . . . 20, 22, 23, 62, 110
mind . . . . vi, viii, xi, xiv, xvii, 6, 8, 11-13, 18-20, 22, 23, 25-28, 30-32, 43-45, 47, 51, 52, 54, 56-60, 62-64, 66-69, 71, 72, 74-79, 84-90, 92, 93, 96-118
Mind Only 74, 76, 77, 105, 106, 112
mindfulness . . 10-13, 96, 97, 110
mindness 110
Mind-Only . . . . xvii, 88
miraculous powers 20, 24
mire of desire 31, 52, 66
Mṛigaśhīr 5
monk 17, 119
Moonlight 28
most senior bodhisatva . . xii, xiii
muni 99, 111
my own all-knowing . 30, 51, 61

Nāḍī Kāśhyapa 5
Nāgārjuna . . . . xiv, 121
Nanda 5
nature of dharmas 70
nirmāṇakāya 20, 56, 92, 94, 105, 107
nirvāṇa . . . 46, 58, 59, 66, 81, 94, 105, 107
no time in superfact 89
noble one . . . . iv, vii, xvii, 36, 47, 55, 56, 61, 105, 111, 121
non-bliss of mind 13
non-conducive side . . 80, 82, 84, 85, 90, 91
non-dwelling nirvāṇa 58
non-virtue 58, 90, 99
not slip back . . . . . xii, 42, 43, 47
Nyagrodha tree 19
ocean of becoming . . . 31, 52, 67
offering to the buddhas 30, 52, 64
ṛiṣhis 30, 32, 51, 53, 57, 73
ṛiṣhis having the god's eye . . . 30, 51, 57
one life hindering 56
ordinary beings 7, 67, 111
Ornament of Manifest Realization 61
Ornament of the Great Vehicle Sūtra Section 68, 74, 77, 78
Other Emptiness xvii, xxi, 75, 121
outflow 111
Padma Karpo . . i, ii, iv, vi, x, xiv-xxii, 14, 49, 55, 81, 82, 92-94, 115, 117, 119-121
Padma Karpo's Collected Works . . . . xx, 121
pāramitā . . 15, 16, 32, 33, 53, 54, 71, 80-86, 88, 89
pāramitā of absorption 33, 54, 88
pāramitā of discipline . 32, 53, 83
pāramitā of generosity 32, 53, 80
pāramitā of patience . . 32, 54, 84
pāramitā of perseverance 32, 54, 85
pāramitā of prajñā . . . 33, 54, 89
pāramitās . . . . xiv, 31, 33, 53, 54, 67, 71, 72, 74, 77-79, 81, 82, 92
patience . . 15, 17, 22, 26, 32, 54, 77, 84, 85
peaceful nirvāṇa 58
perfect application 44
perfect compassion 44, 45
perfect giving 44, 45
perfect intention 44
perfect loving kindness . . 44, 45
perfection of behaviour . . 83, 82
perfection of liturgy 82
perseverance . . 10, 15, 17, 23, 25, 26, 32, 33, 54, 74, 77, 78, 84, 85, 91
perseverance of a bodhisatva 33, 54, 91
Petitioned by the King of Men or What Sūtra 89
phenomena 7, 11, 12, 20, 22, 32, 42-44, 47, 53, 62, 72-74, 76, 100, 101, 107
possessions . . . 25, 32, 53, 78, 80
possessor of knowledge and its feet 18
post-attainment 103, 111
prajñā 11, 16, 17, 23, 33, 54, 68-70, 72, 74, 77, 78, 80, 89-91, 111
prajñā apprehending superfact 68
prajñā arising from contemplation 70
prajñā arising from hearing . . 70

prajñā arising from meditation 70
Prajñāpāramitā .. xvii, 26, 44, 46, 47, 70, 76, 88
pratyeka 61
prostrate .. 20, 21, 30, 31, 51, 52, 55, 57, 64
prostrate to all buddhas 31, 52, 64
provisional and definitive meaning 111
provisional meaning 56-58
proximate afflictions 84
purity of the three spheres .. 64
Pūrṇa 5
Rāhula 4, 5
Rājagṛiha 41
rational mind 62, 77, 89, 100, 112
reading the sūtras iii
realization .. viii, xvi, 61, 74, 81, 98, 112, 113
reference and referencing .. 113
references 72, 81, 103, 113
referencing sentient beings .. 79
refuge 66, 113
rejoice 30, 52, 64
rejoice in all merits .. 30, 52, 64
remembered past lives 7
renunciation 69, 88, 97
riches of the noble ones .. 21, 22
root afflictions 84
roots of virtue 7, 45, 84
rope of becoming 31, 52, 66
rules of discipline 32, 53, 82
saṅgha .... vi, 57, 66
saṅgha of the noble ones 57
saṃsāra ... xvi, 15, 23, 42-44, 46, 47, 55, 58, 59, 81, 88, 94, 98, 100, 101, 105, 107, 109, 112, 113, 116
saṃsāric existence 10, 64
Sāla tree 19
Samantabhadra .... xiii, xiv
Samantabhadra's prayer . xii-xiv, xviii, 63, 121
Sanskrit and diacriticals ... iii, xxi
satva and sattva 98, 113
second turning of the wheel . xvii
self of phenomena 72, 73
self-knowing 75, 77
sentient beings 7, 22, 24-29, 31-35, 43, 52, 53, 55, 59, 62-67, 69, 74, 77, 79, 80, 82, 86, 89, 90, 99, 102, 107, 108, 110, 113, 115, 118
shamatha 11, 68, 96, 114
signlessness 26, 89
six extra-perceptions 31, 53, 57, 68
six migrator sentient beings . 31, 53, 67
six pāramitās .... xiv, 31, 33, 53, 54, 67, 74, 77, 78, 82, 92
sixth world-leading buddha .. xiii
skilful means . 26, 29, 33, 44, 45, 80, 86, 93, 112
skill at thorough dedication 44, 45
skilled in insight 8
solitude 9
special arousing of mind 67
special intention 8, 19, 114
spiritual friend 70
Stack of Jewels ... iii, v-ix, 36, 47, 51, 84
Stack of Jewels Bodhisatva's Piṭaka Sūtra 84
Stack of Jewels Sūtra 51
statement and reasoning 71
steady and delighted applications 32, 54, 84

Sthiramati 5
study and translation of Tibetan texts 122
sublime vi
suchness 62, 76, 88, 104
Sudhana xiii
sugata 18, 62, 63, 114, 115
sugatagarbha . . 62, 63, 115, 116
Sukhāvatī Prayer xii
Sumati 5
superfact . . 68, 89, 104, 105, 116
superfactual 45, 79, 97, 104, 115, 116
superfactual and fictional truths 79
superfactual truth 116
superfice, superficies 116
superficies 32, 53, 61, 62, 72, 75, 77, 87, 90, 101, 102, 116
superficies of grasped-at and grasping 75
supports for study . . . . iii, iv, xv, xxi, 119
supreme enlightenment . . xiv, 31, 52, 63, 65
supreme nirmāṇakāya . . . 20, 94
supreme of great healers 55
supreme wisdom 31, 52, 65
Surendrabodhi 37, 54
sūtras connected with Other Emptiness xvii
Tangyur xiv
tathāgata 6, 7, 18-21, 24, 35, 42, 43, 62, 88, 90, 115
tathāgata, arhat, truly complete buddha 6, 18, 19, 24, 35, 42, 90
tathāgatagarbha 62, 63, 115, 116
teacher of gods and men 18
teaching dharma . . 5, 31, 35, 41, 52, 65
ten levels 31, 52, 65, 92
ten virtuous actions 33, 34
tenth bodhisatva level xiii
tenth level 33, 54, 91, 92
tīrthika 16, 21, 72, 88, 117
Tīrthika texts 72
tīrthika ways 16, 21
the authentic 9, 25, 46, 116
The Bodyless Dakini Dharma . 121
the childish 15
The Condensed 70
The Condensed Prajñāpāramitā in Verse 70
The Dharma Sanctuary of Great Maitreya 94
the eight worldly dharmas . . . 80
the element 62, 116
the five dregs 34
the four absorptions 12
the four āyatanas 12
the general story of the two sūtras iii
the great burden 35
the great ṛiṣhis 32, 53, 73
The Mother 77
The Noble Great Stack of Jewels . . . . iii, v, vi
The Noble One Called "Point of Passage Wisdom" 121
The Noble One Petitioned by the Householder Uncouth 121
the non-analytical cessation . . 12
the seven limbs . . . . xiv, 66
the seven limbs for accumulating merit xiv
The Stack of Jewels Bodhisatva's Piṭaka Sūtra 84
the story behind the prayer . . 56

The Sūtra Petitioned by the King of Men or What 75
the tathāgata . . . 6, 7, 18-20, 24, 35, 42, 43, 62, 88, 90
the ten levels 31, 52, 65, 92
the three doors of emancipation 26
the vehicle of definite goodness 61
the word Noble vi
thing . . xviii, 33, 61, 73, 96, 103, 105, 110, 111, 116
things . vii, ix, xvi, 14, 22, 23, 28, 32, 43, 53, 65, 71-75, 80, 88, 93, 99, 100, 104, 108, 113, 116, 117
third truth of the noble ones . 88
third turning of the wheel . . . xvi, xvii, 115, 116, 121
third turning of the wheel sūtras xvi
thirty-two marks of a great being 19
thorough dedication 44, 45, 56, 59, 63, 67
thorough processing 10
three bad places 58
three doors of complete emancipation 33, 54, 89
three great bodhisatvas xiii
Three Jewels . . . . x, 4, 6, 18, 57, 113, 114
three kayas 116
three kāyas 92, 107
Three knowledges seeing in direct perception . . . 33, 54, 89
three prayers xiii
three realms 70, 87, 112
three types of karma . 30, 51, 60
three vehicles 79, 106
three worlds 23
Tibetan grammar 103, 120
Tibetan texts . . iv, xix, 114, 120, 122-124
tirthika 117
topics and non-topics 14
total affliction 59
total collapse of all things . . . 32, 53, 80
Translated Treatises . . . . . . xiv, xix
Translated Word . . xix, xx, 66, 73
transmission of the dharma . . viii
Treasury of Abhidharma 59
true meaning of pāramitā . . . 81
truly complete buddha . . ix, x, 6, 18, 19, 24, 35, 42, 90, 98, 102, 103, 106
turn the wheel of dharma . . . 16, 31, 52, 65
turned definitely to the Prajñāpāramitā 44, 46, 47
turning of the wheel . . . xvi, xvii, 115, 116, 121
Tuṣhita 56, 94
twelve links of interdependent origination 46, 97
two sutras petitioned by Maitreya vi
two types of formatives 58
two types of pāramitā of the bodhisatva 81
types of perseverance 85
Śhākyamuni . . . ix, x, xii, xiii, 18, 20, 91, 93
Śhākyamuni Buddha . . . ix, x, xii, xiii, 18, 20, 91, 93
śhamatha 8, 68-70, 110, 114, 117
Śhāriputra 4, 5
śhīla 78, 82

śhrāvaka 4, 42, 61, 67, 68
śhrāvaka monks 42
śhrāvakas 4, 30, 51, 57, 67
ultimate authentic statement .. ix
unborn phenomena 76
unending enlightenment 30, 51, 61
unfluctuating karma 60
unimpeded wisdom 89, 90
universal guide 20
unmentionable 83
unsatisfactoriness 10, 31, 52, 65, 113, 117
unsatisfactoriness of sentient beings 31, 52, 65
unsurpassed driver who tames beings 18
unsurpassed offering 64
unsurpassed, truly complete enlightenment ... 7-14, 24-29, 33, 34, 42-45, 47
un-outflowed 83, 111, 117
un-outflowed discipline 83
Upananda 5
Uruvilva Kāśhyapa 5
utmost discernment using prajñā 11
Vajra Vehicle 70, 103, 106
Vajra-Like Concentration ... 13, 33, 54, 88
Vāranāsi 16
Varga 4
Vāṣhpa 5
vehicle of definite goodness 59, 61
Vimala 5
Vinaya Āgama 59
vipaśhyanā 8, 68, 114, 117
Vitality-filled 5, 17, 24, 29, 35, 36
Viśhālamati 5
vows of personal emancipation 82
vows of the enlightenment mind 68
Vulture Peak Mountain 41
well-related words 17
wheel of dharma .... xvii, 16, 31, 52, 65, 112
White Lotus 94
white urna 21
wisdom .. xiii, 31, 43, 44, 47, 52, 61, 63, 65, 68, 69, 72, 75-77, 83, 87, 89, 90, 98, 100, 101, 104, 108, 110, 111, 113, 115-118
wisdom of complete liberation 83
wishlessness 26, 89
without avarice 32, 53, 80
without being wearied ... 42, 44, 47
without laziness 32, 54, 85
workability 11, 114
working to benefit others ... 10
world-leading buddha .... x, xiii

www.ingramcontent.com/pod-product-compliance
Lightning Source LLC
Chambersburg PA
CBHW022008160426
43197CB00007B/334
9789937572620